The Nile

Robert O. Collins

The

Nile

Yale University Press / New Haven & London

Frontispiece: Sunset on the Nile at Malakal

Designed by Nancy Ovedovitz and set in
Adobe Garamond type by Integrated Publishing
Solutions, Grand Rapids, Michigan. Printed in
the United States of America by R.R. Donnelley
& Sons, Harrisonburg, Virginia.

Library of Congress Cataloging-in-Publication Data

Collins, Robert O., 1933–
The Nile / Robert O. Collins.
    p.   cm.
Includes bibliographical references and index.
ISBN 0-300-09764-6
1. Nile River Valley.   I. Title.
DT115.C65 2002
962—dc21   2002009382

A catalogue record for this book is available
from the British Library.

The paper in this book meets the guidelines for
permanence and durability of the Committee
on Production Guidelines for Book Longevity
of the Council on Library Resources.

10 9 8 7 6 5 4 3 2 1

For Janyce
who came with me to drink the waters of the Nile

Contents

Maps

Preface

I first saw and drank from the Nile in 1956. In the years that followed I have returned many times, traversing much of its journey from the springs in Burundi and Ethiopia and their tributaries to the Mediterranean Sea. Rivers, their flow, power, and beauty, have always fascinated me. As a western river guide in the 1970s and 1980s I navigated the rivers and rapids of the American West, which seduced me to run the cataracts of the Nile. These adventures were interspersed with teaching history at the University of California, Santa Barbara, especially History 143, The Nile Quest, and writing the history of the Sudan and the upper Nile.

In retirement I have sought to write of this great river as a whole—including its origins, history, geography, geology, hydrology, and the peoples who live by its banks—for those interested in rivers and the Nile. There are hundreds of books about the Nile with a heavy concentration on Egypt and its monuments, but none for the general reader about all aspects of the river. My purpose has been to distill the voluminous academic, social, and scientific literature into a comprehensible and flowing story of a great river from its remotest springs to the Mediterranean. The goal is similar to something said by the popular British historian George Macaulay Trevelyan seventy years ago: "There are several kinds of reading public of which the more select is the more important, but of which none is wholly negligible. . . . [P]erhaps the highest ideal of history will always remain the volume that satisfies both the learned and the general reader."

One of the difficulties in writing about the Nile basin is the hundreds of languages spoken, the transliteration of which has been deeply influenced by outsiders. Consequently, deciding how to spell names is a curse, and often chaos, particularly when the documentation and oral traditions are in African, Asian, and European languages. The result has been confusion in the literature rather than clarity. The principle applied here aims for consistency of spelling by using the Anglicization or the English equivalent for place names, people, or events recorded in different languages. These choices are often arbitrary, guided more by common usage than a standard system of transliteration. Perhaps to the dismay of Orientalists and those with Arabic sympathies, I have eliminated all the diacritical marks except where the exclusion would create yet another conundrum for the reader. Thus *al-Khartûm* is *Khartoum,* but I have used *Ge'ez* and *Ja'aliyyin.* The *Encyclopedia of Islam* provides a standard transliteration for those who need or demand it.

There is also the problem of measurement. Most of the scientific community has accepted the metric system, but most of the English-speaking public still thinks in inches, feet, and miles. I have thus adopted an unholy compromise between the two systems, giving length and area in the English system of feet and miles. Volume is quite different. Very few English readers have any reasonable conception of an acre-foot or a milliard, so I have employed cubic meters to describe amounts of water—most of which are important only as a relative comparison of volumes.

The Nile

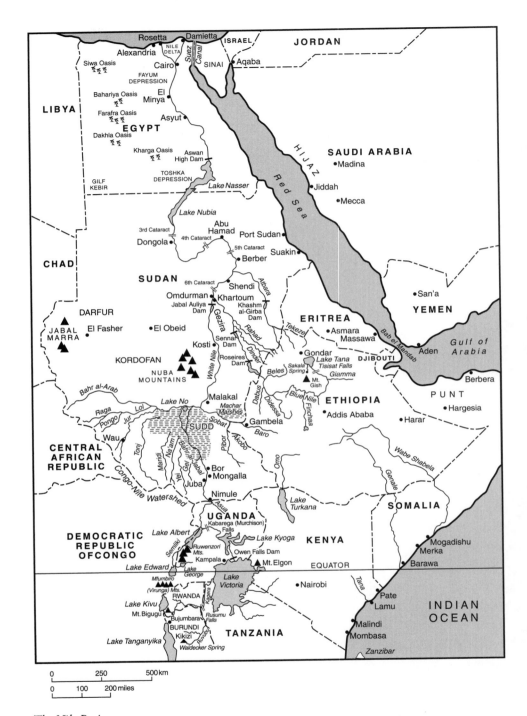

The Nile Basin

Introduction

In 1957 the American literary naturalist Loren Eiseley wrote: "If there is magic on this planet, it is in moving water." There is certainly more magic to be found in the Nile River and its valley than anywhere else in the world. The river bubbles from remote springs in Burundi and Ethiopia, and it descends over falls and rapids and through swamps and plains to make the longest journey of any river in the world, more than 4,230 miles, before emptying into the Mediterranean Sea. From its southernmost source, a spring on a hill in Burundi known as Kikizi, its headstreams tumble over rocks and dash the moss and variegated vegetation with crystalline sprays. Streams become rivulets, thousands of them descending, some in peace, others in tempest, to become rivers.[1]

The Nile and its basin actually consist of many rivers. Each of these has its own distinctive character and panache, but most often recognized are the two main branches: the White Nile, with its ultimate sources in Burundi, and the Blue Nile, which rises in the highlands of Ethiopia and follows a more precipitous course, carrying most of the Nile's water. The river's basin is customarily divided into distinct regions that correspond to the different topography through which it passes on its long journey out of equatorial Africa to the Mediterranean Sea. In the south the Nile begins as many small rivers on the high Lake Plateau of East Africa. From the lakes it plunges down as the Bahr al-Jabal, the Mountain River, into the swamps of the southern Sudan known as the Sudd, from which it emerges into the broad expanse of the White Nile and its great meeting at Khartoum with the Blue Nile from Ethiopia. From the confluence the Nile flows majestically through the deserts of Nubia and Egypt to the Nile delta. It is an ancient river but one that is still evolving in many ways.

South of the equator the streams that form the Nile flow vigorously down from many mountains and hills. The numerous tributaries from Burundi and Rwanda eventually converge into the Kagera River, which cascades over Rusumu Falls and then flows slowly into Lake Victoria, the second largest freshwater lake in the world. There are many other lakes on the plateau, some small, others large—Lake George, Lake Edward, Lake Albert, Lake Kyoga—that contribute large quantities of water, but it is from the northern end of Lake Victoria that the Nile directly flows, as the Victoria Nile. It pours over the Owen Falls Dam and then into Lake Kyoga, after which, in a spectacular drop, it crashes down from the lip of the great African Rift Valley at Kabarega Falls (formerly Murchison Falls) to its bottom at Lake Albert. Reinforced by the waters of Lake George, Lake Edward, and Lake Albert, the Victoria Nile flows out of the Lake Plateau as the Albert Nile to the border of Uganda at Nimule, where it becomes the Bahr al-Jabal, or the Mountain River.

The Bahr al-Jabal deserves its name at first, for it plunges over one cascade and rapid after another, formed by boulders and rocks tossed into its narrow valley by numerous tributaries. But after a hundred miles the steep highlands recede until the horizon is broken only by isolated jabals, or hills. The landscape becomes a plain, and the river slows as it flows through flatlands, and then comes almost to a standstill at its greatest obstacle, the Sudd—hundreds of miles of clogged swampland filled with aquatic plants that imprison the sluggish current. Some of these plants are tall, such as the towering papyrus; others cling to the waters of the lagoons, including the beautiful and indestructible water hyacinth. The clumps of aquatic vegetation are an unstable, ever shifting landscape, and these waters are the home of the hippo, the crocodile, and the four-hundred-pound Nile perch. There are large flocks of birds that come down the Nile corridor and more exotic ones that are permanent residents. Hordes of mosquitoes are everywhere. The river can hardly move at all in this Stygian swamp, so it sits, and in the steamy heat near the equator more than half of the water of the Bahr al-Jabal evaporates away into the atmosphere. Efforts to make the Sudd navigable for steamers have required prodigious human effort and dangerous machinery to clear a way through this great barrier to equatorial Africa.

But the river eventually struggles out of its swampy prison, much reduced, and into the shallow Lake No, which also receives the meager water of the Bahr al-Ghazal surviving its own passage through the great swamp. All lakes have but one outlet, and from Lake No it is the beginning of the White Nile—named for the color of its water farther downstream, for at the swampy northeastern end of the lake the river still has a sickly hue from the decomposing vegetation of the Sudd. Seventy-five miles from

Lake No the White Nile is replenished by the massive flow of the Sobat River from Ethiopia, forming a majestic river again after the trial in the swamps. At the confluence with the Sobat, near Malakal, the White Nile is restored and flows gently north once more, broad and mostly clear, through the vast plains of the Sudan for five hundred miles until it meets its counterpart from the east, the Blue Nile.

The Blue Nile rises at about six thousand feet in the Ethiopian highlands. Its ultimate source is a spring, considered holy by the Ethiopian Orthodox Church, from which a stream called the Little Abbai plunges north to Lake Tana. The Blue Nile—called the Great Abbai in Ethiopia—pours out of Lake Tana from its southern shore, flowing to the southeast, and soon creates its own spectacular drama as it drops over the high precipice of Tisisat Falls. After the falls the river describes a broad arc, curving until it, like the White Nile, is flowing roughly north to Khartoum. Following the summer monsoons the Blue Nile runs freely and swiftly down valleys and deep canyons that in places lie four thousand feet below the surrounding plateau. In these chasms the sun's rays penetrate only sparingly to the rapids and cataracts at the bottom, where the turbulent water defies those who wish to cross and challenges those trying to pass downriver. Fed by many tributaries that also run in deep ravines, the Blue Nile is the major source of water downstream: more than four-fifths of the water that reaches Egypt comes from Ethiopia. In the highlands it is an exhilarating river. Eventually the plateaus and mountain massifs end, and the river reaches the plains of the Sudan, where it flows more slowly but still powerfully.

North of Khartoum the river is the Nile, the White and the Blue united. It is a majestic, mature river that alternates between gentle stretches and rapids—the famous cataracts. The first one encountered going downstream, known as the sixth cataract, lies in wait only fifty miles below Khartoum. Two hundred miles north of the grand confluence at Khartoum the Atbara River crashes down after the rains from the Semyen Massif in Ethiopia. The Atbara is the last major tributary of the Nile, and in its spate it is the most powerful demonstration of moving water in the whole basin, a sudden tumultuous, thundering wall of water that, when spent, leaves stagnant pools as memorials to its hydraulic energy. Below the Atbara the river begins a large, sweeping S-shaped curve, flowing grandly through the Nubian and Egyptian deserts, where no rain or other rivers provide relief from the dessication. It is here that the Nile has made possible the world's oldest continuous civilizations in a hostile and unforgiving desert. The kingdom of Kush and the Egypt of the pharaohs—as well as the Greeks, Romans, Arabs, and all their successors—have always been totally dependent on the Nile for their survival.

The most prominent feature of the Nile's hydrology is the annual flood, which is produced by the waters of Ethiopia—the Sobat, the Blue Nile, and the Atbara. Monsoon rains in summer fill the hundreds of rivers of Ethiopia, and these waters soon make their way downriver in a rush. The river usually begins to rise in May in the northern Sudan, June in southern Egypt at Aswan. It reaches its maximum level in August and September, decreasing thereafter until at its lowest from roughly December to April; some tributaries dry up altogether. That the flood will happen each year is completely predictable, as is the approximate date of its onset. What is never predictable is its volume. In good years enough water would come down from the Ethiopian highlands to overflow the river's banks and make the surrounding basin land fertile for crops. The nutrients deposited as alluvial sediment were as important for the cropland as the water itself. In bad years the mountains sent too much water crashing down, destroying everything in its path. People resigned themselves to their fate when a great Nile flood swept away their homes, monuments, and temples. But the worst years were when there was not enough, and then the land became caked and barren, hard as cement, and people silently succumbed when the waters did not flow and famine stalked the land.

Much of this regimen has changed since 1971, with the completion of the Aswan High Dam in Egypt. The dam has created an enormous reservoir, called Lake Nasser in Egypt, which stretches for more than three hundred miles and backs up well into the northern Sudan, where it is called Lake Nubia. The dam provides protection against the greatest, most destructive floods, while also producing huge amounts of hydroelectric power, and the reservoir stores enough water to irrigate the surrounding land all year round, even in the driest years. The High Dam has been a great benefit to Egypt, but it has come at great cost, including the forced relocation of tens of thousands of Sudanese Nubians. The dam is also generating surprising environmental effects, some foreseen and some not, and these are certainly not all beneficial. They include decreased fertility in the surrounding agricultural lands, serious erosion downstream, inundation of the delta with seawater, increases in soil salinity and waterlogging, increased seismic activity from the weight of the reservoir on fault lines, and decreases in fish populations in the Mediterranean Sea. Taken together, the costs of these effects are staggering. The water and silt in the reservoir are also undermining the dam itself, and the silt is filling the lake. The dam is now predicted to have a useful life of five hundred years, but few Egyptians are concerned about life five centuries in the future. Most are convinced that the dam has impounded the Nile waters within the sovereign territory of Egypt for their use and security from nature or malevolent designs by upstream African riparians. All other environmental costs are irrelevant.

From the dam the Nile flows due north, relatively straight and placid, for about five hundred miles. The river's annual overflowing of its banks has created a floodplain of rich and productive soil, although this prosperous land is exceedingly narrow—at most a few miles in width. Beyond it on both sides is desert. At the end of the Nile in upper Egypt is Cairo, the great and storied city of the Egyptians. Just north of Cairo the Nile delta begins, an enormous triangular region of flat alluvial plain, the most fertile soil in Africa, more than fifty feet deep and built up over thousands of years by the flooding river and its deposits of nutrient-laden silt from upstream. The delta is everywhere sliced through by hundreds of canals fanning out over an area a hundred miles long and 150 miles wide and dotted with lakes, shallow lagoons, and salt marshes along the Mediterranean coast. This fertile plain, along with the narrow strip of alluvium on either bank of the river upstream, has supported the prosperity of Egypt for five thousand years.

In all, the Nile inhabits a basin of astonishing geographical diversity. No other river in the world begins in volcanoes and mountains with glacial snows and ends in arid deserts. Near the Lake Plateau the river is fed by the volcanic Virunga Mountains on the Congo-Nile watershed, one of which, Mount Nyirangongo, erupted as recently as January 2002. To the north, on the equator, tower the Ruwenzori Mountains, known from antiquity as the Mountains of the Moon for their alien equatorial snows and glaciers, concealed behind thick clouds and mists, and unobserved by Europeans until the end of the nineteenth century. In the gigantic uplift of the Ethiopian highlands, source of the Blue Nile, singular peaks thrust themselves skyward as tall as those surrounding the equatorial lakes. In a dramatic fall unequaled in any other river basin, the Nile drops from the heights through tropical rain forest to the depths of the low-lying swamps in the labyrinth of the Sudd and the Machar Marshes. Once it recovers it flows sedately through savanna lands, mostly open grassy plains dotted with small trees and occasional woodlands. Beyond this region lies the Sahel, a strip of arid grasslands between the savanna and the desert. North of the Sahel the Nile passes through the great Sahara desert of Nubia and Egypt, where the river brings the only source of life in the otherwise desolate wasteland. And just past the desert are the rich alluvial lands of the delta.

This geographical diversity is matched by the diversity of peoples living in the Nile basin. At the southern beginnings of the Nile on the slopes and valleys of the green

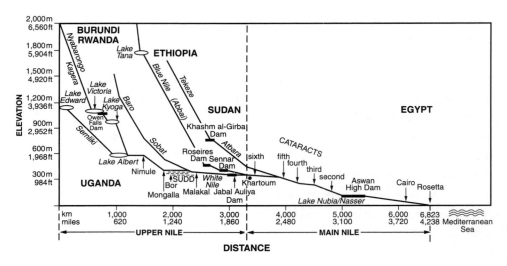

The Descent of the Nile (Source: Paul Howell, Michael Lock, and Stephen Cobb, eds.,
The Jonglei Canal, *1988, reprinted with the permission of Cambridge University Press)*

hills of Africa live the Hutu, the Tutsi, and the Twa pygmoid hunters, Bantu cultivators, Hima pastoralists—all with different origins in other places, speaking different
languages, and with different occupations, each having their own traditional way of
making a living for themselves in the Nile Valley. Farther north on the fertile fields of
the Lake Plateau live yet another distinctive people, an amalgam of the Bantu cultivators who came from the highlands of Cameroon and Nigeria in the west thousands of
years ago and Luo herdsmen who arrived from the southern Sudan in the fifteenth
century, bringing with them cattle, sheep, and goats. The human diversity of the Nile
is perhaps best symbolized by the Nilotic people to the north, in the Sudan, who are
known as Nilotes—and who themselves encompass dozens of different ethnic groups,
including the Shilluk, the Dinka, and the Nuer peoples. They speak languages of the
Nilo-Saharan family and are tall and proud, and fiercely independent. Their reluctance
to be pushed off their land or controlled by outsiders has been the despair of imperial
authorities for two centuries and continues to be for the independent government of
the Sudan today.

In the region around Khartoum and to the north there is even more diversity—the
Nuba people on the summits of hills above the White Nile, and the Ingessna, Hamaj,
and Shankalla living near the Blue Nile in the turbulent borderlands of the Sudan and
Ethiopia. The Sudanese people have a convoluted heritage all their own that embod-

ies the many different physical and cultural characteristics and mixtures of all. The northern Sudan is mostly dominated by Arabs and Nubians; the south, the African part of the Sudan, includes Bantu, Luo, Nilotic, and the Nuba peoples. They all become Sudanese when they are issued a passport, but otherwise the Sudan is a melting pot that has percolated for centuries, filled with people who are still searching for their multicultural identity. And the Egyptians, most of whom claim to be of pure Arab blood, in truth are also an amalgam—since ancient times a mixture of the dynastic pharaohs, Greeks, Romans, Turks, Arabs, Jews, French, English, and still others—all of which makes them distinctively Egyptian. No other river of the world embraces such human diversity.

Similar diversity is found in the enormous variety of plant and animal life in the Nile basin. The Virunga volcanoes of Rwanda are the home of the mountain gorilla. In the western Rift Valley gazelles feed on grass around the lakeshores, where they share space with hippos who surge forth at night to rummage for their forage. The Nile crocodile is ever present, basking in the sun on sandbars and waiting to attack the unwary fish, fowl, and humans who come to the waterside. The crocodile is no longer found in Egypt but flourishes throughout the rivers and swamps of the upper Nile in competition with the prolific bird life. The Nile has always been a great corridor for migratory flocks that breed in the equatorial lakes—crowned pelicans, egrets, flamingoes, gulls, and Nile geese. The slopes of the Ruwenzori Mountains are the home of the elephant, the buffalo, and the leopard. Lions and pigs roam up to eight thousand feet. Here earthworms grow to three feet and canaries can measure fifteen feet from peak to tail. The great swamp of the Sudd is the home of the shoebill stork, the ancient Bog Bird of this primordial land. Many species of waterbirds feed in profusion on the plentiful fish, which include the remains of the Nile perch, the predator of the Nile. The grasslands east of the Sudd are the home of the last great free-roaming herds in their thousands of tiang, hartebeest, and gazelles who make their annual migrations, like the Nilotic inhabitants, to follow the water. Downstream from the Sudd animals become more domestic but equally diverse—cattle, goats, sheep, and beyond Khartoum the camel.

Diversity on the Nile is not limited to fauna. The species of plant life in the Nile basin number in the thousands, particularly in the hothouse environment of the equatorial regions of the Lake Plateau, the Sudd, and the southern Sudan. The mountains of the Lake Plateau have produced a prolific variety of plants from the lower elevations to the higher. In the Ruwenzori with its heavy rainfall there are five distinct zones, the highest being the Scenecio forest at above twelve thousand feet, with a luxuriant growth of hoary leaves covering the ground and the trees. Around the lakes and in the Sudd downstream forests of papyrus fringe the swampy lagoons, whose surfaces are covered with numerous aquatic plants that breed in profusion in the heat and humidity—swamp grass, Nile cabbage, and the plant known locally as *um suf* and *bus*. The most pernicious and domineering plant is the ubiquitous water hyacinth, which first appeared from the Congo River in the 1950s and has become the dominant aquatic vegetation from Lake Victoria to the Jabal Auliya Dam thirty miles south of Khartoum. Downstream from the great confluence the waters of the Nile support domestic crops of sorghum, millet, wheat, and cotton, and the famous date palms of Nubia.

The environments of the mountains, swamps, and savannas of the Lake Plateau and the upper Nile basin have produced an extraordinary variety of plants, and the highlands of Ethiopia have similarly created fauna and flora distinct from those of the plains below. The Blue Nile and its tributaries are the home of crowned cranes, the yellow-billed duck, and the black-headed heron. Huge catfish and larger hippos flounder in the waters of Lake Tana, along whose banks stand the tall *warka* fig trees of great antiquity. The steep ravines and chasms cut by the tributaries to the Blue Nile are filled with luxuriant flowers, the red globes of the Ethiopian lilies surrounded by myriad swarms of butterflies unknown on the Lake Plateau and the upper Nile. These canyons are also thick with scrub forest, and on the narrow but fertile floodplain of the Blue Nile tamarisk flourishes. On the cleared land patches of teff, the millet grown only in Ethiopia and the staple foodstuff, is cultivated in the rich soil deposited by the river. On the plateau above the river arabica coffee flourishes in the cool, moist uplands where it first appeared in history. All this topography and its plants are not found on the plains, which to the Ethiopians confirms that they are unique in their home on the river.

The Nile has also been a river of great mystery. The Greek historian Herodotus and the Roman emperor Nero sought to find its sources far in the heart of Africa, and failed. The Greek astronomer and geographer Ptolemy speculated about the river's origins. The Scottish explorer James Bruce visited Lake Tana in Ethiopia in 1770. The Englishman John Hanning Speke reached Lake Tanganyika and Lake Victoria, which he proclaimed the origin of the Nile in 1862. Later in the nineteenth century the famous African explorer Henry Morton Stanley was one of many Europeans who realized that Speke's answer wasn't the whole story and were searching for the ultimate source of the Nile—a quest that had by that time become one of the great challenges of the century. It was not until the middle of the twentieth century that the true sources of the Nile were finally located and identified as such.

Today the Nile is also a dammed river, from beginning to end. For thousands of years the Egyptians had dug extensive canals and built modest earthworks to divert the river's water into fields that they could farm. Following the Arab conquest of Egypt in the seventh century c.e., the Fatimids and the Mamluks sought to improve on the irrigation works of the Greeks and Romans. After many centuries, however, it was Muhammad Ali, the Turkish viceroy of Egypt in the nineteenth century, who began a program of modernization that included building a huge network of barrages, or small diversion dams, and canals in the delta to increase the country's productivity and prosperity. The British, who occupied Egypt in 1882, took construction on the river to another level, and they soon began clearing canals, building barrages, and damming the river in an effort to eliminate in Egypt the feared floods and drought caused by the unpredictability of the Nile. The earliest result was the construction of the first Aswan Dam, in 1902, which submerged forever the first cataract of the Nile. The dam at Aswan, proclaimed a wonder at the time, was only the beginning of a relentless obsession. In the Sudan dams were built at Sennar on the Blue Nile and Jabal Auliya on the White Nile in the years between the two world wars; the Khashm al-Girba Dam on the Atbara River and the Roseires Dam on the Blue Nile followed in the 1960s. The Owen Falls Dam obliterated Ripon Falls, just below the mouth of Lake Victoria, in return for hydroelectric power for Uganda in 1954. Many other dams throughout the Nile basin have been planned but never built, for reasons mostly political and financial.

All these dams were dwarfed by the extraordinary engineering achievement of the Aswan High Dam, completed in 1971, and its great reservoir. In their years of colonial occupation of Egypt, the British had developed schemes for a complex system of structures that would control the unpredictable flood of the Nile, protecting against the devastation in the years of excessive flood and conserving the river's water for the years of dearth. Their plans mostly centered on damming the equatorial lakes and creating reservoirs far upstream that could alleviate the harmful effects of either too much or too little water, as well as digging canals that would bypass the voracious Sudd and allow the river to flow without losing most of its water to constant evaporation. Part of the beauty of this intricate scheme was that, in the bucolic atmosphere of the equatorial lakes and Lake Tana, the loss of water from evaporation is equaled by gains from precipitation. Together, these plans were intended to release Egypt from the tyranny of its dependency on such a volatile supply of water.

But in the 1950s the revolutionary government led by Gamal Abdel Nasser sought a grand monument in Egypt, not upstream in uncontrollable foreign lands, that would free the country of its dependency altogether through the construction of a great dam at Aswan, a dramatic gesture that eviscerated all the finely wrought plans of the British. In the years following completion of the dam, the reservoir indeed contained more than sufficient water to make the Egyptian desert bloom along its banks and in its delta. But in the relentless heat of the desert, the reservoir loses tremendous amounts to evaporation. Worse, in their hydrologic calculations the dam builders did not account for the fickleness of nature and the river that came to pass at the end of the twentieth century. In the middle years of the 1980s the Nile no longer flowed in abundance, and despite many theories no one knew why. By 1988 the great reservoir had shrunk so low that it seemed electricity for homes and industry would have to be sacrificed for water to drink and irrigate. Then, just when Egypt was on the brink of catastrophe, torrential rainfalls previously unknown in the twentieth century ended the drought, but in its place disastrous floods surged through the confluence at Khartoum and down the river. Lake Nasser swelled to spectacular heights in the late 1990s that threatened the structural integrity of the High Dam. The awesome pressure of billions of cubic meters was relieved by spilling the excess down a diversion canal into the Toshka depression, but the invincibility and security symbolized by the dam was shattered. It could help protect against years of extended drought or terrible floods, but it was clear that it could never free Egypt from the tyranny of its dependence on the river's unpredictable flood.

Egypt's and the Sudan's absolute dependency on the Nile has been dictated by nature—through geography, geology, and climate—over which they have no control. The Egyptians and the northern Sudanese live in a desert. Without the waters of the Nile, ancient or modern humans could not have survived, let alone multiplied, in a barren land of rock and sand and wind. Egypt is not alone, for all the countries of the Nile basin face the same problem of dependency and demand for water. These themes dominate the past, present, and future of the Nile and those who live on its plateaus and savannas, in its swamps, and by its banks. The magic of moving water in the Nile has cut canyons through high mountains and plateaus and forced its way through swamp and desert to the Mediterranean Sea, where a multitude of different peoples have sought to live by its shores in the security the waters have provided. The never ending struggle to survive on this long and great river continues despite the triumphs of contemporary engineering, all of which are ephemeral when measured against the long millennia of geological time and perpetual dependency on the Nile's waters.

1 The Tyranny of Dependency

Hail to thee, O Nile, that issues from the earth and comes to keep Egypt alive! . . .
He that waters the meadows which He created . . .
He that makes to drink the desert . . .
He who makes barley and brings emmer into being . . .
He who brings grass into being for the cattle . . .
He who makes every beloved tree to grow . . .
O, Nile, verdant art thou, who makes man and cattle to live.
—Hymn to the Nile, Papyrus Sallier II

The Nile is one of the natural and romantic wonders of the world and the longest river, flowing 4,238 miles over thirty-five degrees of latitude. Its basin is broad, embracing nearly 2 million square miles of equatorial and northeast Africa—one-tenth of the African continent—but the quantity of freshwater conveyed by the Nile out of equatorial Africa and the Ethiopian highlands is a mere cup (2 percent) of the Amazon, perhaps a glass (15 percent) of the Mississippi, or at best a pitcher (20 percent) of the Mekong. If the measure of a river's greatness is the volume of water it carries, the Nile is more correctly compared with the Rhine. The Nile's volume is in fact huge in absolute terms, but the river's distinction among all others in the world is not its volume but its rich and colorful history, its profound role in shaping human civilization in Africa, and the absolute dependency on the river and its vagaries of those who live in its basin.[1]

The Nile was born 160 million years ago, when the continents drifted apart, leaving the oceans and aulacogens, or rifts, to mark the separation of wandering tectonic plates. Not surprisingly, after this global surgery, the scars beneath the earth's crust were so thin that when the intense heat of tectonic transfiguration cooled the aulacogens subsided, becoming trenches for the rivers of the Americas—the Amazon and the Mississippi—that flowed into the Atlantic. In Africa the Nile emptied into the Indian Ocean. The vast African landmass remained in place during this period of continental drift, and taking advantage of its stability the earth's crust once again buckled, 25 million years before our time, to uplift the highlands of Ethiopia and excavate the Rift valleys of eastern Africa and the Red Sea. These massive upheavals and fractures diverted the Nile from its course to the Indian Ocean, but the river lacked the power to breach the Nubian swell, the rock dike in the northern Sudan that blocked its way to the north, enabling the expansion of the Mediterranean Sea. The passage of the Nile to the sea required another 10 million years and physiological changes in the planet.

Fifteen million years ago the global climate underwent one of its periodic shifts, establishing the seasonal pattern of rainfall that, even today, brings predictable precipitation to the Ethiopian highlands from the south Atlantic and the Indian Ocean. Five million years ago surface evaporation caused the Mediterranean Sea to begin shrinking, and the Strait of Gibraltar pinched shut. Rainfall, in the form of a seasonal deluge, increased, and as a result the water plunging from the highlands to the sea cut a deep canyon through what is now Egypt, creating roughly the present course of the Nile. When the sea returned to its previous size, the dam at Gibraltar was breached, and the same monsoon that had excavated the canyon now filled it with the soil of the Ethiopian plateau.

The modern Nile emerged following the retreat of the glaciers eighteen thousand years ago, during the late Paleolithic period. Rising surface temperatures in the oceans created a new pattern of heavy rainfall in Africa, enabling the continent to recover from the aridity of the Ice Age. Humans prospered and evolved with the regeneration of the land, lakes, and rivers. Plentiful moisture from the south Atlantic crossed the equator northward in pursuit of the retiring glaciers to transform the region, now known as the Sahara desert, into a verdant land with lakes and rivers, rich in grass and forests. Farther south on the Nubian highlands, the Lake Plateau of equatorial Africa, and the Ethiopian highlands, the rain fell in greater quantities, creating the modern Nile with its annual regimen of surging high water in the summertime, what is called the Nile flood.[2]

The rainy period lasted roughly six thousand years, a mere instant in geologic time but decisive in the formation of the Nile, for the volume of water became so constant and so great that it absorbed the independent rivers of Africa into an integrated basin. Lake Victoria, which hitherto had no outlet, overflowed, and the White Nile became a mighty river, receiving even the waters of Lake Turkana, which is today isolated in the eastern Rift Valley. Then the rainfall began to decline, and the wet phase came to an end some six thousand years ago, leading to unrelenting desiccation in the Sahara and turning it into the arid wasteland it is today. Lakes disappeared or were reduced to morbid marshes. Rivers ceased to flow and became dry wadis. Grass vanished, and animals died. Humans, following their primordial instincts for survival, left the desert to seek the water by the banks of the Nile.[3]

Following this climatic adjustment, the amount of water forming the Nile became determined by the meeting of moisture-laden trade winds from the south Atlantic with dry winds from the north. The confrontation takes place in a band of low pressure that straddles the equator for several hundred miles of latitude north and south. This region where the trade winds collide is known as the intertropical convergence zone (ITCZ), and what the collision produces is rain. The location of the zone itself fluctuates seasonally by hundreds of miles to the north and south, a movement that is determined by the eccentricity of the earth's orbit, variations in the sun's path through the galaxy, and solar activity that has controlled the weather systems of the earth.

Warming of the global climate over millions of years produced an increase in water supply, in Africa as elsewhere. When the ITCZ moves north, rainfall carrying water from the Atlantic Ocean is deposited in the rain forest of the Congo, the Lake Plateau of equatorial Africa, the Nilotic plains of the southern Sudan, and the western escarpment of the Ethiopian plateau—all of which contribute to the White Nile. When the southeast trade winds prevail, surging north and west from the Indian Ocean to the Ethiopian highlands, they produce the Blue Nile. The southerly winds begin to retreat each year in October, forced back by the winter winds from the north bringing dry air from the great landmass of Europe and the steppes of central Asia. When the southerly winds are spent, the rainfall they have dropped determines the amount of water the Nile will carry for the coming year. This amount, in turn, establishes how large the river's annual flood will be. And the size of the flood—too much, not enough, or, with luck, just right—is the critical factor that makes dependency on the Nile a tyrannical master.

Following the climatic wet phase more than five thousand years ago, hunters and gatherers were forced out of the Sahara by its desiccation, and they migrated to the east until they found water and settled along the banks of the Nile. The ancient civilizations they built in Egypt and the Sudan endured longer than any of those built by invaders and inhabitants of the Nile from Asia and Europe during the past two thousand years, yet all were equally dependent on the river. The waters gave life in flood and death in drought, dominating the daily routines, seasonal rhythms, structures and methods of governance, and supplications for salvation by those in upper Egypt, the Sudan, the upper Nile, and the Lake Plateau. The Nile flood, awaited and worshiped by those who depend on it, is decided by forces beyond their control, and whether it gives or denies the waters is the tyranny of dependency.

The refugees who came out of the desert and settled by the banks of the Nile became bound by the regimen and ritual of the river in a way of life that their ancestors had never experienced in the African interior. In the vast region that is now the Sahara, limitless space and a profusion of animals and natural vegetation had required little organization to support a small society. Living by the Nile meant exchanging the vulnerable independence of the hunter for the permanence and security of the cultivator, dependent on the waters. The Nile flood has inundated the northern Sudan and Egypt annually for five thousand years, providing water for crops and renewing the soil with nutrients from the Ethiopian highlands. Throughout the ages, the flood's arrival has been awaited with both confidence and apprehension. On one hand, the Nile is the most predictable of rivers; unlike other great rivers, the date of its flood is rarely capricious. On the other hand, the constancy of the flood's appearance is utterly unrelated to its volume—no one has ever been able to know how much water the Nile would provide from one year to the next. In the years of low flood, it would not provide sufficient water or deliver nutrients, and the result was famine and death. Years of high flood meant entire fields and villages would be destroyed.

In the spring, rain clouds roll out of the south Atlantic across the tropical African rain forest of the Congo and over the plains of the upper Nile to loose their power and water on the Ethiopian highlands. By May the Ethiopian rivers and Nile tributaries are full and flowing. Farther north in Egypt the Nile is a diminished stream. Then, as if by magic or divine decree, the Nile begins to rise at Aswan in June. With implacable regularity, in the many millennia during which every ruler has made measurements, the Nile has never risen in Egypt before 17 May or after 6 July. The river surges with growing volume, strength, and speed for 110 days (the annual average in the twentieth century), reaching its maximum height and volume in September. Whereas in June the flood would take twelve days to flow the six hundred miles from Aswan to Cairo, in September it could complete its journey in only six days.[4]

The arrival of the Nile in Egypt, whether low, high, or normal, would always be greeted with rejoicing, especially once the river rose high enough to overflow its banks and water the fields, usually during the second week of August. Dynastic Egypt held celebrations and commemorated the flood in statues and hieroglyphic inscriptions to the god Hapi. Although a lesser god, Hapi was revered as the personification of the Nile's fertility. The Egyptians depicted him as a Falstaffian character with a protruding belly and pendulous breasts, a god of the people, unlike the central deity of the Egyptian dynasties, Osiris, whose death and resurrection assured the renewal of life with the beginning of the Nile flood. The tears of Isis, the mourning wife of Osiris, were dropped into the river, raising the waters and securing the rebirth of the crops that had died after the harvest of the previous year. The cultivators, farmers and peasants, were uncomfortable with royal rituals. They preferred to sing hymns to Hapi, for he had no temples or official cult; they cast their annual offerings into the rising waters with simple and sincere supplications.

The Greek and Roman successors to the Egyptian pharaohs also recognized and revered the implacable regimen of the Nile, dutifully acknowledging its regularity on coins and statuary. The Coptic Christians of Egypt traditionally celebrated the rise of the Nile on 17 June, the Night of the Drop, when the archangel appealed to the Lord to raise the river. This Christian tradition of pagan origins was readily adopted by the Muslim rulers of Egypt, who on the same date would send the *munadee el-Nil,* the herald of the Nile, through the streets of Cairo to announce the daily rise of the river.

The problem was the complete unpredictability of the flood's volume. Since the amount of water has determined the conditions of life in Egypt, the Nile's fluctuations have been an obsession of both the ancients and the moderns. Throughout geologic time the record has been inscribed in stone and sand by fossils, disclosing the river's hydrology during the many epochs before human settlement by its banks. People began to measure the water's rise and fall almost as soon as they arrived, carving graduated scales into large rocks or stone walls, forming instruments that came to be called nilometers. The difference between excess and scarcity as measured on the nilometer was only five feet, the average height of a man in antiquity. The Egyptians learned very early to construct a series of barrages, or small dams, and canals that allowed them to irrigate the fields surrounding the river, but if it did not rise high enough to flood the land, productive cultivation failed under the desert sun. If the Nile rose too high, the resulting inundation destroyed villages, towns, temples, and fields. The nilometer became the instrument that measured the welfare of the state and society.

The oldest known nilometer measurements are carved on stone fragments from a diorite stela known as the Palermo Stone, owing to its present location in the Palermo

Museum, on which were recorded the Nile flows from predynastic Egypt to the end of the Fifth Dynasty (2480 B.C.E.), in the Old Kingdom. These readings are difficult to convert with precision into modern measurements. They were recorded at the Memphis nilometer called the House of Inundation, which has disappeared, taking with it the means of determining its original baseline. It remains unknown whether the foundations of the nilometers of dynastic Egypt rested on the bottom of the Nile, on the ground level of its agricultural basin, at the level of its low water, or at the level necessary to inundate the fields. The nilometer at Memphis and others constructed at early Egyptian temples along the length of the river may have resembled more permanent structures that have survived from the later dynasties of the New Kingdom as well as the Greeks and the Romans. These nilometers were constructed in substantial chambers on temple grounds by the river. Covered stairways led to the stone columns, scaled in cubits, that descended to the ground or the low-water level. Movable measuring devices, usually plumb lines sequestered in the temples, were used by the Greeks, the Romans, and eventually the Arabs, but they may have been employed in dynastic Egypt as well.

The method of measuring the Nile was improved and stabilized with the construction of a nilometer at the southern tip of the island of Roda, opposite Old Cairo, in 715 C.E., seventy-five years after the Arab conquest of Egypt. The Arabs had realized that they could not consolidate their rule without a reasonable system of taxation and tribute. These state revenues, however, were dependent on the Nile, and their calculation required measuring the river. During the exceptionally high flood of 861, the Roda nilometer was destroyed, then rebuilt and placed in the custody of Abu al-Raddad. His descendants remained the guardians of Roda for another thousand years as a familial symbol of stability on the Nile during a parade of rulers, parvenus, and proconsuls who presumed to govern in the pursuit of their own prosperity.

The nilometer at Roda consisted of a well with three openings at different levels. In the center was an octagonal marble pillar with a scale inscribed in cubits. (An Egyptian cubit was about eighteen inches.) When the Nile reached sixteen cubits, inundation of the fields could begin. By the time the waters reached eighteen cubits, the middle lands were flooded, and at twenty cubits the high land was irrigated. The readings from Roda replaced the numerous and antiquated nilometers, particularly the House of Inundation in Memphis, to become the official register for the level of the Nile for the next twelve centuries. The completion of the first Aswan Dam in 1902 rendered Roda obsolete. Although its readings continued to be recorded, the official measurements of the Nile were moved to Aswan where the Nile entered a more regulated Egypt. (Upon the completion of the second Aswan Dam in 1971, the measurements were moved to Dongola in the Sudan, where the Nile today enters its great reservoir.) Remembered, but no longer relevant, Roda has been preserved as a favorite museum in modern Cairo.[5]

Early measurements of the Nile cannot be regarded as infallible benchmarks. Over the centuries the conquerors and rulers of Egypt, not surprisingly, tampered with the scales that defined their resources. Not all these revisions were devious, for the accumulation of Ethiopian silt during the centuries raised the level of the riverbed, the baseline from which measurements were taken, which required the adjustment of the beginning of the scale. The zero level most certainly was recalibrated frequently, although there is no record of when. Furthermore, official measurements were likely recorded by lowly clerks, who may have been illiterate and hardly interested in the tedious transcription of worn and soiled texts. Even shifting calendars complicate assessment of Nile records. After

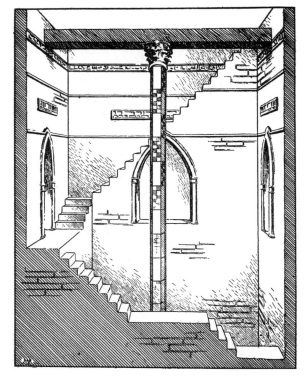

The Roda nilometer at Cairo (Reprinted from William Popper, The Cairo Nilometer, *© 1951, the Regents of the University of California)*

the Arab conquest the Muslim lunar calendar was used for official purposes, but the sun, not the moon, determines the dates for the rise and fall of the great river. Because the major source of revenue was the land tax based on the harvest, the fiscal year was arranged according to the Nile flood and, hence, the solar year. Often, private individuals cut their own marks in the stones of buildings, cliffs, temples, and the steps of river fortifications—many of which remain visible today, thanks to Egypt's arid climate—but these unofficial measures were recorded in different and often indecipherable units for personal purposes. These are all frustrating conundrums in the search for accuracy, but the records offer a vibrant and unique chronicle spanning thousands of years, an achievement unequaled by any other civilization in history.

The nilometers proved their worth. Not only were they the instruments by which the state calculated the acquisition of its resources, but they are invaluable tools by which to reconstruct the history of Egypt and Kush throughout the millennia. The pharaohs of the first five Egyptian dynasties (3050–2480 B.C.E.) were the beneficiaries of abundant waters from the Nile until the rainfall from the south Atlantic gradually declined to its present configuration. The first period of low Nile was recorded about 2200 B.C.E., at the end of the Sixth Dynasty, when Egypt's resources were no longer able to sustain the authority of the central government. Dynastic Egypt disintegrated as the provincial patriarchs sought to exert their autonomy from the pharaoh and exploit the cultivators and what remained of the harvest. Famine was widespread, and cannibalism was recorded. For two hundred years Egypt, from the first cataract at Aswan to the Mediterranean, dissolved into a chaos known today as the First Intermediate Period, or dark age, from which it emerged only when the waters of the Nile once again began to flow in profusion. Prosperity returned the kings to power in the twentieth century B.C.E. Amenemhet I (1938–1908 B.C.E.) founded the Twelfth Dynasty and became the first pharaoh of the Middle Kingdom.[6]

The geologic and written evidence during the subsequent two hundred years of the Middle Kingdom (1938–1786 B.C.E.) shows average Nile floods (comparable to those of the nineteenth century C.E.). These substantial flows made economic prosperity possible and supported the strong central governments of the pharaohs of the Twelfth Dynasty. Armed with the abundance a resurgent Nile provided, these pharaohs were able to embark on imperial adventures south of Aswan against the Nubians in the Sudan. Following the death of Amenemhet III, circa 1797 B.C.E., dynastic Egypt again disappeared for two hundred years into another dark age, known as the Second Intermediate Period, during which low Niles deprived the state of resources. Without the means to govern, the central authority could not defend Egypt from the invasion of the Asiatic Hyksos, who seized the Nile Delta and occupied Memphis in 1647 B.C.E., establishing their rule as the Fifteenth Dynasty. Few records survive from the dark age, but those that do describe hard times. The drought of 1740 B.C.E. appears to have been the historical event described as the biblical seven years of famine in Genesis.[7]

The revival of dynastic Egypt by the pharaohs of the New Kingdom (1550–1070 B.C.E.) coincided with three hundred years of good Nile flows. The prosperity from the land sustained more than sixty years of omnipotent rule by Ramses II (1290–1224 B.C.E.), along with his imperial adventures and his massive stone monuments. Perhaps the drastic reduction of the Nile flood after the death of Ramses II was retribution for his hubris, but during the subsequent dynasties, the Twentieth and the Twenty-first, the Nile no longer provided the water to support the empire, the state, or society.

With the river's diminution, the pharaohs' authority dissolved into feudal anarchy, and banditry, wanton destruction, and civil war plagued the land. The two and a half centuries from 1200 to 945 B.C.E., sometimes called the Third Intermediate Period, were by far the darkest in the long history of dynastic Egypt. Without water, neither the competent nor the corrupt could govern, and Egypt disintegrated into precincts ruled by warlord officials.

The failure of the flood during this third dark age has been recorded geologically, in the encroachment of the desert from the Egyptian colonies in Nubia, and historically, in the exodus from the Ramesside capital of Avaris in the delta. Scarcity produced inflation, particularly in the markets and the granaries of the state, which were administered from the temples. These sacred sanctuaries were religious centers that also provided for the welfare of the hungry and the homeless. In times of starvation, these refuges were no longer inviolable from assault by those ravaged by famine, so they had to be secured with walled fortifications. The decline of the state and society invited incursions by the Libyans from the west and the Nubians from the south. The nomadic Libyans soon discovered that an exhausted Egypt was best exploited by conquest rather than pillage; they became the new pharaohs for two hundred years. The Nubian kings of Kush, who followed the Libyans, ruled Egypt for a hundred years, and their success was determined as much by the return of the Nile flood as by their military strength and administrative abilities. Assyrians with superior iron weaponry defeated the pharaohs from Kush, who were driven out of Egypt in 655 B.C.E.; the Kushites found sanctuary south of Aswan, in Nubia, where they continued to rule and measure the Nile flow for another thousand years. For all five dynasties—three Libyan, one Nubian, and one Assyrian—ruling for four hundred years, prosperity and stable government depended on good Nile floods.[8]

Alexander the Great's conquest of Egypt in 332 B.C.E. marks the end of dynastic Egypt, as well as the close of the consistent record of the Nile flood for a thousand years, until the arrival of the Arabs in the seventh century C.E. The Greek rulers, and later their Roman successors, possessed and built nilometers, for they were as concerned as the pharaohs about governmental matters that depended on the flow of the Nile, but few of their records survive. The Nile flood obviously fluctuated during these centuries. There was a low Nile in 99 and highs in 67, 91, and 111 C.E., but no consistent evidence about the flood exists other than the continued presence of a powerful central government and a citizenry always ready to complain but not reduced to starvation. Geological sediments are not very helpful in the short measure of contemporary time, and no dramatic climatic change can be demonstrated for this period. Egypt's welfare during these centuries is best understood through descriptions of life by its inhabitants and rulers rather than the records of their nilometers.

The centuries of domination by the Greeks and Romans appear to have been blessed with rainfall. Even the deserts seem to have been sprinkled more regularly by thunderstorms. The revival of the Ramesside gold mines in the Wadi Allaqi by the Greek Ptolemies and the Romans and the heavily traveled caravan routes from the Nile to the Red Sea could not have been established without abundant water in the wadis and wells. During these same centuries the Mediterranean littoral was a fertile fringe on the desert hitherto ignored by dynastic Egypt. The availability of more water in the deserts than in the past seems to have resulted in increased activity along the ancient trans-Saharan caravan routes, where commerce was still carried by horse and oxen that consumed copious quantities of water. (The camel did not arrive until the fourth century.) The amount of land under cultivation increased twofold, and the population doubled from that during the reign of Ramses II, to some 5 million. The Greeks and Romans introduced new technologies, including the *saqia,* or waterwheel, which improved on primitive irrigation methods, and Egypt became a major exporter of surplus grain to Rome. Although these were impressive achievements, they were still subject to the Nile's vicariousness in its floods. The rhetoric of rulers, despite technological triumphs, could not produce water.

The decline of Rome contributed to that of Egypt. Emperor Diocletian was the last Roman ruler to visit the Nile, and his legacy was a severe system of taxation firmly imposed throughout Egypt in 313 C.E., less than two decades before the founding of Constantinople as the capital of the Greek-speaking East and the rival to Rome, capital of the Latin-speaking West. Constantinople's imperial gravity absorbed Egypt into the Byzantine orbit for more than two hundred years (395–641 C.E.), but the emperors of Byzantium were never able to neutralize the centrifugal force of the Christian Coptic Church, ruled by its powerful patriarchs at Alexandria. This was more than a simple struggle between church and state; it was a deep cultural conflict between the indigenous past of the dynastic Egyptians and the Hellenism of the Greeks. The centralization of authority was enforced by the presence of the bureaucrat, the soldier, and the tax collector, whose calculations were based on the measurements of Nile water. Political, religious, and social instability abounded. The failure of the Nile flood during the last half of the sixth century and the first half of the seventh contributed to the gradual subsidence of the northern delta, returning the soil to the sea. The combination of these calamities reduced the land under cultivation in Egypt by half and, following the great plague of 542–600, the population similarly declined. The details of these catastrophes remain obscure, but by the time the Arabs invaded Egypt in 639, the population had diminished through disease and famine to a mere 2.5 million.

After the death of the prophet Muhammad, the Arabs, inspired by Islam and the practical profits of imperial conquest, swept out of the deserts of Arabia in their jihad against the Byzantine empire. They defeated the Byzantine forces in the Fayum in 640 and at Babylon (Old Cairo) in 641. On 29 September 642 the Arab general Amr ibn al-As marched into Alexandria, and by 644 the Arabs had occupied Egypt. They had to govern an impoverished land in desperate need of the Nile waters. The success of their rule, like that of their predecessors, was determined as much by the Nile flood as by their religious enthusiasm, military superiority, and administrative abilities.

During the first three centuries of the Arabs' administration, ample floods helped them consolidate their rule. Two severe low Nile floods occurred in 650 and 694; others were below average, but not until the tenth and eleventh centuries did the river's failures outnumber the normal or high flows. The fourth lowest Nile flood in history was recorded in 967, during a generation of dearth between 945 and 977 that resulted in extensive loss of cultivation and encouraged yet another invasion. In 969 the Fatimids, Berber and Shiite Muslims from the Maghrib region of North Africa, conquered Egypt and established their new capital at modern Cairo in 973. Their rule was greatly facilitated by a full Nile, although it did not last: between 1052 and 1090 the Nile almost disappeared. Devastating in their consistency, the low floods resulted in cannibalism, disease, and plague. By the end of the eleventh century another million Egyptians had perished, reducing the population of the Nile Valley between Aswan and the Mediterranean to half what it had been in the most prosperous centuries of the pharaohs.[9]

The calamity that befell Egypt in these years, memorialized in the name of the Fatimid caliph al-Mustansir, was overcome not by its rulers but by the return of a full Nile. Normal flows graced the end of the eleventh century and most of the twelfth century, from 1090 to 1195; the fourteenth century experienced excess flows, especially during the great flood of 1359–1360, when "the people went out into the desert beseeching God to reduce the level of the Nile." Thereafter the irregular records from Roda and other nilometers provide a mosaic, rather than a detailed dossier, on the state and social conditions of Egypt during the Mamluk dynasty. From the fifteenth to the nineteenth century, a fragment in time compared with the millennia of dynastic Egypt, the Nile flow appears to have been in decline, but the measurements are inconsistent and unreliable, the registry of hard times without the good.[10]

In the seventeenth and eighteenth centuries the Nile was extremely low. Its diminished flood was accompanied by severe drought throughout all the arid and semiarid plains that stretch across Africa from the Nile to the Atlantic. The waters did not return to abundance until the nineteenth century, when there were exceptionally high floods in 1800, 1809, and from 1818 to 1820. Giovanni Battista Belzoni, an irrepressible Italian who enthusiastically plundered the monuments of upper Egypt, described the great flood of 1818 on 17 September: "We saw several villages in great danger of being destroyed . . . their unfortunate inhabitants were obliged to escape to higher grounds. . . . Some crossed the water on pieces of wood, some on buffaloes or cows, and others with reeds tied up in large bundles. . . . In some parts the water had left scarcely any dry ground, and no relief could be hoped till four and twenty days had elapsed [when the flood traditionally began to recede]." An even bigger flood, the highest of modern times, occurred in 1878.[11]

The vagaries of the Nile flood, particularly its lows, have led to some paranoid beliefs. Foremost among these is the fear that those who live upstream can command the lives of those downstream, an article of faith that has been inscribed on the soul of Egyptians for millennia. The Ethiopians, who collect the waters from the south Atlantic in their highland sanctuary, have always been thought to represent the greatest threat. The expansion of Islam by the Arabs in the seventh century isolated their Christian enemies in Ethiopia in a religious rivalry that persists to the present day. The Muslim rulers of Egypt became convinced that the failure of the flood was the result of the machinations of the emperors of Ethiopia to divert, obstruct, or impound the flow of the Nile. The medieval kings of Europe, latent Crusaders, regularly sought to improve their international presence by sending bellicose demands to the sultans of Egypt to stop molesting the Coptic Christians. The rulers of Egypt had little reason to fear their Christian subjects—they were divided between Copt and Roman just as the Muslims were divided between Shiite and Sunni—but no ruler of Egypt could ignore threats to cut off the water by the emperors of Ethiopia, whom they did not know and with whom they did not regularly communicate.

Literary allusions to this fear of diversion abound. The Arab chronicler al-Macin wrote in the thirteenth century that the emperor of Ethiopia had turned aside the Nile waters until the sultan of Egypt sent an embassy bringing a handsome bribe. This was a myth, but it was believed after disastrous low Niles and the death of a third of Cairo's population in 1200. The last of the Zagwe kings of Ethiopia claimed to have diverted the Nile waters when Egypt suffered three years of famine during the reign of the powerful Mamluk sultan al-Zahir Baybars (1260–1277). The greatest of the Solomonic emperors that succeeded the Zagwe, Zar'a Ya'qob (1434–1468), responded to Muslim persecution of Egyptian Christian Copts by sending a delegation carrying a threatening letter to the sultan. "And are you not aware, you and your Sultan, that the River Nile is flowing to you from our country and that we are capable of preventing floods that irrigate your country? Nothing keeps us from so doing, only the belief in God and his slaves. We have presented to you what you need to know and you should know what you have to do."[12] In his epic poem *Orlando Furioso,* published in 1516, the Renaissance poet Ludovico Ariosto wrote:

> And the Egyptian Sultan, it is said,
> Pays tribute and is subject to the king,
> Who could divert into another bed
> The river Nile, and thus disaster bring
> On Cairo, and on all that region spread
> The plight of famine and great suffering.[13]

And in his opera *Aïda,* Giuseppe Verdi sought to demonstrate the tragedy of hostility between the two countries with his tale of the star-crossed love of an Egyptian army commander for an Ethiopian princess. Commissioned by Khedive Ismail to write the opera for the opening of the Suez Canal in 1869, Verdi failed to meet the deadline. Ismail and the Egyptians had to wait until 1871 for its first performance at the new Cairo opera house.

In spite of the popular notion, however, low floods in actuality have never been attributable to the devious schemes of malevolent Ethiopian rulers to divert the Nile. Only now, at the beginning of the twenty-first century, do the Ethiopians appear capable of making the idle threats of their historic rulers a reality, through dams for development and hydropower in their highlands. The Egyptians will regard any diversion of the Nile by Ethiopia as a hostile act, but even with dams the Ethiopians are unlikely to exercise the kind of control that causes apprehension downstream. The flow of the Nile will still be determined by nature—albeit with more influence by humans in the future than ever in the past.

The twentieth century experienced the most severe fluctuations in precipitation of any century in the past five thousand years. The Nile refused to flow in 1913, 1984, and 1987, some of the lowest years ever. It also experienced some of its most impressive highs in 1946, 1954, 1961, 1963, 1996, and 1998. These acute aberrations are partly the result of sophisticated instruments that have allowed more accurate measurement. Nature is still responsible for this erratic behavior, some of which is now understood to include the influence of such natural climatic phenomena as El Niño. More and more, however, all these natural variations are exacerbated by the effects of human civilization. Greenhouse gases produced by industry have brought about a dramatic revolution in the pattern, quality, and quantity of the earth's precipitation. Even more decisive is the astounding increase in the population of the Sahel and the Nile basin, which has caused relentless destruction of the primordial land cover through clear-cutting, animal grazing, and the construction of large reservoirs to impound water. The insatiable demands of an increasing population require ever more water for domestic use, whether from wells or the river. Expanding irrigation schemes and nascent industries have drawn off increasing amounts of water. Nature is not impervious to these egregious intrusions.

The fluctuations of the Nile flood during the twentieth century, though extraordinary in extent, were not new in the history of Nile flows. Because the timing of the Nile's annual rise and fall was as predictable as the sun, the moon, and the stars, the rulers and the ruled of Egypt have always desperately sought to forecast its volume. Their efforts were always unsuccessful, but five thousand years of failure did not deter twentieth-century British and Egyptian hydrologists from seeking the answer through more advanced instrumentation, more accurate measurements, and more sophisticated analysis.

In 1882 the British occupied Egypt in order to secure the Suez Canal, the strategic link to their vast Oriental empire. Government by the British was more administrative than exploitative, but they too were totally reliant on Egypt's agricultural productivity, which depended on the Nile. At the beginning of the nineteenth century, Muhammad Ali, the Ottoman viceroy of Egypt, had introduced year-round irrigation, from which he and the country prospered beyond all expectations. By the end of the century, however, the irrigation infrastructure required extensive renovation that the British consul-general Sir Evelyn Baring, Lord Cromer, argued could be achieved only through scientific administration by professional British officers, who would rid the state of Turkish-Egyptian financial corruption and devise long-term techniques to regulate the Nile's waters. To accomplish Egypt's regeneration, Lord Cromer brought Sir Colin Scott-Moncrieff and other British hydrologists from India. By 1902 this intrepid band of British engineers had built a network of barrages and canals, culminating in the dam above Elephantine Island at Aswan, to control the flow of the Nile for diversion schemes downstream. This was an astonishing achievement, on which the prosperity of Egypt still depends, yet concern over how to predict the river's volume from year to year persisted.

Before and after World War I the Egyptian Ministry of Public Works recruited new men from Oxford who were interested in how mathematics, statistics, and probability theory could be applied to the Nile and the search for a pattern by which to forecast the size of its floods. The most formidable and relentless hunter in this quest was Harold Edwin Hurst. A modest mathematician and physicist, Hurst joined the Egyptian survey department in 1906. That same year its director, Sir Henry Lyons, an engineer from the Royal Military Academy at Woolwich who had personally recruited Hurst, published *The Physiography of the River Nile and Its Basin,* the most comprehensive account then available of Nile hydrology. The skill of Hurst at calculations and equations attracted the attention of his superiors, and by 1915 he had been appointed director-general of the physical department of the Egyptian Ministry of Public Works.

In 1921 Hurst presented his first analysis of the Nile's periodicity. Although he never presumed to predict its volume, he was able to demonstrate that the flow of the Nile did not jump from one extreme to another year by year, rising and falling like a yo-yo, but in fact ran in a definite pattern with a cycle of fifty to a hundred years. This periodicity of volume, which came to be known as the Hurst phenomenon, convinced both Hurst and the Egyptians that the waters of the Nile could be stored in reservoirs during periods of high flow for use in the period of low water that inevitably would follow.[14]

After half a century of studying Nile flows and their periodicity, Hurst proposed such a storage scheme—a series of dams throughout the Nile basin, most importantly in the highlands of the Lake Plateau, that would level the differences between high and low floods, eliminating the effects of the periodic cycle. By the middle of the twentieth century, however, Gamal Abdel Nasser, Egypt's new president, was determined to see the Nile conserved in his country, not elsewhere, through the construction of one grand structure—the Aswan High Dam. This was not at all the kind of well-planned storage scheme that Hurst had in mind, and its effects have been quite different, but during his final years in Egypt he nevertheless calculated the volume of water necessary to impound behind the great dam. The dam did what Nasser wanted: end Egyptian dependence on the Africans upstream who possessed but did not control the Nile waters.[15]

Hurst's analysis was determined more by the recorded past than by the unpredictable future. Many believed, particularly in Egypt, that the Nile was now in the hands of the engineers, when in fact nature is still in command. Volcanic eruptions, El Niño, solar flares, cyclical tides, and differences in patterns of rainfall in the two distinctive basins of the White and the Blue Niles have demonstrated that the Aswan High Dam may have ameliorated the effects of the Hurst phenomenon but has certainly not eliminated it. Hurst died in 1978, just before the onset of the lowest Nile flows in history. The Nile's greatest failure now threatened the very integrity of the vast reservoir behind the dam at Aswan designed to banish periodicity.

2 *The Lake Plateau*

The springs of the Nile flow between the two mountains, Crophi and Mophi,
and these springs are bottomless, half the water flows to Egypt and the north,
the other half toward Ethiopia and the south.
—*Herodotus,* The Histories

In 1935, Dr. Burkhart Waldecker fled the persecution of the Jews in Nazi Germany and sought sanctuary at the Musée Léopold II in Elizabethville, now Lubumbashi, in the Belgian Congo. In return for asylum he lectured, also finding time to pursue his passion, the ultimate source of the Nile. Two years later Waldecker stumbled on a spring atop a hill known as Mount Kikizi, 6,724 feet above sea level and 4,202 miles upriver from the Mediterranean. The Africans, the Rukwabagara people of Burundi, did not know what to make of Dr. Waldecker; they described him as "a mysterious man like no other European we have known for he has no porters, scratches himself, and has only two canteens." In the gully below the spring through which a stream called Kasumo flowed downhill, Waldecker scrawled in his best academic Latin on the rock wall: CAPUT NILI MERIDIANISSIMUM, the southernmost source of the Nile.[1]

From the spring atop Kikizi the waters flow down the Kasumo River northward to the Mukusenyi River. These currents are fed by innumerable streams until they reach the Ruvyironza River. The Ruvyironza winds for thirty miles through the exquisite green hills of Africa described by Hemingway until it meets with the Ruvubu River, which rises in the highlands of northwest Burundi. The Ruvubu is an ample river, free

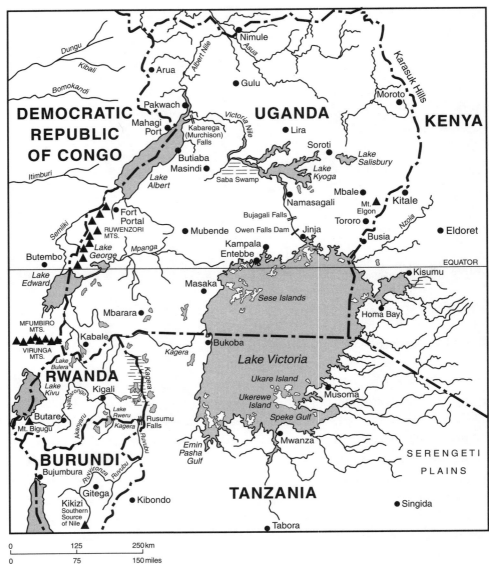

The Lake Plateau

of aquatic plants, flowing steadily north and east to its confluence with the Nyaba-rongo River.

But the southernmost source of the Nile on Mount Kikizi is not the source farthest from the Mediterranean. Northwest of Kikizi stands another peak, Mount Bigugu, which is part of the Congo-Nile watershed east of Lake Kivu. Below its summit at 9,691 feet springs another small stream, the Lubyero, which flows down the mountain to meet with the Lukarara River. The beginning of the source on Bigugu lies 4,238 river miles from the Mediterranean, which makes it 36 miles longer than the spring memorialized by Waldecker at the top of Kikizi. Such distinctions are more amusing than critical, for the difference is so slight in the course of the world's longest river as to be all but meaningless. The streams from the two springs, the ultimate sources of the Nile, come together when the Lukarara River, flowing east from Mount Bigugu, joins the Nyabarongo flowing north from Kikizi.[2]

The confluence of the Nyabarongo and the Ruvubu forms the Kagera River, which tumbles vigorously eastward for a short distance before it pours over the Rusumu Falls. After the fall the Kagera turns northward along the fault line marking the boundary between Tanzania and Rwanda, passing through swampy lakes before abruptly angling eastward where its placid surface is broken by the rapids at Kyansore Island. Kyansore, the traditional home of the sacred drums of the Banyankole people, marks the last cataract between the high country to the west and the vast inland basin of Lake Victoria to the east. After the cataract the Kagera finishes its journey of 250 miles and empties into Lake Victoria on its western shore.

Neither of the mountains that the Nile springs from, Kikizi and Bigugu, has a dramatic watershed. They are otherwise undistinguished hills among many in this region, a place of jagged topography with thousands of springs and streams that form complex drainage patterns. If the Nile requires a distinctive watershed, the Virunga Mountains, a range of volcanoes known in Uganda as the Mfumbiro, "the mountains that cook," are the most visible. They are eight sentinels that stand more than 10,000 feet tall on the parapets of the watershed between the basins of the Congo and the Nile. Six of the volcanoes are extinct, and among these are the highest of the peaks, Mount Karisimbi, which dominates the others at 14,787 feet, and Mount Mgahinga, the home of the mountain gorilla. In the remaining craters of the two live volcanoes, Mount Nyirangongo and Mount Nyamulagira at the western end of the chain, the magma bubbles at fifteen hundred degrees Fahrenheit. At 9:30 A.M. on 17 January 2002 the lava burst from the flanks of Nyirangongo to engulf the city of Goma below, driving thousands of Africans into the countryside. The Virunga Mountains rose up

Rusumu Falls on the Kagera River

more than a million years ago during the tectonic dispersal of the African continent, creating a formidable dam fifty miles across the deep trench of the western Rift Valley. Rising as a bulwark against the south Atlantic monsoon, the Virunga volcanoes receive 150 inches of rainfall a year. On their southern slopes the water flows down into Lakes Kivu and Tanganyika, and thence westward into the Congo and eventually the Atlantic; on the northern slopes it descends in torrents to Lake Edward at the bottom of the western Rift and on to the Mediterranean Sea.

The Rift Valley is one of Africa's most dramatic features. Far in the geologic past the continent was rent by the movement of the earth's crust as Asia separated from Africa some thirty million years ago, creating a deep ditch along its spine from south to north. The present configuration of the Rift was established only a million years ago, during the Pleistocene epoch, and begins in the Mozambique Channel. The great trough snakes up the valley of the Zambezi River to Lake Malawi, where it bifurcates. The eastern branch, known as the Great Rift, runs north through the highlands of Kenya and Ethiopia to the Red Sea, up the Gulf of Aqaba to the Dead Sea and the Jordan River, disappearing into Mount Hebron, the southern bastion of the mountains of Lebanon. The western Rift slices north through Lakes Tanganyika, Kivu, Edward, and Albert, ending in the Sudd, the swamps of the Nile. All the lakes of central and eastern Africa, except Kyoga and Victoria, lie at the bottom of these two trenches, confined by their imposing escarpments thrust upward when the valley floor sank.

The clouds of the south Atlantic monsoon collide with the escarpment of the western Rift, where they release the water that falls as rain and then flows northward down the Nile. The water that pours off the northern slopes of the Virunga Mountains is collected in Lake Edward, straddling the Congo-Uganda border at the bottom of the Rift. Lake Edward is sometimes called the Bird Lake, so named for its permanent residents in their thousands—pelicans, flamingoes, egrets, and gulls—and its migrating tourists, the Nile geese. All are attracted by the blue-green waters that make this lake one of the most beautiful in the world. Its splendor at the end of the day inspired the great British hydrologist Sir William Garstin to compose a dramatic description in his official government report of 1904: "Sometimes at sunset when the sun dips behind these mountains the peaks stand out in deep purple masses against a sky flaming crimson and orange, and again blending into tints of rose and salmon colour."[3]

The outlet from Lake Edward, at its northern end, is the Semliki River. It flows

Lake Edward, the Bird Lake

The Semliki River in the western Rift Valley, looking toward the Democratic Republic of the Congo

northward down the Rift, at the foot of the towering Ruwenzori range, forming the link between the Virunga Mountains of equatorial Africa and the Nile. The Semliki plunges over rocks and rapids as it falls a thousand feet in one hundred miles through a deep, narrow valley lined with luxuriant trees and plants. It is a violent river that empties into a dense papyrus swamp at the southern shore of Lake Albert, which lies nestled at the bottom of the western Rift.

The Ruwenzori range is Africa in all its immensity, grandeur, and romance. The ancient Greeks and Arabs called these the Mountains of the Moon, for their snowy peaks and dense, almost constant cloud cover. The existence of snow-capped mountains in the interior of Africa was common folklore among the cosmopolitan Greek merchants on the East African coast two thousand years ago. The Greek geographer Claudius Ptolemaeus, known as Ptolemy, claimed in 140 C.E. that the great Nile flowed from fountains in the *Lunae Montes,* the Mountains of the Moon, rather than the twin peaks of Crophi and Mophi, south of Aswan, as Herodotus had argued. But no European laid eyes on the Mountains of the Moon for another two thousand years, until the age of the imperial explorers in the nineteenth century.

In 1888 a medical officer with Henry Morton Stanley's third expedition to Africa, Thomas Heazle Parke, said that he "distinctly saw *snow* on the top of a huge mountain." Stanley "pooh-poohed the idea," considering it ridiculous that equatorial peaks might be covered with snow. Even his Zanzibari porters "tried to persuade us that the white covering which decorated the mountains was salt." During his march to the East African coast a year later, Stanley and the survivors of his expedition were passing through the Toro kingdom in the foothills of the Mountains of the Moon in western Uganda. On 2 April 1889 the clouds parted long enough to present Stanley with a grand finale for his last African expedition. Rising into the sky before him was "one great chain of snow capped peaks extending one over another into the far distance," a member of the party wrote in his diary. "It was a beautiful sight. The great expanse of snows shining in the sun right in the middle of central tropical Africa. As the sun sank, it turned the snow a rosy colour."[4]

Overwhelmed by this Wagnerian drama, Stanley inquired of the local Ankole people the name of these mountains. They were called the Ruwenzori, "the place whence the rain comes." In retreat on a disastrous expedition, Stanley readily accepted the Ankole name, which he translated as Rain-Maker, rather than following the fashionable Victorian custom of naming African lands, lakes, and rivers after European aristocracy. As the most controversial of journalists and the most famous African explorer of the nineteenth century, Stanley conveniently ignored Parke's observation of the previous year and claimed that he was the first to discover the Mountains of the Moon.

To the people who live high on the misty slopes of the Ruwenzori, they are known as *Gamalga gafumba biri,* "the great leaf in which the clouds are boiled," a more sublime description than Rain-Maker. The mountains rise through dense forests and remote alpine meadows, soaring into swirling mists on icy crags, glaciers, and snow-capped peaks on the equator. They stretch for only eighty miles along the eastern escarpment of the western Rift, but they are unique. They are the only mountains in eastern and central Africa that are not volcanic. They are home to six distinct environmental zones, more than any other mountain range in Africa. In the Ruwenzori elephants wander at 5,000 feet, lions prowl near 8,000, and the leopard is found at 15,000 feet, the snowline on the equator. Their summits rise to 16,000 feet, and their slopes are obscured three hundred days of the year by the rains from the south Atlantic that annually dump more than two hundred inches of water on their flanks. Here in the Ruwenzori earthworms grow to three feet long, canaries reach fifteen feet from peak to end of tail, and flowers and trees are giants in a land of cliffs. The streams that disappear over the sheer precipices are blown to mist by the winds of the Mountains of the Moon.

When the waters from the Virunga and the Ruwenzori reach Lake Albert, the northernmost lake in the western Rift, they merge with those from the Kagera basin and Lake Victoria from the east. The Africans had sensibly called Lake Albert the Luta Nzigé, "the brightness of the lake that kills the locusts," in commemoration of the drowning of those voracious insects as they attempted to cross the waters of the Rift. In 1864 a rich and remarkable Victorian, Sir Samuel White Baker, with his beautiful Hungarian wife, Florence, reached the shores of the lake and in an effusive outburst of patriotism named it for Prince Albert, Queen Victoria's beloved, deceased consort. Since independence, the Africans have understandably renamed a number of lakes and falls as a way of reclaiming their heritage. Lake Albert was one of them. In a display of exuberance Mobutu Sese Seko, the president of Zaire from 1965 to 1997, named the lake for himself, although it has yet to appear on the maps of Uganda, the Democratic Republic of the Congo, or the other states of the Nile basin.

Lake Albert, one hundred miles long and about twenty miles wide, is only 160 feet deep, a shallow lake whose surface is swept by the winds blowing down the tunnel of the Rift, producing tropical squalls that whip the surface into treacherous waves. Its narrow shores, constricted by the heights of the escarpments in the Congo to the west and in Uganda to the east, cannot accommodate any substantial population. Lake Albert has not been a significant factor in the history of the African peoples who have occupied the Lake Plateau, for they were cultivators and herdsmen, attracted more by the fertile fields above the Rift than the waters of the lake at its bottom. On its limited shores there are those who extract salt, others who fish, a few who cultivate the land below the escarpment. The dilapidated port of Butiaba is the only significant town that commands the lake. Twenty-five miles north of its rotting piers Lake Albert receives the water that arrives from the Kagera basin and Lake Victoria.

Lake Victoria, the Victoria Nyanza, is the second largest body of freshwater in the world, a shallow saucer only 260 feet deep but with a vast surface area of nearly 27,000 square miles. It rests on the Lake Plateau between the eastern and western Rift valleys, two thousand feet above their lakes and four thousand feet higher than the Mediterranean Sea. The shoreline of Lake Albert is as straight as the fault of the Rift. The coastline of Lake Victoria rambles around its sprawling waters in numerous bays. Clusters of fertile islands of idyllic beauty dot the surface—the Sesse Islands in the northwest, the Buvuma archipelago in the north, and the Ukerewe isles in the southeast. In sun-

Lake Albert at the bottom of the western Rift Valley

light the expanse of Lake Victoria sparkles a brilliant blue that deepens when the rays of the equatorial African sun break through the dark thunderclouds that frequent the lake. Like the shallow waters of Lake Albert, those of Victoria are lashed into dangerous turbulence from squalls. Waterspouts occasionally descend with destructive force.

In the middle of Lake Victoria on its western shore, the headwaters of the Nile arrive from the Kagera River. The Kagera has collected the waters from Waldecker's spring on the hill of Kikizi and those from the slopes of Mount Bigugu and all the thousands of streams in its catchment basin in Burundi, Rwanda, and Uganda. The volume is great; the loss is enormous. After the drop at Rusumu Falls, the Kagera passes through swamps and meanders through its delta at Lake Victoria, in the process surrendering 75 percent of its water to evaporation on the way to the lake. It is the largest river from the basin of Burundi and Rwanda, but its contribution is insignificant, only 20 percent of the waters of Lake Victoria. There are many other minor rivers and streams that flow into the lake from the south and east around its perimeter, which add another unimpressive 20 percent. The vast surface of Lake Victoria, shimmering in the heat of the equator at four thousand feet above sea level, lying between the Rift valleys and fed by the monsoons of the south Atlantic and the Indian Ocean, has its own discrete climate from that of the highlands that surround it. The average water temperature is seventy-nine degrees Fahrenheit, the same as the swimming pools at the fashionable hotels in Kampala, Khartoum, and Cairo. Heat, moisture, and wind combine to form billowing clouds over the lake, producing showers and violent thunderstorms that account for the other 60 percent of the water of Lake Victoria.[5]

The outlet from Lake Victoria is situated on its northern shore at Jinja, the beginning of the river known as the Victoria Nile. John Hanning Speke in 1862 became the first European to discover the spot, watching the water drop sixteen feet from the lake into three separate channels to begin its northward course, and he proclaimed this the true source of the Nile. The rapids were a modest geological formation that Speke named Ripon Falls, in honor of George Frederick Samuel Robinson, the first marquis of Ripon, president of the Royal Geographical Society, and in time the viceroy of India. Speke was later castigated by his critics for prostituting the names of distinguished Victorians, including the queen, after lakes and rivers in a barbarous land, but they most certainly would not have been amused if he had named the source of the Nile after Mutesa, the ruler of Buganda who, in his unquestioned authority over the falls, had allowed Speke passage and made possible his discovery. Like Waldecker, today Speke is remembered only by a plaque at the site of his discovery bearing an ambiguous description—"John Hanning Speke on 28th July 1862 FIRST DISCOVERED THIS SOURCE OF THE NILE"—and an obelisk in London's Hyde Park with the inscrutable inscription "Speke, Victoria Nyanza and the Nile 1864." Everyone was too polite to claim that this was *the* source of the Nile, so they concealed their doubts through careful wording.

Ripon Falls has been submerged since 1954, when the Owen Falls Dam was constructed across the Victoria Nile just below the lake's outlet. From the dam the river flows in a northwesterly direction, tumbling over a series of rapids between high wooded cliffs to the town of Namasagali. From there the river proceeds broad and navigable until it gradually widens into the labyrinth of Lake Kyoga. This body of water is more swamp than lake. It has a number of shallow arms running east and west, but its open water is surrounded by marshy inlets and papyrus swamps that infiltrate the low-lying land among the undulating country around it. Some of the passages are navigable; most are not. The profusion of aquatic plants and the recent appearance of the infamous water hyacinth have choked the channels, forming an alliance with evaporation at the equator that consumes more than half the rainfall that pours into the thousand square miles of its basin to fill the streams and rivers to the south and the slopes of Mount Elgon to the east.

The navigable Nile passes along the western edge of Lake Kyoga to Masindi Port and sixty miles downriver turns to the west through the Karuma rapids, after which its passage is stately between high cliffs and over and around rocks, reefs, and islands. On either bank the forests and parklands of the Lake Plateau fall away from the cliffs as the gradient descends and the channel narrows, until the Victoria Nile disappears over the Rift at Kabarega Falls, formerly known as Murchison Falls. As the river approaches the brink, it is compressed into a cleft in the rock wall of the escarpment less than 20 feet wide and plunges 140 feet to the valley floor. The rock walls rising above the spray are festooned with luxuriant vegetation and drenched by the mist and a thunderous roar. In the pools and eddies below, neither the hippopotamus nor the crocodile is seen. Even the ubiquitous birds of Africa are absent. In the sunlight a rainbow spans the chasm and illuminates thousands of sparklers from the water quivering on the sheen of dark green gneiss, carbon-colored mica, and white crystalline quartz.

Ripon Falls, the outlet of Lake Victoria, in 1920 (Photograph, Underwood and Underwood, London)

At the bottom of the Rift the current is sluggish and flows around depositions of silt and sandbanks, expanding into a marshy delta with many channels that are inhabited by birds, crocodiles, and hippopotamuses. This delta is where the Victoria Nile enters Lake Albert, a scene that Garstin again waxed eloquent in describing: "As the sun sets the nearest hills become a deep purple, whilst the higher ranges are bathed in a rose-pink glow. The water is full of opalescent tine and reflects each one of the many hues of the sky. Lines of feathery papyrus in dark green borders frame the broad river channel, and beyond the calm lake stretches a deep shade line reflecting the distant ranges. As the sun sinks behind the mountains the rosy tints of the western sky deepen into flame, while the outlines of the hills are marked in indigo in a strong and gorgeous contrast."[6]

This vision is not reflected on the surface of Lake Albert. The Victoria Nile flows into the lake at its northern end and, almost indecisively, promptly flows right back out again as the Albert Nile. It is not an auspicious beginning. The water is green and stinks from algae. Beyond the lake the river is a morass of decaying aquatic vegetation. Swamps and lagoons obscure the banks. The river expands to fill the valley, but its surface is afloat with ambatch, papyrus, and the ubiquitous water hyacinth. Its bottom is mud. On the horizon the escarpments of the Rift recede into the Sokare Hills to the west and the Didinga and Imatong Mountains to the east. The Lake Plateau comes to an end as the Albert Nile flows into the southern Sudan, which has its own history and hydrology distinct yet not divorced from the lakes and land of equatorial Africa.

Kabarega Falls, known to the Victorians as Murchison Falls, drops 140 feet into the western Rift Valley and Lake Albert through a chasm 18 feet wide (Photograph © Kazuyoshi Nomachi/Pacific Press Service)

The history of the Lake Plateau has been dependent more on the research of linguists and historians of oral traditions than the excavations of archaeologists. Deprived of ruins, which in the lower Nile are preserved by Saharan desiccation, archaeologists on the Lake Plateau have only those remains eroded by the rains of equatorial Africa. There are no written records, no hieroglyphs, and no accounts from travelers. When Pharaoh Djur of the First Dynasty went up the Nile into Nubia in 2900 B.C.E., the Cushitic peoples were migrating down the Rift Valley from the Ethiopian highlands. They were different from the indigenous people of the Lake Plateau, the Khoisan-speaking hunters and gatherers commonly known as the Bushmen. The migrants spoke a Cushitic language that belongs to the greater Afro-Asiatic family and is related to those of their contemporaries in dynastic Egypt, the Berbers in northern Africa and the Semitic speakers, Arabs and Hebrews, of the Middle East. The Cushites were a pastoral people who raised cattle, sheep, and goats and occasionally cultivated with little enthusiasm.

Unlike most of Egypt beyond the narrow cultivable banks of the Nile, the expansive and fertile parklands of the Lake Plateau between the Rifts are well watered, and there the indigenous Bushmen and the Cushitic emigrants had space. Their populations were small, and plentiful land enabled them to live peacefully in a symbiotic relationship. Over the course of the first millennium B.C.E., they were joined on the highlands between the lakes by a new people, the Bantu.

The Bantu came from the plateau on the border between Cameroon and Nigeria, southeast of the Benue River, during the five centuries of exceptionally high and "joyful" floods in Egypt, from 945 to 525 B.C.E. Like the Cushites, who had come from the north, they brought with them from the west a different language, different culture, and different crops. They spoke languages known today as Bantu that are related by common vocabulary and grammar to those of eastern, central, and southern Africa. The Bantu who came to occupy the Lake Plateau had, quite sensibly, wandered eastward along the northern savanna fringe of the tropical rain forest of the Congo to the lakes of equatorial Africa. They were farmers whose social and political organizations were limited to the homestead and the village. Their numbers were not great. They became settlers in a newfound fertile land with abundant rainfall. On the Lake Plateau their history has been more a mosaic through time than the detailed diorama of dynastic Egypt.[7]

The local hunters and gatherers, the Bushmen, required greater space than could be accommodated by Bantu cultivators, and over the centuries they quietly disappeared in search of more favorable hunting grounds in central and southern Africa.

The pastoral Cushites were neither as mobile nor as willing to move as were the Bushmen. They were few and insecure. Their political organization in clans was not in competition with the sedentary farmers of the Bantu homestead and village. There was undoubtedly tension between the two, but an abundance of land facilitated the evolution of a peaceful relationship. The Bantu and the Cushites exchanged goods, Bantu crops in return for Cushitic products from animal husbandry. The language of trade, however, was that of the settlers, whose increasing numbers in time resulted in the adoption of the Bantu languages by their pastoral neighbors, in an evolving process of linguistic accommodation and cultural assimilation.

The Bantu were farmers who also fished. They possessed iron technology and were dependent on the rain from the south Atlantic to grow their yams, beans, and sorghum. These crops rapidly exhaust the soil, which must therefore lie fallow to wait for regeneration or be abandoned in favor of new land. Not surprisingly, the Bantu preferred to move on from their homeland in the Benue Plateau rather than await the revival of the soil by means and time they knew not. Their numbers were modest, and the African continent was large. Their methods of agriculture produced a pattern of shifting cultivation that has been one of the principal explanations for the extensive migrations of the Bantu over the past two thousand years.

The arrival of the Bantu on the Lake Plateau has been characterized by insouciant academics as the moment when "the Bantu met the banana." The banana is indigenous to Southeast Asia and appeared in eastern Africa long before Herodotus described the source of the Nile in 460 B.C.E. It came via the ancient trade routes that extended from Indonesia, Malaysia, and India. From the East African coast it may have traveled up the Zambezi and along the coast, but more likely came down the Rift from Ethiopia to the Lake Plateau. The first written description of the banana in Africa comes from a Greek merchant in Adulis in 525 C.E., long after it had passed into the interior. Adulis was the ancient trading entrepôt on the Red Sea for the kingdom of Aksum in the Ethiopian highlands. It is now covered by sand, but only a few miles from the modern port of Massawa in Eritrea the site remains the window on the sea for landlocked Ethiopians.

The banana quickly became the principal foodstuff on the Lake Plateau, for it was ideally suited to the climate. Unlike the yams, beans, and sorghum brought by the Bantu from West Africa, banana cultivation requires little labor for clearing land, planting, or weeding. It produces a yield ten times greater than the savanna crops from West Africa. It is more nutritious and simpler to prepare than yams. After the harvest its rotting hulks are left to restore the soils of the Lake Plateau as a fertilizer that the rains from the south Atlantic do not provide. One variety of the banana was used as a vegetable and for baking, grinding into flour, and brewing into beer. The banana flourished on the Lake Plateau, replacing yams and sorghum as the staple crop. With a secure supply of food, the Bantu began to settle down rather than move, and their population increased from one season to the next and one generation to another. They became farmers committed to the land, which encouraged greater social organization around a permanent village. The village became a local political unit and then a kingdom, leading eventually to state building by those with the necessary acumen, leadership, and leisure.[8]

Sometime roughly a thousand years ago another new group appeared on the Lake Plateau, the Cwezi. They arrived from the north, bringing cattle, and then vanished, leaving behind ruins and legends. They appear in the traditions as harbingers of change, like other pastoral emigrants, the Hima and the Luo, who followed in subsequent centuries. They are remembered in Bantu folklore and myth as revered mediums whose authority stemmed from their religious powers. As the Bantu peoples became farmers and created permanent settlements their traditional gods apparently no longer provided satisfactory answers, but the leaders of the Cwezi clans offered spiritual solutions that were much appreciated and remembered. Among the ruins left by the Cwezi are extensive concentric earthworks at Bigo, overlooking the Katonga River, that are twelve feet deep and six miles long. There is no definitive explanation for the purpose of these ditched embankments. Similar but more modest remains attributed to the Cwezi are found at Kasonbo, Munsa, and Kibengo on the southern shores of Lake Albert. Whatever their purpose, the Cwezi symbolized the end of the Bantu migration and the evolution of more centralized political organization, without which their monuments could not have been constructed. By the end of the fifteenth century the Cwezi had disappeared into legend, but on the Lake Plateau they are remembered as real and spiritual intermediaries between the Bantu past and their impending confrontation in the sixteenth century with the latest pastoral emigrants from the north, the Hima and the Luo.

The appearance of the Hima in the southern hills and the Luo on the parklands in the north changed the political configuration of the Lake Plateau dramatically and permanently. The Hima belonged to the Tutsi ethnic group and spoke a Cushitic language. They drifted down the Rift from southern Ethiopia, seeking new pastures for their cattle, and found their way to the Lake Plateau before the sixteenth century. They were few in number, hundreds not thousands, but they were tall in physique and arrogant in bearing, setting them apart from the Bantu cultivators on the Lake Plateau.

Later European visitors were struck by the physical distinction of the Tutsi, describing "their gigantic structure, their high foreheads, the curve of their nostrils, and their fine oval faces," and finding in it evidence of the "noble traits" of a ruling class. A similar observation contrasted them with the local Bantu farmers, the Hutu people, and spoke of the locals as "ungainly figures . . . who patiently bow themselves in abject bondage to the later arrived yet ruling race, the Tutsi." These physical differences have been used for hundreds of years as justification for the imposition of Tutsi authority over the Hutu.[9]

The Tutsi were organized into clans, each one with firm allegiance to its ancestral founder and his descendants. There was no comparable structure among the Bantu households and villages on the Lake Plateau. The leaders of the Hima clans of the Tutsi and their rebellious sons asserted their authority from the summit of many thousand hills in the region, and the clans with their few but loyal followers established commercial relations with the Hutu owners of the land. In return for the recognition of their authority, the Tutsi accepted the economic and social environment of the Bantu in the southern Lake Plateau, trading milk and meat for beans and bananas, and losing their Cushitic language to that of the Bantu. Although they were the minority—roughly 15 percent of the population—the social and political organization of the Tutsi, along with their imposing physiques and wealth in cattle, enabled them to assert their dominance over the local Hutu. But there was most surely a greater intermingling of rulers and subjects than either will admit today.

During the sixteenth century in Rwanda and the seventeenth in Burundi a single clan became an aristocracy and its chief became king, the *mwami,* who ruled over two very compact states—each one smaller than a modern-day county of California. The land around the southern source of the Nile was a peaceful panorama of green hills, fertile valleys, and deep blue lakes surrounded by the peaks of the Virunga volcanoes. The first Europeans who came into this country at the end of the nineteenth century were enchanted by its sublime beauty, describing it as the Switzerland of Africa. The languid charm of this bucolic scene, however, obscured the deep ethnic cleavage between the small minority of Tutsi, the Hima rulers, and the vast majority of the Hutu, their Bantu subjects.

In Rwanda the transformation from clan to state is attributed to Ruganzu Bwimba, a Tutsi who, according to the traditions, established a petty principality in the sixteenth century near Kigale, the present capital of the republic of Rwanda. The origin of the kingdom of Rwanda, however, was the work of the mwami Ruganzu Ndori (circa 1600–1624) in the seventeenth century. Like the great chieftains of highland Scottish clans, he sought to assert his authority over rivals on their hills and the lowlanders in the valleys. In difficult and circumscribed terrain, it took another two hundred years for Rwanda to evolve from clan to principality to kingdom through conquest, political organization, and control of the economy. The last independent Tutsi chiefs surrendered to Mwami Mutara Rwogera in 1852, and the kingdom was centralized during the reign of Mwami Kigeri Rwabugiri (1860–1895). Once intimidated by the mwami and incorporated into the state, the Tutsi chieftains on the summits of a thousand hills became the ideal instruments of the monarchy for ruling the Hutu cultivators. The last of the free Hutu communities on the Uganda frontier succumbed to Mwami Yuli Musinga (1896–1931) in the 1920s. The Hutu farmers became peasants who supported the Tutsi aristocracy, political subjects of the mwami and economic serfs of their Tutsi overlords in the inequitable transfer of wealth between those with cattle and those with crops.

South of the Akanyaru River, the kingdom of Burundi followed a similar pattern roughly a century later than Rwanda. Under the leadership of its founder Ntare Rushatsi (circa 1657–1705), Burundi evolved from a principality to a small kingdom through conquest, political organization, and the resources from the land—the cattle of the Tutsi clans and the crops from their Hutu subjects. The nineteenth-century mwami of Burundi Ntare Rugaamba (circa 1795–1852) consolidated his kingdom by the spear and asserted his authority over not only his thousand hills but the eastern savanna of Tanzania.

None of these kings at the end of the nineteenth century had any knowledge of where their waters flowed except that they went north to an end they knew not. Nowadays their successors at the southernmost sources of the Nile realize that Rwanda and Burundi are upstream riparians and members of the larger whole of the basin, residing at the beginnings of a resource upon which millions downstream are dependent. Following modern independence, however, when the Tutsi monarchies were dissolved in Rwanda, in 1961, and Burundi, in 1966, ancient ethnic antagonisms boiled over. In recent decades these green hills have been covered in blood and defiled by the ferocity of ethnic cleansing between Tutsi and Hutu. The bloodletting and genocide have immobilized the development of the Kagera basin.

Around the time the Tutsi began state building in the south during the sixteenth century, the Luo people left their homeland in the southern Sudan and crossed the Victoria Nile with their cattle to settle among the Bantu of the northern Lake Plateau. Like the Tutsi, the Luo were primarily interested in grazing land for their herds, and there was ample pasturage and water on the highlands above the equatorial lakes. They settled among the Bantu farmers of the Lake Plateau, who exchanged crops for milk, meat, and manure from their cattle. Like the Tutsi the Luo were convinced that pasture could best be acquired through political rather than religious authority, and they possessed institutions for asserting this control that the Bantu did not. The leaders of certain clans held accepted and unchallenged prestige, giving them the means to impose centralized rule over a more egalitarian and dispersed majority through accommodation rather than conquest. These ruling clans of the Luo came to be known collectively as the Bito.

The Luo speak a Sudanic language of the larger Nilo-Saharan lingusitic family that in the Nile Valley is squeezed between the Afro-Asiatic languages—dynastic Egyptian, Arabic, Hebrew, and Cushitic—and the Bantu languages of the south that belong to the Niger-Congo peoples. The Luo language is related to that of the Nubians of Kush and their Christian kingdoms south of Aswan. They are also the linguistic cousins of the Nilotic Dinka and Nuer in the southern Sudan and the Maasai of Kenya and Tanzania. Their traditions are many; their records are few. Their origins, according to legend, are in the vicinity of Rumbek, a contemporary administrative center in the Bahr al-Ghazal of the southern Sudan. From this cradle land some of the Luo at the end of the fifteenth century began to move. Others stayed home. The intricate but massive traditions of their wanderings had no Homer, but the themes are not dissimilar to an African odyssey.

Family disputes among brothers who aspired to the leadership of the clan resulted in its dispersal. Such family quarrels, intensely personal, are often a transparent disguise for the struggle for control of wealth—cattle, pasture, water, women—and, of course, sibling rivalry. At the end of the fifteenth century two dissident brothers, Nyikango and Dimo, from the principal clan of the Luo, went north from Rumbek. They passed west of the swamps of the Nile through the plains of the Bahr al-Ghazal to Wipac on the northern shore of Lake No, where the Nile tributaries from the Congo-Nile watershed meet the Bahr al-Jabal from the equatorial lakes and the beginning of the White Nile. Wipac is still remembered as the place of the parting of the clans.

At Wipac the brothers quarreled. Nyikango remained and founded the Shilluk kingdom at Fashoda on the White Nile. Dimo returned to Rumbek and the vast plains of the Bahr al-Ghazal. A younger brother, Gilo, also fell out with Nyikango and went east, where there were more fraternal disputes. Gilo went south, leaving behind those Luo who are today the Anuak people in the salient at the base of the Ethiopian escarpment. At Pubungu on the Bahr al-Jabal, north of Lake Albert, the remaining brothers once again decided to go their separate ways. One brother went east to settle on the sparsely inhabited eastern shores of Lake Victoria in Kenya. Gilo went south across the Victoria Nile, to the northern Lake Plateau, where he changed the structure of Bantu society forever. The peregrinations of these legendary leaders have produced the mythical heroes of the Luo people.

The Luo who settled on the Lake Plateau with their cattle were small in number, perhaps several thousand. The Bantu accepted the authority of the Bito clan leaders, and the Luo people became assimilated into the Bantu majority's speech and customs. Their cattle became the symbol of wealth, and the Bantu banana became the staple of the state. In the seventeenth century the clan ruler, the *mukama,* of Bunyoro-Kitara became a strong feudal king with a well-established state between Lake Albert and Lake Victoria. Like the Tutsi kingdoms in Rwanda and Burundi to the south, Bunyoro was surrounded by troublesome tributary kingdoms, in Buddu, Bugungu, Bwera, Busoga, and Buganda. The mukama of Bunyoro sought to gain control over these numerous clan leaders, who for their part were determined to defend their autonomy, leading to a frustrating struggle for power through the seventeenth and eighteenth centuries.

After two centuries of expansion and endless rivalries between the leaders of clans, powerful personalities appeared in the nineteenth century to transform the political structure from a loose confederacy of autonomous tributaries of a feudal king into centralized states. In the northern part of the Lake Plateau these leaders were Kabarega (1870–1895), mukama of Bunyoro-Kitara, and Mukabya Mutesa (1856–1884), *kabaka* of Buganda. The success of these kings in the nineteenth century and not before has produced abundant and ambiguous explanations. They were concerned with politics and culture and most of all the acceptance of their authority, not with controlling the waters of the Nile. They protected those who fished in the river or paddled Bugandan war canoes on Lake Victoria, but these gestures were more symbols of authority than any concern about the Nile.

Kabarega, following another Luo fraternal dispute—this one with his eldest brother, Kabigumire—secured the throne as mukama of Bunyoro in 1870. Kabarega was determined to transform the authority of the mukama into a centralized monarchy like those of Rwabugiri in Rwanda and Rugaamba in Burundi. His army ruthlessly subdued hostile tributaries in Busoga, Busongora, Bukonjo, Bwamba, Bubiri, Bulega, Bugungu, Chope, and Toro, but it could not prevail against the powerful kingdom of Buganda. In the seventeenth century Buganda, situated on the shores of Lake Victoria, had been a petty principality of Bunyoro-Kitara, but during the next two centuries its kabakas sought, like all the other vassals, to expand their authority whenever the mukama of Bunyoro was preoccupied with more immediate concerns.

In the nineteenth century Kabaka Suna II laid the foundation for a more centralized state by creating a loyal bureaucracy and challenging the power of the hereditary aristocracy. Suna II and his royal officials intimidated these leaders of other Bito clans into recognizing his absolute authority and that of his son and successor, Mutesa I. Under Mutesa I, who reigned from 1856 to 1884, Buganda became the most powerful state of the northern Lake Plateau.

State building on the Lake Plateau in the nineteenth century had little to do with the Nile waters. An Englishman, Sir William Garstin, was the first to recognize the hydrologic unity of the highlands and the lakes. He arrived in Cairo in 1892 as the inspector general of irrigation at the Egyptian Ministry of Public Works. Unlike other British hydrologists working in Egypt, Garstin was less interested in the canals of the Nile delta than in the hydrology of the Nile basin. He was a most affable gentleman, but he also possessed one of the most perceptive minds of the century about the Nile and how its waters flow. After making an initial reconnaissance to the upper Nile in 1901, he understood the unity of the highlands and their lakes in relation to the rest of the Nile basin.

Garstin, however, retired in 1906, and he was succeeded by Harold Edwin Hurst, who dominated hydrologic study and planning for the next forty years. Hurst was more concerned with ways to assure a sufficient supply of water in Egypt, and with him Garstin's concept of the Lake Plateau fell out of favor. The concept of the Lake Plateau as an integral but independent part of the Nile basin was not revived until late in the twentieth century. When the former European colonies on the Lake Plateau gained their independence, mostly in the 1960s, it led to emerging nationalism in these new countries, followed by decades of political instability and civil conflict in the region. Only toward the end of the twentieth century were these fires subdued, and with a more peaceful outlook there has been a revival of the concept of a regional East African community of political and economic union. Late in 2001 presidents Daniel arap Moi of Kenya, Yoweri Museveni of Uganda, and Benjamin Mkapa of Tanzania formalized the creation of the East African Community, designed for the cooperative integration of the economic, monetary, and transportation systems of the three states. Greater regional cooperation in East Africa has led to the rehabilitation of Garstin's notion of the Lake Plateau as a hydrologic basin. A hundred years after him the Lake Plateau, homeland of the Bushmen, Bantu, Cwezi, Hima, and Luo, has a chance to put his ideas into practice.

3 *The Sudd*

No-one who has not seen this country can have any real idea of its supreme
dreariness and its utter desolation. To my mind, the most barren desert
that I have ever crossed is a bright and cheerful locality compared
with the White Nile marshland.
—Sir William Garstin, 1909

The Lake Plateau ends at Nimule, a former imperial border post whose whitewashed buildings with galvanized iron roofs command the Albert Nile from lofty bluffs. Today it is a frontier fort held intermittently by Africans and Arabs during their interminable warfare for control of the southern Sudan and the upper Nile. Here the Nile turns sharply to the left, 120 degrees, and plunges northwest over the rocks that come down from the western escarpment of the Rift, the Kuku Mountains, and the placid Albert Nile is transformed into rapids and whitewater, the Bahr al-Jabal, or Mountain River.

The Bahr al-Jabal is indeed a river of the mountains, tumbling through a narrow valley strewn with outcrops that divide its precipitous flow into tortuous channels for the next hundred miles, including sheer drops like the Fola rapids. The banks become cliffs and the valley a narrow gorge, where the river churns like a millrace of boiling turbulence, then collects its waters in pools below as it prepares to plunge once again over more rocks deposited from the Kuku escarpment. The Bahr al-Jabal is a river of awesome beauty. Its walls are deep black vertical strata covered with bright green creepers, and the mimosa trees that cling to stony banks and rocky islands are ablaze with white and pink flowers that contrast with the deep blue African sky above and the

The Fola rapids of the Bahr al-Jabal below Nimule

violent whitewater below. In the west the escarpment towers upward in an unbroken but declining wall; in the east an undulating plateau rises in tiers to the horizon. Throughout its descent the Bahr al-Jabal receives additional water from its tributaries, which flow in deep ravines that enter from either bank. These are barren in the dry season and flood during the rains, when they become torrents washing down the boulders and making the rapids and the Nile impossible to navigate.

In spite of the geologic obstruction from its irregular tributaries, the Bahr al-Jabal continues its northward course and the landscape begins to change. The western escarpment of the Rift disintegrates into a few isolated hills, the jabals of the Sudan. In the east the Rift also subsides and is replaced by scattered peaks jutting up from the edge of the Lake Plateau. Between these receding ridges the Bahr al-Jabal slides over the Bedden rapids, the last rocks that impede the Nile until it reaches the stones of the Sabaluqa gorge fifteen hundred miles to the north. Free of rocks and their dikes and dams, the Bahr al-Jabal has a brief moment of freedom to flow through undulating flatlands of forest and bush until confronted by Jabal Rejaf, known locally as Logwek. This perfect cone juts into the sky 374 feet above the surrounding equatorial plain on the west bank of the Mountain River. It is the historic sentinel that marks the end of navigation from the north and the entry to the Lake Plateau and Africa in the south.

North of Jabal Rejaf on a modest ridge that absorbs the morning sun lies the regional capital of the southern Sudan, Juba. Like Nimule, Juba was an imperial creation: an administrative center for the southern Sudan built in 1930 to replace the malarial stations of a forgotten Egyptian imperial past downriver, at Gondokoro, Lado, and Mongalla. Juba was the last bucolic outpost of empire on the upper Nile. Its administrative buildings were constructed from local ironstone. Its hotel is a conglomerate of quaint cottages surrounded by paths festooned with bougainvillea and lined with the empty beer bottles of its former guests. During World War II, its quay on the Bahr al-Jabal made possible the shipment of thousands of tanks, trucks, and weapons from the mouth of the Congo to Cairo along the African Line of Communications. In 1956 British engineers constructed a bridge across the Nile at Juba, a departing gesture to commemorate the independence of the Sudan, linking Equatoria with the Lake Plateau, the only crossing of the Nile south of Kosti, nine hundred miles downstream.

Today Juba is a fortified camp of the Sudanese government, a beleaguered garrison of Arab Islamic imperialism surrounded by African insurgents. Its population of troops and refugees, over a hundred thousand, is supported more from the air than from the Nile: the Juba airport can be defended, but the Bahr al-Jabal cannot. Those who ply it are vulnerable to enemies hidden on its banks, as with any waterway, but in this case defenseless government steamers on the Mountain River must confront an even more difficult adversary to their navigation, the Sudd.

Jabal Rejaf, the end of navigation on the White Nile and the Bahr al-Jabal

The Sudd, a gigantic swampland through which the Nile slowly makes its way for more than four hundred river miles, begins at Bor, an administrative post situated precariously on the east bank of the Bahr al-Jabal sixty miles downstream from Juba. By the time it gets here, the power of the Mountain River is exhausted. Its banks disappear into swamps that stretch beyond the horizon. Meandering slowly through twists and bends that drink up what is left of its current, it is a dying river making its way through a labyrinth of desolate wasteland. Before it leaves the Sudd, the river loses more than half its water to evaporation. Neither trees nor jabals disrupt the monotony of this endless swamp.

The Sudd is one of the most formidable natural obstacles in the world. For two thousand years it frustrated every pharaoh, emperor, and pasha hoping to discover the source of the Nile in equatorial Africa. Until 1841 no one had passed through this primordial bog. Since then, the Sudd, as if in retaliation, has sought to prevent any further penetration by Christianity, Islam, commerce, or civilization. In the twentieth century all four were dependent on an open channel up the Nile to the Lake Plateau. Free navigation of the Bahr al-Jabal was essential for the ivory and slave traders of the nineteenth century. An open river will be even more important for those who seek to extract the large oil reserves from beneath the Sudd in the twenty-first.

In the Sudd, thick papyruses rise above the aquatic plants that remain below, imprisoning the river, but their green walls are regularly ruptured by blue water from countless lagoons that flow through thousands of spillways into the narrow channel that was once the Mountain River. West of a diminished Bahr al-Jabal are the open waters of Lakes Fajarial, Shambe, and Nyong; to the east flows a discernible channel, an aquatic alley, known as the Atem River. A less definitive but longer Bahr al-Zaraf, the Giraffe River, leaves the Bahr al-Jabal at Shambe and wanders a similar northward course. It is more a sluggish stream than a river that meanders northeast for two hundred miles to the White Nile. Its waters come not from the Lake Plateau but from the rains that storm out of the south Atlantic to fall on the vast expanse of swamp and grass of the Sudd, where they creep eventually into the Bahr al-Zaraf. North of where the Bahr al-Zaraf parts from the Bahr al-Jabal, Zaraf Island rises a few feet above the dreary landscape. Its sandy soil supports trees that form its skyline and bush beneath that have given sanctuary to outcasts, outlaws, and southern Sudanese insurgents, but it remains an isolated atoll in the center of a sea of swamp, the Sudd.

In the Sudd the air is close, steamy, and fetid with decomposing vegetation. There are few sounds—the cry of the fish eagle, the unremitting buzz of mosquitoes, the splash of a Nile perch. There are few birds except the antediluvian shoebill stork, *Balaeniceps rex,* which stands forlornly among the reeds brooding on life and death in this Serbonian bog. The Sudd is that elusive geologic formation that leaves no markers from its past. It is an ever-shifting maze consisting of millions of aquatic plants that combine, break up, and recombine, forming a vast swamp that expands and contracts with the Nile flow. It derives its name from the Arabic word *sadd,* or barrier, for the huge clumps of aquatic vegetation that come together to all but completely block the Bahr al-Jabal and the Bahr al-Zaraf, as well as any other rivers and streams that find their way into it. The Turks, Arabs, Sudanese, and Europeans who came up the Nile in the nineteenth century feared these islands of aquatic vegetation, which they called *sudd,* or obstacle. Today "the Sudd" is the name for this whole region of permanent swamps, including the surrounding Nile floodplain and its seasonal wetlands.

These clusters called sudd are conceived in the shallow lagoons on either side of the tortuous channels in this part of the Nile, where the river is immobilized for hundreds of miles in the great swamp. Nowhere else in the long course of the Nile do its waters flow so imprisoned by reeds and congested with aquatic plants that bed their roots in the compost below. In the spring the thunderstorms from the south Atlantic raise the level of the lagoons, and the wind comes right behind the rain to convulse their placid surface. Clumps of aquatic vegetation on the rising water break free from the bog below, their roots a tangled web of humus whose weight is the ballast that keeps them upright as they float. They drift aimlessly around the lagoons and congregate as islands until wind and current and chance propel them through a thousand spillways into the constricted channels of the Bahr al-Jabal and the Bahr al-Zaraf. Floating downstream, clumps of sudd are soon trapped at the sharp bends of a labyrinthine channel, where they quickly bury roots in the decomposition of the river bottom to anchor the tall reeds and recumbent aquatic plants.

Once secured, sudd entangles other sudd until these floating islands cover the surface of the Nile. Forced below the obstruction into a constricting aperture, the sluggish current increases in velocity, thereby sucking each new sudd into the hole until it is plugged by a solid block of earth, roots, and reeds compacted by the expanding pressure of the river. So great is the force of moving water that it frequently thrusts the sudd barricade above the river, and as it accumulates ever more floating islands, its enlarged surface is serrated into ridges and furrows. Once the Bahr al-Jabal and the Bahr al-Zaraf become completely closed, their waters can find an outlet only by spilling into the lagoons on either side to rise and cut a new channel around the obstruction that, in turn, will become a new barrier from fresh masses of sudd. This repetitive process represents the eternal competition for control between moving water and immobile land, which inevitably succumbs to the water's power. Ultimately the force of water, assisted by the pressure of wind, is so great that the sudd dam will burst. The power of pressure from the river breaches the obstacle of tangled vegetation and its captives—four-hundred-pound Nile perch, hippos of even greater weight, and emaciated men working to clear the river—until its force is spent in the twisting channels and lagoons on either side, where this contest between water and land begins again.

The lagoons and lakes of the Sudd rise and fall, expand and diminish, with the amount of seasonal rainfall and the flow of the Mountain River carrying the waters from the equatorial lakes and the torrents below Lake Albert. The lagoons are about ten feet deep, but their size has changed dramatically in the twentieth century. Lagoons in the northern region of the Sudd, beyond Adok, began to shrink during the first half of the century, and those in the south, upstream from Shambe, grew during the latter half, particularly in the 1960s when massive rainfall on the equatorial lakes precipitated unprecedented flows downstream. Every lagoon has its own character. Some belong to a river channel; others are isolated from the stream by walls of papyrus, behind which they rise and fall with the rain, seepage into the surrounding swamp, and the overflow from the reservoirs behind impermanent sudd dams. Large

Papyrus and other aquatic plants in the Sudd

lakes, such as Shambe, Fajarial, and Nyong, have their own channels to the river, but they do not drain the considerable volume of their dead water, which has remained relatively unchanged in the past century.

From time immemorial the Sudd has diverted, obstructed, and eclipsed the flow of the Nile from the equatorial lakes. It has also thwarted the quests of explorers and the imperial ambitions of rulers. There are no records in dynastic Egypt or the kingdom of Kush of anyone ever having passed through the Sudd. In 61 C.E. the Roman emperor Nero, an avid geographer, sent two centurions up the Nile. Upon returning they reported finding only an impenetrable swamp, a pestilential piece of real estate that the Roman empire did not need. For the next two thousand years, no one else sought to enter the Sudd.

But in November 1839 a corpulent Turkish naval captain, or *qapudan,* named Salim sailed south with explicit instructions from Muhammad Ali, the charismatic ruler who had dragged Egypt into the modern world, to open the Nile for his imperial ambitions in Africa. The expedition departed from Khartoum, sailed up the White Nile, and returned after it was blocked by sudd obstructions on the Bahr al-Jabal. Muhammad Ali was obsessed, like so many before and after him, with the possibilities for commerce, dreams of empire, and curiosity about the source of the Nile, so he sent Salim back up the Nile in November 1840. Commanding ten dhahabiyah—large Nile sailing vessels—the Turk brought with him a ragtag collection of officers, including two Kurds, a Russian, an Albanian, a Persian, two French engineers, a French collector, and a paying German passenger, Ferdinand Werne. At the end of January 1841 the expedition emerged from the Sudd on a free-flowing Bahr al-Jabal at Gondokoro, north of Jabal Rejaf, the end of navigation and the entry to the Lake Plateau. The party returned to Khartoum late the following April.

Salim never found the source of the White Nile, but he had demonstrated that the Sudd couldn't isolate equatorial Africa forever. The southern Sudan and the Lake Plateau were now open to imperialists bringing civilization, commerce, and religion—Islam, in the case of the Turkish, Egyptian, and Sudanese imperialists, and Christianity in the case of the Europeans. Merchants of every cultural, ethnic, and religious persuasion were the first to follow Salim up the Bahr al-Jabal and the first to lose their identity in order to survive in the turbulent frontier beyond the Sudd. They were few but tough traders—Turks, Europeans, Arabs, Sudanese—who organized regular expeditions that passed through the Sudd to barter cloth, beads, and wire for African ivory. Their profits were substantial. In 1863 the traders launched more than 120 dhahabiyah up the Nile to diversify an expanding commercial enterprise whose attractive profits now came from slaves rather than ivory.

The missionaries soon joined the merchants. In 1846 Pope Gregory XVI created the Vicariate Apostolic of Central Africa and the Congregatio de Propaganda Fide to organize the missionary activities of the Catholic Church, sending four priests to bring Christianity to the newfound pagans in the upper Nile basin. The first band of missionaries, led by a Slovene named Father Knoblecker, founded the Austrian mission station near Gondokoro in 1850. During the next decade they died from malaria, and the mission was abandoned in 1860 as the thriving trade in slaves overcame the hazards of health for those more interested in the material than the spiritual world.

The dhahabiyah of merchants and missionaries at first meandered through the channels of the Bahr al-Jabal to Gondokoro and the beginning of the Lake Plateau. In 1855, however, an Egyptian Christian Copt, Habashi, employed by John Petherick, the British trader and consul in Khartoum, discovered the mouth of the Bahr al-Ghazal at Lake No. This was not a majestic encounter. The turgid flow of the Bahr al-Ghazal through the Sudd led him out of the swamps to Mashra al-Raqq, the port of the king, and the gateway to the savanna of the ironstone plateau that gradually rises south and west to the Congo-Nile watershed. The following year Petherick navigated the Bahr al-Ghazal. In 1857 Antoine Brun Rollet followed Petherick. He had amassed a fortune from trade in the Sudan, and as the Sardinian vice-consul in Khartoum he was a respected correspondent of the Geographical Society in Paris, which advocated sending steamers and building railways to the interior of Africa, beyond the Sudd to the Congo. The opening of the southern Sudan and the Lake Plateau had begun.

In their dhahabiyah powered by the north wind, steamers with paddle wheels, and later hydrofoils, these travelers frequently had to cut a passage through the sudd obstructions. Often the accumulated aquatic plants were sufficiently pliable to pole, pull, and push the boats over the barrier. When none of these efforts were successful, sudd accumulating downstream of the vessel would imprison it. Unable to proceed upstream and unable to retreat downstream, crew and passengers in their dhahabiyah and later more powerful steamers had no recourse but to hope for rescue. To abandon ship meant certain death in the Sudd, with its swamps stretching endlessly beyond the horizon. Relief expeditions did not always arrive in time to save the occupants of a stranded vessel from starvation. There are reports of fragile steamers being crushed by the implacable pressure of the river, building its blocks of sudd, and legends of cannibalism when rations came to an end.

After Salim Qapudan had opened the river to the traders and missionaries in 1841, sudd obstructions were more a nuisance than the formidable obstacle they became at the end of the century. No one has ever predicted with any credibility sudd obstructions from one year to the next, let alone one decade to another, but they appear to have favored commerce, Christianity, and Islam rather than British, Egyptian, or Sudanese imperialism. In the 1860s and 1870s officials serving Khedive Ismail, the ruler of Egypt, encountered many delays, hardships, and death as they sought to pass through the Sudd on their way to incorporate the Lake Plateau in the expanding Egyptian empire.

Samuel White Baker and his wife, Florence, made their first journey up the Nile in 1863 as wealthy Victorian travelers, and they passed through the Sudd without difficulty, reaching Gondokoro in forty days. The khedive, hoping to complete the imperial conquests of his grandfather, Muhammad Ali, appointed Sir Samuel to lead a large expedition in 1869. Sir Samuel and his wife returned to the upper Nile, seeking to suppress the Nilotic slave trade and to acquire—by peace or by war—Equatoria, the Lake Plateau, and the source of the Nile. Despite twelve hundred Egyptian and Sudanese troops, British engineers, and a fleet of steamers, Baker was unable to break through the sudd obstructions in the White Nile to reach Lake No and the Bahr al-Jabal. He and his flotilla had no alternative but to enter the Bahr al-Zaraf and hope to continue their passage to the Lake Plateau. His boats were trapped; his men died. He retired to clear water at Tawfiqiyah on the northern fringe of the Sudd. In December 1870 he returned to the Bahr al-Zaraf. After three months of unremitting toil and heavy losses of men and material, the expedition breached the last sudd barrier to the open water of the Bahr al-Jabal downstream from Gondokoro. This kind of determination to succeed was very Victorian, and very expensive, but Baker's herculean efforts demonstrated that those who seek to dominate the upper Nile and the Lake Plateau must clear the channel through the Sudd. This reality is as true today as when Baker Pasha arrived at Gondokoro to expand the empire of Egypt into the heart of equatorial Africa.

The governor-general of the Sudan, Ismail Pasha Ayyub, personally led a sudd-cutting party of several hundred soldiers in 1872 to clear the Bahr al-Jabal, but their success disappeared within a few years, and the river was blocked once again. In 1878 an unusually high flood was reported as the reason for the massive sudd obstruction that closed the channel for two years, despite all efforts to pass through the barrier. Without an open channel Egyptian administration in Equatoria could not be sustained, nor imperial ambitions pursued on the Lake Plateau. Between 1878 and 1883 only nine steamers passed through the Sudd from Khartoum, and these brought no merchandise. Commerce in equatorial Africa disappeared in proportion to the risk of a hazardous and increasingly impassable river. When river traffic declined, sudd formations remained undisturbed in the channels. In 1878 the commercial community at Lado, the new Egyptian administrative outpost upstream, across the river from Gondokoro, had been reduced to three indigent traders. Ismail could not retain, let alone expand, the empire into equatorial Africa if he could not support his administrative and military officers south of the Sudd.

Even in the face of a desperate financial situation and opposition from his European fiscal controllers, Khedive Ismail was determined to pursue the imperial dream of his grandfather. He sent yet another formidable expedition through the Sudd in 1879, only months before he was forced by the European powers to abdicate the khediviate. The expedition left Khartoum under the command of Ernst Marno. Like so many Europeans who have appeared in Africa, Marno had come for adventure, and after arriving in Khartoum from Vienna, in 1867, he spent the next decade making himself useful to those in the Egyptian administration who employed his talents for difficult projects that required discretion. Under his direction a fleet of steamers and an army of laborers opened the Bahr al-Jabal after months of enervating effort and heavy losses. During his return Marno paused at the mouth of the Bahr al-Ghazal, the river of Petherick and Brun Rollet that would open the way west. His curiosity was not misplaced, for he was able to rescue Romolo Gessi, another of the khedive's European officials, whose flotilla had been immured in sudd for three months. Marno came from downstream as Gessi was trying to cut his way from upstream. When Marno found them, on 5 January 1881, they had eaten everything, including their dead colleagues.

In spite of his rescue by Marno, Gessi had lost a hundred men, and he himself died of malaria at Suez on his way home to Italy. Gessi and his men were doomed to fail; no expedition can cut through sudd from upstream. Every block of sudd hacked from the upstream side of the barrier and dragged free will float serenely down the imperceptible current and wedge itself behind those attempting to cut their way downriver. Every successful sudd-clearing expedition has attacked the obstructions from the downstream side. Here the current, no matter how sluggish, will usually carry the dislodged clumps of aquatic vegetation away, ultimately to sink many miles downriver in the broad expanse of the White Nile.

Except for minor obstructions in 1881 and 1884, the Bahr al-Jabal remained open until 1895. Only the inscrutable vagaries of the Sudd can account for fifteen years of a river free of obstructions. After Marno's expedition no sudd-clearing parties patrolled the Sudd, and the steamer traffic was hardly sufficient to keep the channel clear. From 1881 to 1885 the Sudan was convulsed by the violent upheaval precipitated by Muhammad Ahmad, known as al-Mahdi, another Muslim reformer of the nineteenth century determined to revive Islam throughout the Sudan. He and his followers, the Ansar ("helpers"), scored their greatest triumph in 1885 when they captured Khartoum, in the process killing Charles George Gordon, the British governor-general there. By the time of the Mahdi's death later that year, they had successfully destroyed the Turkish, Christian, and European presence in the Sudan.

Three years later his successor, the Khalifa Abd Allahi, ordered a strong flotilla under the command of Umar Salih to replace Egyptian imperialism with Sudanese Mahdism in Equatoria and the Lake Plateau. For the next seven years the khalifa was able to support his Ansar on the upper Nile through a fleet of river steamers captured from the Egyptians plying between his capital at Omdurman and the end of Nile navigation at Jabal Rejaf, fifteen hundred miles to the south. But in 1895 the Bahr al-Jabal was again overwhelmed by sudd.

In 1896 Said Sughaiyar left Rejaf to return down the Bahr al-Jabal to obtain arms and supplies in Omdurman for Umar Salih. Below Bor his men hacked at the aquatic vegetation from May to June, only to die from hunger, exhaustion, and fever. Unable to cut a passage from the upstream side of the sudd, Said found an alternative channel and in his last steamer reached the White Nile and Omdurman. Upon hearing Said's description of the daunting Sudd in the south, and threatened by a more formidable Anglo-Egyptian army from the north, the khalifa decided to abandon his Islamic frontier. The Ansar who remained beyond the Sudd in Equatoria would have to fend for themselves against hostile Africans and the advancing Europeans—Belgian, British, and French—in their rivalry to control the waters of the Nile and thereby the Sudan, Egypt, and Suez.

In 1882 Great Britain, in response to a nationalist revolt, had invaded Egypt to protect its interests there, following which its forces remained in occupation of the country to prevent any further threats to the khedive's government. British supremacy in Egypt and eastern Africa could not be sustained without control of the Nile waters from their beginnings to the Mediterranean. France, however, the historic rival of the English, had designs of its own in Egypt and the continent. The Suez Canal had originally been a French engineering success (which the khedive of Egypt later sold to Britain), and control of the upper Nile would complete an expanding French empire stretching across Africa from Dakar to Djibouti, as well as block Britain's plans to extend its empire southward from Egypt to Uganda. Théophile Delcassé, France's influential undersecretary for colonial affairs, was dazzled by a proposal made in 1893 by Victor Prompt, a distinguished French hydrologist and classmate at the Ecole Polytechnique of the president of France.

The idea was to seize Fashoda, just north of Malakal on the White Nile, and build a dam that would obstruct the river, depriving the British and the Egyptians downstream of the Nile's waters. The French concocted an elaborate plan to send troops marching from the Atlantic all the way across Africa, two thousand miles, to capture the upper Nile at Fashoda. To lead the expedition they chose Captain Jean-Baptiste Marchand, who left Marseilles for Africa in June 1896. The French expedition to Fashoda was another of those bizarre schemes that characterized the Scramble for Africa by the European powers at the end of the nineteenth century. There was not a stone within a hundred miles of Fashoda with which to build a dam on the unobstructed, horizontal Nilotic plain, but even the most provincial republican deputy in France and the most officious bureaucrat in Paris were captivated by the romanticism of the quest.

Marchand and his intrepid band, the *tirailleurs sénégalais,* struggled against all human and natural odds, making their way across the continent and up the Congo, crossing over the watershed into the Nile basin in December 1897 and establishing Fort Desaix, near the confluence of the Busseri and the Sue rivers. From the height of land these rivers rush through the upper reaches of the ironstone plateau during the rains to become the river Jur. In May 1898 the rains returned from the south Atlantic, the rivers rose, and Marchand and his tirailleurs continued to follow the flow, maneuver, and chop their way through the sudd of the Jur and Bahr al-Ghazal to Lake No, the White Nile, and Fashoda, where they arrived on 10 July 1898. Marchand had no illusions that his heroic attempt to acquire the waters of the Nile for France could be sustained by Paris from either the western Sudan or northeastern Africa through the Sudd.

Meanwhile, of course, reports of Marchand's progress reached London, and the British concluded that it had now become necessary to conquer the Sudan to prevent the Nile from falling into the hands of the French. They sent General Horatio Herbert Kitchener, with an Anglo-Egyptian army of twenty-five thousand men, up the river to the Sudan to secure the river, and along the way to avenge the death of Gordon and destroy the Mahdist state. Both objectives were enormously popular with Parliament and the British public. On 2 September 1898, Kitchener's army defeated Khalifa Abd Allahi on the sandy plain of Karari, north of Omdurman. This decisive battle brought an abrupt end to the Mahdist state, and with it expired Sudanese imperialism in equatorial Africa for the next half century.

Three days after his victory on the battlefield of Karari, Kitchener was confronted at Khartoum by a greater challenge than the khalifa and the Mahdist state. On 5 September two Sudanese steamers returned from Fashoda riddled with bullets of French manufacture. Marchand was astride the Nile. The prime minister, Lord Salisbury, had sent handwritten instructions urging Kitchener on to Fashoda, where he and his formidable flotilla arrived on 19 September. Kitchener had 25,000 troops, artillery, and a fleet of steamers and gunboats; Marchand had a dozen French officers and 125 tirailleurs. Marchand was recalled, and the crisis that had hurled the two great liberal powers of the West to the brink of war disappeared into the eternal swamps of the Nile. In deference to French sensibilities after their humiliation, the British removed the name Fashoda from the map of Africa, replacing it with the more acceptable but pedestrian Kodok.

The ability to govern Egypt requires control of the Nile waters. Lord Cromer, the British consul-general in Cairo, understood this fundamental principle, and after Fashoda he became in effect the pharaoh of Egypt and the Nile basin. Kitchener, within a month of his confrontation with Marchand at Fashoda, established an advance post at the confluence of the Sobat and the White Nile. South of the Sobat River all the tributaries of the White Nile—the Bahr al-Jabal, the Bahr al-Zaraf, and the Bahr al-Ghazal—were impassable. Until a channel was cleared to Equatoria and the Lake Plateau, the British could hardly assert their claims to the basin of the upper Nile. The time had come to forge the last link in Britain's African chain of imperial possessions from Cape Town to Cairo by opening a passage to bind the upper Nile and its waters to the empire. Lord Cromer was determined to resolve these "big questions" of the Nile waters because they were critical to the success of his programs of fiscal reform and economic development in Egypt and the security of the Suez Canal for Great Britain. In February 1899 he ordered his friend Sir William Garstin, the affable and perceptive undersecretary of state for the Egyptian Ministry of Public Works, up the Nile to observe and report on the means to secure it.

Upon his return to Cairo in the spring of 1899, Garstin was tactful but blunt. He told Cromer that there could be no future control of the Nile waters unless an expedition was sent at once to clear the sudd from the Bahr al-Jabal. Garstin and Cromer both knew that the increasing numbers of Egyptian peasants, the fellahin, would require additional water for cultivation, which was essential for the stability of Egypt and consequently for the security of the British at Cairo and Suez. New water for Egypt would have to come from the equatorial lakes, or perhaps from the western tributaries, an enigma that had diverted the search for the source of the Nile since the eighteenth century. After he made a second tour in 1901 and another more extensive reconnaissance in 1904, Garstin was convinced that the only way to bring more water to Egypt was to carve a passage through the Sudd.

Money was available; labor was not so easy to come by. Prisoners taken at Karari had to be supplemented with convicts from the Omdurman jail, which together provided no more than five hundred men. Always perfunctory, and now imperious after having been made the first earl of Khartoum and Broome, Kitchener gave orders for the British governor of Omdurman to round up another five hundred suspicious characters. On 16 December 1899 the expedition left Omdurman in five steamers under the command of Major Malcolm Peake Bey, five British and twelve Egyptian and Sudanese officers, eight hundred conscripts, and a hundred women to attend to domestic needs. On the last day of 1899, they began attacking the sudd of the Bahr al-Jabal. Three weeks into the twentieth century two blocks of sudd, each a half mile long, had been dislodged, but Peake and his Sudanese had just begun.

Tormented by mosquitoes, overcome by heat exhaustion, and debilitated by suppurating skin ulcers and the deadly dysentery, the Sudanese would first cut the sudd into four-foot squares with axes, hoes, and swords. They would then burn the papyrus and aquatic plants on the surface of each block, and a steamer would ram the block at full speed to jar it loose. If this failed, they would drive telegraph poles in three sides of the block and wrap a steel hawser around them with pronged pikes. Under full power the steamer would churn back and forth, belching smoke amid the screams of straining winches and taut cables in the fetid air. Suddenly, the block would pop. The steamer would pitch, recover, and, panting, pull the torn sudd into open water. It was a bizarre and dangerous scheme, using the best of British technology by the last of the Victorians at the end of their century.

As Peake and his Sudanese chopped, burned, and ripped their way through block after block, the Bahr al-Jabal released the phenomenal pressure of impounded water behind its sudd dams. After a most stubborn piece was extracted in January the Nile rose more than three feet. In March a huge block suddenly broke loose and swept the dam busters—steamers, barges, and men—downstream. The Bahr al-Jabal rose six feet as the sudd lugubriously passed Peake's steamer for the next thirty hours. Back in 1873, when the governor-general Ismail Pasha Ayyub had been attempting to clear the White Nile, a similar sudd plug exploded, and one of his officers described the effects: "The hippopotamuses were carried down, screaming and snorting; crocodiles were whirled round and round, and the river was covered with dead and dying hippopotamuses, crocodiles, and fish who had [been] crushed by the mass." By the end of

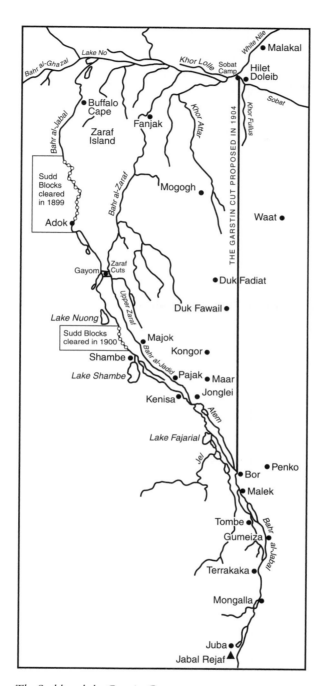

The Sudd and the Garstin Cut

March 1900 eighty-two miles of the Bahr al-Jabal had been opened, but in April the rains returned from the south Atlantic, flooding the upper Nile and making further work impossible. The expedition was recalled so it could refit and return during the next dry season to attack yet more formidable barriers, particularly the infamous Block 15, twenty-two miles of sudd.[1]

In January 1901 a second expedition left Khartoum to break the sudd barrier at Block 15, but it did not succeed either. As the steamers dragged sudd downstream, the pressure from the waters impounded in the lagoons on either side of the Bahr al-Jabal could no longer be contained by a fragile fence of papyrus and aquatic reeds. The sudd broke out of its imprisonment with all the exuberance of freed slaves, carried by the power of flowing water against which any river steamer, then and now, is impotent, particularly when the winter wind blows steadily upstream to conspire with the water. The combined power of the dry, cold northern winds from Asia and the water released from the lagoons in torrents will often force the sudd upstream rather than down the channel of the Bahr al-Jabal, whose sluggish current cannot compete. In 1902 a third expedition was launched to clear the sudd with no more success, and it was not until 1905 that more men and more steamers finally eliminated Block 15, opening the Bahr al-Jabal to the Lake Plateau.

Garstin, in 1904, proposed a different way of channeling the waters from the Lake Plateau to Egypt and avoiding the tremendous losses in the swamps. He recommended bypassing the Sudd altogether by digging a canal that would slice a straight line from Bor to the White Nile, at its confluence with the Sobat. His idea became known as the Garstin Cut, and later the Jonglei Canal. But the scheme became bogged down for another three-quarters of a century amid rival proposals to bring down the water and numerous logistical and technical difficulties. In any case, for the half century following the opening of the river in 1905, lower flows—combined with regular steamer traffic, whose wash would dislodge aquatic plants—kept the Bahr al-Jabal open except in the occasional years of high water, 1918 and 1926, when sudd blocks three and four miles long had to be extracted. The way to the south was now clear, but the way west for the British conquest of the vast Nilotic plain that rises to the Congo-Nile watershed, the Bahr al-Ghazal, remained as unknown as its streams and rivers.

At the end of the nineteenth century the Nile quest, the conquest of the Sudan, and the confrontation at Fashoda had resulted in British domination of the Nile basin, but the imposition of imperial authority could not disguise imperial ignorance of the basin's geography, its people, or its waters. The Nile is a basin with many faucets.

The least known at the beginning of the twentieth century was its western watershed in the Bahr al-Ghazal. Slave traders—Arabs, Turks, and Sudanese—had come from the north into the Bahr al-Ghazal for African slaves, a practice that had mobilized British abolitionists to end the trade on the upper Nile. Marchand had come over the Congo-Nile watershed and down the rivers of the Bahr al-Ghazal to Fashoda, where he was challenged by Britain and sent home. King Leopold of the Belgians, sovereign of the Congo Free State, was another imperial rival of the British, and he too dreamed of an African empire stretching from the Atlantic to the Mediterranean. As part of his grand scheme to occupy the headwaters of the Nile, he sent his officers to establish an enclave on the Bahr al-Jabal at Lado. This was another challenge the British had to dispute, which led them to the Bahr al-Ghazal.

The Bahr al-Ghazal is the name for a river, a province, and a region the size of France. Its area is the largest drainage basin in the whole of the Nile Valley, spanning ten degrees of latitude, or seven hundred miles. From the north the wadis of Darfur and Kordofan disappear in spate into the Sahel. From the south the waters flow down the northern slope of the Congo-Nile divide. The watershed is an undulating plateau upon which the south Atlantic monsoon drops its rains from May to October, there to sustain lush parklands and rivers that cut ravines through which their waters tumble over rocks and rapids. These waters are hidden from the sun by the triumphal arches of the forests towering above the luxuriant growth of reed and bamboo by the torrents below. Farther downstream the rivers, red with the laterite of the ironstone plateau, meander through the great Nilotic plain, where the gallery forests of the watershed become parklands that turn to savanna whose grasslands stretch to the horizon, broken only by clumps of the small heglig tree, *Balantis aegyptiaca*. The rivers that drain this vast basin have evocative Arab and African names—the Yei (Lau), Na'am (Wohko), Gel (Tapari), Tonj (Ibba), Sue, Busseri, Jur, Kuru, Sopo, Raga, Lol, and the Bahr al-Arab (Kiir). The names of these rivers are unknown in Egypt, for they all lose their water in the Sudd.

The Bahr al-Arab, the Kiir, is unique among these rivers, for it is more a symbol than a purveyor of water. It has the largest drainage basin of any river in the Bahr al-Ghazal or the Lake Plateau. It also has the least water. The wadis of the Sahel in the north are spasmodic. The seasonal rivers from the Congo-Nile divide have a greater volume than the Bahr al-Arab, but they are not its tributaries. Its sluggish waters represent, however, the cultural divide between Arabs and Africans on the frontiers of traditional African religions, Islam, and Christianity. Throughout its long convex passage the Arab Baggara, who call it the Bahr al-Arab, and the African Dinka, who call it the Kiir, have fought for cattle, grass, slaves, and souls from time beyond their oral traditions. Today it remains a shallow, sudd-filled river running red with the blood of Arabs and Africans from hostilities that will be remembered long after its waters are cleansed in the swamps of the Sudd.

The other rivers of the Bahr al-Ghazal cannot claim its cultural or hydrologic importance. They are rivers that are not navigable even in flood and whose waters never reach the Nile. Those from the Yei, Na'am, Gel, and Tonj disappear directly into the swamps. Those that flow from the west come together into the Bahr al-Ghazal river, whose final contribution to the Nile, after the hydrologic accounting from the Sudd, is an insignificant trickle. The rivers of the Bahr al-Ghazal region represent an enormous quantity of water, estimated at 20 billion cubic meters—60 percent of the average flow from the equatorial lakes. The waters contained in these rivers, if they reached Egypt, would increase the volume of the Nile there by 25 percent, which would feed another twenty million Egyptians, but less than 3 percent of it trickles into Lake No and the White Nile. None of it arrives at Aswan. Sir William Garstin was appalled by this enormous loss, as has been everyone who followed him from the Arab north in search of the Nile waters from the African south.[2]

In the nineteenth century the Bahr al-Ghazal had been a province of the Egyptian African empire, supplying ivory and slaves. But by the end of the century ivory was diminishing with the elephant, and slaves were no longer an acceptable commodity. Water was the vital resource, but its flow could not be understood without clearing the sudd, and to the British this meant imposing their authority over the streams flowing from the Congo-Nile watershed. If a navigable river could reach the heartland of the Bahr al-Ghazal, British occupation could be accomplished without British and Sudanese troops and disgruntled African porters slogging into the interior through sodden grass laced by streams and torrents. But too little water half the year and too much during the remainder convinced the British that their fragile administration in the Bahr al-Ghazal, the geographical center of Africa, could not be sustained by such unreliable rivers. They had to go overland, with their imperial bearers struggling under the burden of civilization, just as the traders from Khartoum and their slaves before them had in the nineteenth century.

The Khartoumers had cut paths from Mashra al-Raqq on the western edge of the Sudd into the interior across the black alluvial clay of the upper Nile, the infamous cotton soil. During the rains it indiscriminately sucks the African porter, official, and traveler into its viscous mud. In the dry season its concrete serrated surface slashes their feet and shreds their boots. All the supplies, arms, ammunition, food, and whiskey necessary for the British to control this vast western watershed of the Nile had to be carried by hundreds of African porters along these paths through walls of tall grass cut away and widened into tracks. The Africans were recruited sometimes by persuasion but usually by coercion to carry the impedimenta of imperialism across the cotton soil and the streams and rivers whose waters disappear into the Sudd.

Lake No is a shallow reservoir on the northern fringe of the Sudd and the regulator of the flow of the Bahr al-Jabal and the dribble from the Bahr al-Ghazal. Papyrus and a plethora of aquatic plants surround its elusive shores. The traders who came up the White Nile to pass through the Sudd called this body of open water Mugran al-Bubur, "the meeting of the rivers"—the Bahr al-Jabal and the Bahr al-Ghazal—that they were about to enter. The local Nuer call it Lake Nu. As a reservoir it rises and falls with the rains. As a regulator it controls the volume of water that is released into the White Nile depending on the discharge from the Lake Plateau upstream and the Sobat River below. Water birds feed in profusion, hippopotamuses gambol in its shallow water, and crocodiles bask on the mud flats of alluvial clay. In high water the lake becomes a dam that impedes the sluggish flow of the Bahr al-Jabal into an imperceptible current meandering through a labyrinthine channel whose sharp bends entrap the prolific masses of floating sudd released by the rise of the lagoons.

When the river finally leaves Lake No, from its northeastern shore, and once again flows downstream it becomes the Bahr al-Abyad—the White Nile. From here it is a broad river, although the level plain soon separates it again into lagoons, marshy ponds, and parallel channels like the Khor Lolle. (A *khor* is a modest river or stream that is full and flowing in rains and sluggish in dry season.) Gradually the swampy banks on either side come closer together, and downstream from Tonga the valley becomes more clearly defined. Trees rise on the high ground by the river. To the south, the Bahr al-Zaraf finishes its struggle through the Sudd, and below Tonga it joins the White Nile, where it contributes an additional 30 percent of the waters of the Lake Plateau—much more than the trickle from the Bahr al-Ghazal. By the time the White Nile reaches its confluence with the Sobat River, it is a majestic river, a hundred yards wide, although it still carries a greenish-gray hue left over from the passage through the Sudd.

Once the British empire had established control over the upper Nile, British hydrologists began in earnest the study of Sudd hydraulics, the regimen of this great swamp. In his magisterial reports of 1901 and 1904, Garstin demolished the myth that the Sudd was a "continuous expanse of vegetation floating on the surface," showing instead that it was a maze of lagoons and lakes surrounded and awash with a formidable array of aquatic plants.[3] The topographical surveys of the Nile basin and the Bahr al-Jabal by Captain Sir Henry Lyons in 1906 confirmed Garstin's views. These men were followed by a coterie of British hydrologists committed to Sudd studies—A. D. Butcher in the 1930s, H. G. Bambridge after World War II, H. A. W. Morrice in the 1950s, and J. V. Sutcliffe before the resumption of civil war in the southern Sudan in 1983. Garstin had vision, Lyons instrumentation, Butcher measurements, and Morrice an understanding of the importance of the Sudd as an inseparable part in the conservation and development of the Nile. Sutcliffe, who had begun his Sudd studies in the 1950s, was the last and the most successful in describing Sudd hydraulics, but it is a subject still controlled by the vagaries of nature.

One of the questions the study of Sudd hydraulics sought to answer was the mystery by which billions of cubic meters of water simply disappeared from the swamp. A. D. Butcher dominated Sudd studies for the generation before the Second World War, and his influence remained for another generation thereafter. He argued that the massive loss of water from the Sudd must be attributed to the transmission of moisture from aquatic plants rather than evaporation from surface water. He was wrong. Half a century after his investigations J. V. Sutcliffe and Y. P. Parks clearly demonstrated that evaporation, not transpiration, is the principal cause of the losses. Butcher had done his studies at a time of steady low Nile flows, so he underestimated the rate of evaporation because the floodplain was smaller than normal.

In the Sudd the amount of loss is actually fairly constant, and it does not vary significantly between open water and that covered by aquatic vegetation. The volume of water lost is determined by the extent of flooding over which the evaporation takes place. On a plain of such insignificant slope, the rise of floodwater by an inch or two can inundate hundreds of square miles, exposing them to evaporation that cannot be offset by rainfall. Between 1905 and 1980 the mean annual flow into the Sudd from the Bahr al-Jabal fluctuated between 15 billion and 66 billion cubic meters, an annual average of 33 billion cubic meters. The quantity of water that emerges from the Sudd, after evaporation, has remained the same from one year to the next—16 billion cubic meters, or half the annual average flowing from the Lake Plateau. The 17 billion cubic meters, on average, that evaporates is the equivalent of 20 percent of the water that reaches the High Dam at Aswan. Billions of cubic meters of water can enter the Sudd at Bor, but the amount returned to the White Nile always remains the same.[4] The water lost could irrigate an additional 2.5 million acres in Egypt.

The Sudd itself has nestled for millions of years in the heart of the Nilotic plain, tilting imperceptibly from south to north at less than seven inches to the mile, and ab-

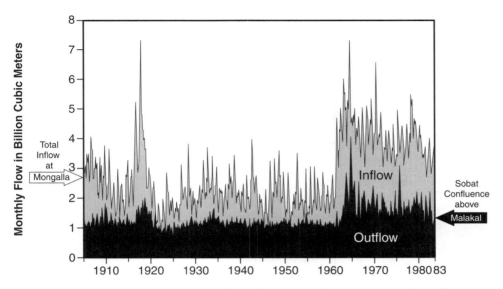

Sudd Flows, 1905–1983 (Source: J. V. Sutcliffe and Y. P. Parks, The Hydrology of the Nile, *1999)*

sorbing the sediments of Africa, now many miles deep. The Sudd governs the Nilotic peoples who surround it, the Dinka and the Nuer, by its two distinct environments, the permanent and the seasonal swamp. The permanent swamp contains the uninhabited lagoons and lakes, whose size and surface are determined by the rainfall from the south Atlantic on the Lake Plateau and the Bahr al-Ghazal. The seasonal swamp is more vulnerable. The volume from the Bahr al-Jabal and the Bahr al-Ghazal determine how much water will spill from the permanent swamp into the seasonal pastures, the *toic,* whose rich forage sustains the cattle of the Dinka and the Nuer.

From May to October the rains come from the south Atlantic, and the Sudd expands to cover the toic, confining the Dinka and the Nuer to their tukuls and the cattle to their barns. At the end of the rains in October, the Nilotes burn the grasslands to produce a flush of new growth; these young grasses are enough for their cattle to eat as they migrate behind the receding waters of the Sudd, reaching the toic by the end of January. During the years of average Nile flow the toic is sufficient to support the pastures on which the cattle and the Nilotes grow fat and fecund in great cattle camps from February to May, when the living is full and easy. This is the time when the Dinka and the Nuer settle disputes, intermarry, exchange cattle, and remember the good times in anticipation of the harsh months to follow.

In the first half of the twentieth century the difference between the permanent and

A Dinka fisherman in the Sudd near Shambe (Photograph © Kazuyoshi Nomachi/Pacific Press Service)

the seasonal swamp was known, but neither had been measured or was understood. In the latter half of the century, Sudd studies by British and Egyptian hydrologists with advanced technology provided new explanations of Sudd hydraulics. The first aerial survey of the Sudd was made in 1930, but the size of both the permanent and the seasonal swamps was calculated with little knowledge about the differential between the inflow from the Lake Plateau and the outflow at Lake No. The Sudd can never be measured with any real accuracy. It expands and contracts with the day, the month, the season, and the year, all governed by the fluctuations in outflow from the equatorial lakes, the rivers of the Lake Plateau, and the Bahr al-Ghazal.

Between 1905 and 1960 the Sudd covered about five thousand square miles. Suddenly, between 1961 and 1964, the equatorial lakes rose more than eight feet from the unexpected rainfall on the Lake Plateau, which produced 170 billion cubic meters of water in Lake Victoria alone. This huge volume of additional water, twice the amount that appears at Aswan every year, was confined within the geological fortifications of the equatorial lakes and had nowhere to go but down the Nile. Overflowing into every crevice, the Bahr al-Jabal surged down its channel, dumping the water into the Sudd. The Sudd expanded until it covered more than twelve thousand square miles, an area the size of Maryland and Delaware. For twenty years, from 1960 to 1980, the discharge from the equatorial lakes doubled, from 27 billion to 50 billion cubic meters annually, a volume of water sufficient to kill thousands of Nilotes and feed millions of Egyptians.

Overwhelmed by the implacable pressure from rising water, the papyrus walls encompassing the lagoons burst into thousands of spillways through which the waters rushed, inundating the surrounding meadows. These seasonal grasslands became part of the permanent swamp. The Dinka and the Nuer lost 120,000 cattle, and without the cattle tens of thousands of Nilotes died. The Twic Dinka called the flood *await-har,* or skeletons, for it left behind only the bare bones of dead trees rising out of their grasslands, now covered in water. Zaraf Island disappeared. Whole villages, such as Jonglei, near the southern end of the Sudd, vanished. Thousands were killed in violent confrontations over the few remaining pastures above the flood. Navigation through the Sudd suffered as well. The excess water produced huge sudd obstructions that closed the Bahr al-Jabal and opened a new channel, which the *ra'is,* the river pilots, called the Bahr al-Jadid, the new river. The new river wanders through an extensive chain of lagoons, rejoining the remnants of the Bahr al-Jabal south of Lake No.

In the upper Nile basin, governance has always been an ephemeral affair. No one comes to the Sudd except to clear its channels, measure its water, or extract its oil. The Dinka and Nuer who live on the surrounding plains are governed by the regimen of the Sudd, and their lives have only been disrupted by those who have made their way up the Nile—Turks, Arabs, British, Sudanese. During the first half of the twentieth century British ignorance of the relationship between the Sudd and its inhabitants frustrated their efforts to govern. During the latter half of the century, Sudanese ignorance of this relationship—along with the dislocations following the great floods of the 1960s—helped precipitate the rebellion of the Nilotes in 1983, when civil war broke out once again between the southern and the northern Sudanese. Since then, the longest-running civil, ethnic, and religious conflict of the twentieth century has decimated the southern Sudan, killing two million Africans and destroying any prospects for developing its natural resources or the waters of the Nile. Sudd studies, of course, have been on indefinite hold ever since. The Dinka and the Nuer who live in the region remain determined to oppose any alien control of their waters, pastures, and plains. After twenty years of political anarchy in the southern Sudan, governance and any rational use of the Nile waters or its oil remain an elusive fantasy.

4 *Land Beyond the Rivers*

Ah, land of whirring wings
which is beyond the rivers of Ethiopia;
which sends ambassadors by the Nile,
In vessels of papyrus upon the waters!
Go, you swift messengers,
To a nation, tall and smooth,
To a people feared near and far.
To a nation mighty and conquering
Whose land the rivers divide.
—Isaiah 18:1—2

Few Nilotes live in the Sudd. They live in the land beyond its rivers, on the Nilotic plain of the Bahr al-Ghazal to the west and the upper Nile to the east. The Dinka and the Nuer are a product as much of their environment as of their genes. Physically the tallest and most supple and graceful of peoples anywhere in the world, their isolation behind the swamps and the enormous size of the land beyond the rivers give them independence of mind, pride, and cultural arrogance. No one has ever ruled them, not even themselves. They are a people who derive truth from experience and despise doubt. Their individuality is exalted by genius; their imaginations are vivid. Their creative arts are more verbal than physical. They regard organization as restrictive and therefore repugnant. Religion evolved from experience, not speculation; philosophy from reality. They frequently confuse rhetoric with leadership. The British anthropologist E. E. Evans-Pritchard's description of Nilotic society as ordered anarchy is as true today as it was when he made it in 1940. When the Turks and Arabs ended their isolation during the latter half of the nineteenth century, the Dinka and the Nuer defied their futile attempts to rule. When the British and the Sudanese sought to impose their imperial administration during the twentieth century, they also failed.[1]

The Turks, who already ruled Egypt, were the first to arrive in the upper Nile, where their firearms threatened the Africans living along the river, who did not have these weapons and had never experienced their power. "The blacks, who stood shortly before in large numbers on the shore, have fled because they saw the Turkish countenance of Sulimen Kashef's halberdiers," wrote Ferdinand Werne, the German engineer who accompanied the voyage commanded by Salim Qapudan that successfully navigated the Sudd to Gondokoro in 1840–1841. "The Turk is pleased at such fear, which is associated with hatred and contempt on the part of the negroes."[2]

During the 1880s, the Muslim reformer Muhammad Ahmad al-Mahdi and his followers, the Ansar, destroyed the rule of the Turks in the Sudan, establishing in its place an Islamic theocratic state. The Nilotes, however, resisted the challenge to their traditional religions, and the Mahdi failed to convert them to either Islam or allegiance to the Mahdist state. Following the confrontation with the French at Fashoda and the defeat of the Mahdist state in 1898, Britain, with Egypt, established rule over the Sudan in an arrangement known as the Anglo-Egyptian Condominium. Technically it was a system of joint governance, but in practice the British were in control, and they too tried to impose their idea of authority on the freewheeling Dinka and Nuer. But even with their machine guns and the "all-seeing eye" of the Royal Air Force, the British were no more successful than the Turks or the Mahdists.[3]

The administrative retrenchment in the Anglo-Egyptian Sudan during the Great Depression of the 1930s, followed by World War II, reduced British administration in the upper Nile to a few beleaguered officials to keep order, the product of a policy known as "care and maintenance." As long as the Dinka and the Nuer behaved, they continued in their traditional way of life unmolested by the burden of modernization. In 1956 the Sudan became an independent republic, and its leaders were determined to replace the benign British administration in the upper Nile with Arabic and Islam. For the next fifty years, the futile efforts of the Sudanese government to incorporate Africa into the Arab Islamic world precipitated the longest insurgency of the twentieth century, and, among the Africans themselves, revived animosities older than memory.

The history of the Nilotes is recorded only in their oral traditions, and their origins remain obscure. By the fifteenth century they had occupied the Nilotic plain east and west of the Sudd. The Dinka and the Nuer are cattle people who—when the pastures disappear in flood, leaving them and their cattle hungry—depend on fish from the rivers and sorghum from the land. The challenge from Turks and Arabs was a combination of imperial aggrandizement and exploitation of the three resources of interest in the Bahr al-Ghazal and the upper Nile in the nineteenth century—ivory, cattle, and slaves. Of the three, slaves were the most mobile and the most profitable. Slavery in the Sudan is as old as the imperial rule of the pharaohs of dynastic Egypt. For five thousand years, slaves from the Sudan have provided the human resources for the armies, harems, and households of Arabia, Egypt, and the Ottoman Empire. When the British occcupied the southern Sudan in the twentieth century, they put a stop to the traditional slave-taking *razzias,* or raids, and the trade in slaves, but they did not put an end to the tradition. Even today, slavery remains an accepted custom among the many different ethnic groups that live in the vast Sudan, beyond the authority of the government in Khartoum.

The British eliminated the slave trade, but their governance of the upper Nile was minimal. They insisted on order, administered by punitive patrols, and reduced the internal conflict between Dinka and Nuer over cattle and pasture land. They introduced new tropical medicines that enabled the few British administrators, known as Bog Barons—paramedics more than doctors—to reduce the spread of epidemic disease among both the Nilotes and their cattle. They imposed harsh punishments for those in possession of unregistered firearms and took a dim view of killing baby elephants. They brought peace and order to the southern Sudan during a half century of imperial rule but little else.

In the years that followed British rule, however, the fierce ancient rivalries between the Dinka and the Nuer have revived in the traditional competition for cattle, pasture, personal power, and—at the end of the twentieth century—leadership of the insurgency movement against the Sudanese government. Without order and pills, the Nilotes suffered great losses of people and cattle in the floods of the 1960s, and two million Dinka and Nuer have died in the past two decades from drought and war. The old rivalries have produced a plethora of expedient alliances—ordered anarchy—dominated today more by personal ambition and the struggle to survive, since the cattle and pastures have been decimated by nature and the security forces of the Sudanese government. Little has changed on the upper Nile in a hundred years, except that the historic internal conflicts between Dinka and Nuer have escalated thanks to the tech-

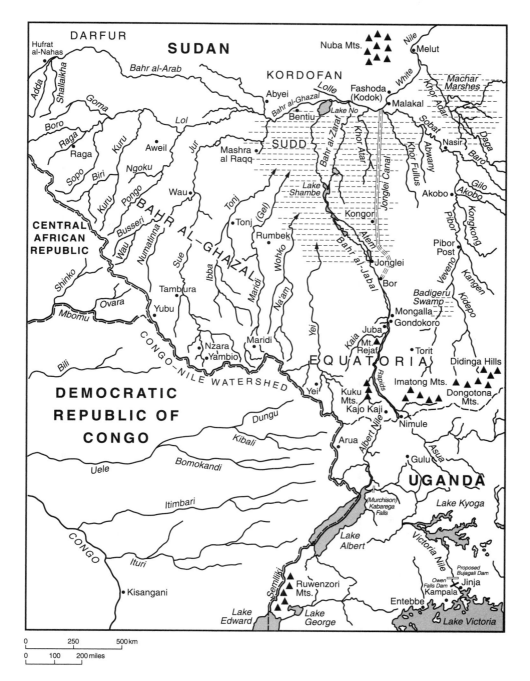

The Southern Sudan

nology of automatic weapons, which kill more efficiently than spears, and the greed produced by the discovery and extraction of oil.

Two centuries before the arrival of Asian and European imperialists on the upper Nile, the Dinka and the Nuer had settled on the Nilotic plain, probably precipitating the migration of the Luo. The origin of the Luo is as obscure as that of the Nilotes, and despite their legendary common homeland in the region of Rumbek in the Bahr al-Ghazal, their relations with the Nilotes have always been ambivalent. Luo traditions include descriptive and legendary accounts, rich in symbolism, of their travels. This voluminous oral literature suggests that the Luo, like the Nilotes, struggled over internal rivalries. Confrontations were decided by the heads of clans, whose authority imposed tribal coherence rather than the individuality so characteristic among the Dinka and Nuer, with whom there was always competition for pasture and uncontested authority in the grasslands. Any migration requires leadership, and the heads of the Luo clans established their own as they traversed a great arc around the Dinka and the Nuer on either side of the Sudd, seeking new lands. North of Lake No on the banks of the White Nile near Fashoda, their legendary leader, Nyikango, founded a new kingdom, and his people became known as the Shilluk.

The Shilluk prospered on the White Nile. They were cultivators of the soil, which meant a sedentary life and the political and social organization to make it productive. Unlike the Nilotes, they had the unity of a single river, the White Nile. Fashoda was the entrance to the land beyond the rivers and the Lake Plateau. The Nilotes now had no competitors for the land beyond the Sudd, but the Shilluk had to absorb the indigenous non-Luo inhabitants on the White Nile and meet the challenge of those coming up the river from the confluence, which helped develop unity of leadership. To assert Shilluk authority in the early sixteenth century, the founding father Nyikango was transformed over several generations into the *reth,* a divine king, who represented the spiritual and secular sanctity of the nation. One of the appealing fantasies of the Nile is the attribution of anything south of Aswan to the pharaohs of dynastic Egypt, including the notion of divine kingship. The last of the pharaohs had been buried for two thousand years before his ghost is supposed to have appeared at Fashoda, the village of the hornless cattle, royal capital of the reth.

By the eighteenth century the Shilluk, under a succession of able reths, had expanded their presence down the White Nile to its confluence with the Blue Nile at Tuti Island. For two hundred years the Shilluk controlled the waters of the White Nile and its crossings. The Baggara Arabs of Kordofan who came to the White Nile were taxed for the water they needed for their cattle. The traders and pilgrims coming from West Africa to the markets of Sennar on the Blue Nile, the Red Sea, and the shrines of Mecca and Medina paid their commercial and religious passage to cross the Nile. Any confrontation over water always leads to conflict at the river, in local courts, or in the staterooms of capitals, all three of which characterized the relations of the Shilluk on the White Nile with the Baggara from the west and the Funj from the east.

A more serious threat to Shilluk domination of the White Nile appeared at the confluence in 1821, when the armies of Muhammad Ali marched up the Nile to conquer the Sudan. By the mid nineteenth century, when Salim Qapudan first penetrated the Sudd, the Shilluk had lost the islands in the White Nile. They retreated before the firearms of the Turks, the Baggara stopped paying tribute for water, and the governor-general of the Sudan sought to consolidate Turkish authority at Fashoda. In 1869 he began to meddle in the selection of the reth, and six years later, in 1875, the Turks ended four hundred years of Shilluk independence. It has never been restored.

Back when Nyikango established his Shilluk kingdom at Fashoda, centuries ago, some Luo clan chiefs—contentious brothers of his—continued their travels eastward, to the rivers that flow down the Ethiopian escarpment and the Nile watershed from the south. At Adonga, on the south bank of the Akobo River, the legendary Oshoda founded the kingdom of the Anuak. Oshoda was no divine king, but he was the keeper of the royal emblems that embodied the spirit of the Anuak and all their ancestors for unknown generations. The emblems confirmed the legitimacy of the holder to rule and have become the symbol of determination to preserve the Anuak nation. Like the Nilotes and the Shilluk, the Anuak have never submitted to those who would rule them, whether the invaders were Nuer, British, Ethiopian, or Sudanese. In their resistance to outside domination, the Anuak have enjoyed three advantages in the twentieth century that the Shilluk and the Nilotes did not possess—frontiers, isolation, and guns.

Rivers do not make good frontiers, and this includes the Nile and its tributaries. Those who live by the banks of a river usually come from the same society. They will typically cross the river daily without concern, but they will seldom proceed upstream and will go down only with trepidation. The rivers of the world can facilitate commercial unity, as do railways and airlines. They do not create cultural homogeneity or political unity when a line is drawn down the middle as a cartographic convenience, dividing life on either shore. The Nile is not divided in this way, but the rivers of the Sobat basin remain today a tragic example of creating boundaries for the sake of expedient map making.

In 1899 Major H. H. Austin and Major Charles W. Gwynn of the Royal Engineers were ordered to define the boundary in the remote frontier between Ethiopia and the Sudan. They had no knowledge of the country, its inhabitants, or their language, the important factors in delimiting a frontier. Austin trekked north from Lake Rudolf, now known as Lake Turkana, in Kenya. Gwynn marched south from the Blue Nile along the Ethiopian escarpment. There was either too much water or too little. Supplies were short, and there was a war in South Africa that these officers found much more appealing than the miserable terrain they were trying to traverse. They resolved their dilemma by drafting the international boundary down the middle of rivers, a solution that, on paper, appeared so sensible that it was duly consummated in the Anglo-Ethiopian Treaty of 1902. In fact, their casual reconnaissance produced another African frontier, like so many drawn in the staterooms of Europe during the partition of the continent, that was a matter of convenience divorced from the realities of the land and its people.

Consequently, the frontier between Ethiopia and the Sudan does not follow the escarpment either above or below its precipitous slope, which is the natural boundary between those who live on the plains and those who live in the highlands. Each ethnic group living on this frontier has a very different environment, culture, and history. The international boundary, unfortunately, follows the rivers—the Akobo, which descends from the Ethiopian highlands to the Nilotic plain, to its confluence with the Pibor, and then down the Pibor until it meets the Sobat River. In following these three rivers, the border forms an enclave in Ethiopia called the Baro Salient. The pastures, swamps, and forests in this area do not belong geographically to Ethiopia, for they jut from the escarpment into the Nilotic plain. The salient is the home of the Anuak, who arrived sometime in the sixteenth century. Here the authority of government, whether in Khartoum or Addis Ababa, remains as irrelevant as ever. With sovereignty defined by a map drafted from expediency rather than understanding, the Anuak and the southern Sudanese insurgents for the past twenty years have exploited the frontier, like their predecessors, to continue in their independent ways—to the exasperation of presidents in the Sudan and Ethiopia who have no authority or control over their borderlands.

The frontier between Ethiopia and the Sudan is more than fifteen hundred miles long, and in the basin of the Sobat it is a wild land that is difficult to reach in the best weather, impossible in the worst. It is even less accessible from the highlands of Ethiopia than from the rivers of the Nilotic plain. The Baro Salient is the traditional sanctuary from disagreeable governance, a status disrupted in this century only by the futile attempts of alien authorities to impose their rule. Even in the remotest regions of Africa, however, no one is ever truly isolated. The flow of Nilotes and their cattle in search of water and grazing, the fugitives from order, and the ubiquitous traders pass across frontiers with little concern for central governments. When the imperial authorities from Khartoum and Addis Ababa tried to impose order on the Sobat frontier, they were sucked into endless border disputes over worthless territory, leaving the Anuak with a remarkable degree of independence, particularly after they acquired guns.

The Ethiopians have been the principal suppliers of firearms in this region for more than a hundred years. In the last decade of the nineteenth century, Emperor Menelik II of Ethiopia assiduously began to acquire modern weaponry, particularly rifles, to oppose Italian ambitions to conquer his kingdom. His defeat of an Italian expeditionary force at Adua in 1896 preserved the independence of Ethiopia for another forty years, and it precipitated a flood of cheap surplus guns, muzzle-loaders and later rifles, from the Ethiopian highlands to the Nilotic plain. The Anuak were eager buyers, hoping to preserve their independence from the Nuer, the Ethiopians, and the British. This technological revolution in the Baro Salient enabled Akwei-wa-Cam, the custodian of the royal emblems, to consolidate his political authority through control of the used firearms.

Around the turn of the century, Austria abandoned the Werder rifle, and European and American syndicates purchased the guns in large quantities for sale in Ethiopia. By 1911 the Anuak had an estimated ten thousand breech-loading rifles; the following year, these turned out to be decisive in the defeat of a large, well-armed patrol of the Anglo-Egyptian government of the Sudan. British arms were soon engaged in a much greater conflict in Europe than frontier skirmishes in the Sudan among savages "who understood no theories but only what they see with their own eyes." But World War I led to another flood of surplus arms, including the French Gras rifle, and between the two European wars the British decided to leave the Anuak to their own devices.[4]

While World War I was being fought, however, Menelik II's daughter Zauditu had become empress of Ethiopia, in 1917. As a woman she was provided with a regent, a relative of the emperor, a young *ras* (prince) named Tafari Makkonen. Ras Tafari sought to modernize Ethiopia, and in the process he became a powerful regent. When Zauditu died in 1930, Ras Tafari was crowned emperor and took the name Haile Selassie I ("Strength of the Trinity"). In spite of the capability he demonstrated as emperor, he was no more successful in asserting his authority over the Anuak of the Baro Salient than the British had been twenty years earlier. His frontier agent, Qagnazmatch Majid Abud al-Askar, a Syrian Druze and adventurer with a pretentious title (Imperial Agent for the Nilotic Tribes of Ulu Baboor and Sayo-Wallaga Provinces), made determined efforts. But the Anuak defeated Haile Selassie's forces in 1934, and the Ethiopians made no further attempts to assert their authority in the land below the escarpment for another fifty years.

The Sobat is a major contributor to the waters of the Nile, but its isolation and incomprehensible frontier discouraged any consistent hydrologic studies. A lone inspector of customs at Gambela represented Britain on the Ethiopian frontier. He was expected to maintain order in the interest of commerce and civilization. Gambela, named after an Anuak notable, was a British enclave of four thousand acres at the bottom of the escarpment, inside Ethiopian territory. An imperial anachronism on the Baro that consisted of a rustic house, a cubicle for the customs office, and storage sheds in need of repair, Gambela was isolated from November to June while the otherwise navigable Baro became a stream or disappeared altogether. For six months each winter Gambela was a hermit's cave. When the rains returned in the summer, it became an island surrounded by flowing water and steamers that could now come to collect the coffee carried down from the highlands.

Since neither the British nor the Ethiopians ruled the borderlands, the most powerful official around was the British inspector of customs, who collected the lucrative tariff on coffee, which was the essential lubricant for all social, commercial, and official affairs in the northern Sudan. For almost thirty years, from 1921 to 1949, two inspectors, Colonel J. F. H. Marsh and J. K. ("Jack") Maurice, dominated affairs on the frontier through their personalities, twenty police, four machine guns, and commercial diplomacy. In October 1956, however, the newly independent government of the Sudan handed over Gambela to the imperial Ethiopian government, as a gesture "for our future relations with Ethiopia." It had remained a sanctuary for half a century that the Anuak never threatened or attacked, presided over by two imperial arbitrators with no power except their respected impartiality in settling the interminable frontier disputes. In the next half century Gambela became an equally important sanctuary for southern Sudanese insurgents.[5]

On the sparkling sunlit morning of 18 August 1955, No. 2 Company of the Equatorial Corps was drawn up on the parade ground at its headquarters in Torit in preparation to proceed to Juba and Khartoum to march in the parade celebrating the independence of the Sudan. The men were all southern Sudanese. Most were illiterate veterans who had never served outside the southern Sudan and had settled comfortably with their families on farms surrounding the garrison town. Rumors were rife that they were being sent down the Nile to be enslaved or imprisoned. When the command was given by their northern officers to move out, they rushed the ammunition stores, armed themselves, and rampaged through the town, killing northern Sudanese and looting their shops. News of the mutiny spread like the wind. In the villages and towns of Equatoria northerners were hunted and killed. Thus began a half century of violence that has decimated the population in the Upper Nile. Not surprisingly, the mutineers of 1955 and the organized liberation movement that evolved from their spontaneous rebellion, the Anya-Nya, sought protection in the rivers, swamps, pastures, and forests on the ungovernable frontier of the Baro Salient, where guns are always plentiful and demonstrable.

After seventeen years of futile conflict, and the deaths of many thousands of noncombatants, the Sudanese government and the Anya-Nya agreed to a peaceful settlement at Addis Ababa in 1972. The agreement granted autonomy to the south, but the government still had no authority in the Baro Salient, which remained a sanctuary for members of the Anya-Nya who refused to accept the terms of the Addis Ababa Agreement. After ten years of tension, the settlement collapsed in 1983, when President Jaafar al-Numayri revoked the provisions for autonomy and religious freedom in the southern Sudan. This provoked a renewal of the civil war against the Sudanese government by the Sudan People's Liberation Army (SPLA), with its headquarters at Bilpam, on the Ethiopian side of the Pibor in the Baro Salient.

The renewal of civil war produced another massive influx of firearms to this volatile frontier, and this time they were far more sophisticated than the Werder and Gras rifles of a prior era. The capitalist arms dealers of the past were replaced by apparatchiks of the Soviet Union, who organized a massive infusion of weapons that soon found their way down the escarpment to the SPLA in the Baro Salient and the southern Sudan. The Soviet decision to support the revolution appears to have been motivated by the opportunity to advance its influence in Africa during the Cold War rather than any political sympathy for the rebels. The ensuing Cold War competition in northeast Africa was an extension of the interest both Russia and the United States had long shown in Ethiopia.

Moscow's infatuation dated from the end of the nineteenth century, when the Russian Orthodox Church became aware of the historic bastion of Orthodox Christianity in Ethiopia. The czar was, after all, the protector of all Orthodox Christians throughout the world, and his ministers were eager to accommodate their French allies in Africa out of a common concern over imperial Germany. An impressive diplomatic mission departed for Addis Ababa in 1895, led by the distinguished explorer Aleksandr Elyseev and accompanied by a scoundrel, Nikolai Stefanovich Leontiev. Menelik responded to the Russian initiative by sending his emissaries to St. Petersburg bearing gifts and the Ethiopian Order of Solomon for the czar. Patriarchs, dukes, and the czar received the Ethiopians. They were entertained at banquets and parades, and their orthodoxy was confirmed in religious services consummated with decorations, rifles, ammunition, and a cash credit for Menelik—all orchestrated by Leontiev. Menelik had few illusions about Leontiev's personal ambitions, but he perversely sought to further his own imperial goals by appointing the Russian as governor of the western frontier, which included the Baro Salient, with instructions to incorporate the Nilotic plain and its rivers into the highlands of Ethiopia.

Leontiev was followed by a succession of Russian missions to assist Ethiopian imperialism among the Luo and Nilotic peoples between the highlands and the Nile. No one on the Nilotic plain—not the Anuak, not the Nuer, and certainly not the British—was prepared to let Menelik's forces loose on the tributaries of the Nile that defined the Baro Salient. A host of Ethiopian troops, led by a ranking nobleman named Tessama, struggled down the escarpment in March 1898 and disintegrated from disease, desertion, and the desolation of the Sobat plain. Only eight hundred Ethiopians were reported to have reached the mouth of the Sobat, where they planted the Ethiopian flag and claimed the Nile waters for Menelik. Having done their duty, they immediately retreated to the highlands. The Ethiopians did not assert their rights to the Nile waters for another century.

The Americans came later than the Russians, and they were practical, private, and more concerned about hydrology than imperialism. In the early 1930s the J. G. White Engineering Company of New York conducted extensive surveys for a dam at Lake Tana on behalf of the new emperor. Haile Selassie intuitively realized the importance of the Blue Nile, but in 1930 neither he nor the Egyptian minister of public works understood the waters of the Sobat and its basin. In the salient, the dilapidated post at Gambela provided the longest register of measurements of the Baro River. The records were useful, for the Baro is the main tributary of the Sobat. But they were of no help in understanding the hydrology of the rivers that flow from the Ethiopian highlands, those on the Uganda frontier south of the Sobat, or the unmeasured and enigmatic Machar Marshes to the north.

Like the Bahr al-Ghazal, the Sobat represents the coming together of tributaries; its basin is formed by the confluence of the Pibor and the Baro, in the northwest corner of the salient. Unlike the Bahr al-Ghazal the contribution of water from the Sobat is substantial, thanks to the Ethiopian connection. Its watershed is the size of Wyoming, and like Wyoming the rivers are half in the highlands and half in the plains. The rivers of the Pibor plain derive their water from intermittent highland streams, like the Kideppo, that tumble down from the Didinga Hills and the Imatong Mountains, the watershed and frontier between the Sudan and Uganda. On the Nilotic plain vigorous streams become sluggish rivers—the Veveno, Lotilla, and Kangen—that meander through ill-defined valleys of cotton soil that bisect the plain between the Bahr al-Jabal and the Ethiopian escarpment. Like the rivers of the Bahr al-Ghazal, they overflow their banks during the rains and spill their waters onto the heat of the plain.

The streams that form the Pibor River come together at Pibor Post, another miserable outhouse of twentieth-century imperialism. Originally known as Fort Bruce, its termite-infested *tukls,* or huts, and ramshackle brick buildings were built in 1912. The place has received little improvement in eighty years, except for the defensive perimeter the Sudanese erected in the 1980s as part of their futile effort to subdue the insurgency on their imperial frontier. As the Pibor flows north, it receives the Akobo River and the Gilo River, which collect more waters from the Ethiopian highlands to the east. The Akobo is the ancestral river of the Anuak, and Akobo Post at its confluence with the Pibor has had little symbolic significance and fewer facilities for a century. As at Gambela during the first half of the century, there were two strong British personalities who dominated affairs at Akobo, Lieutenant Colonel C. R. K. Bacon and Major G. W. Tunnicliffe. They maintained a fragile peace on the frontier that enabled the agents of the Egyptian Ministry of Public Works to come up the rivers from Malakal and measure the waters.

North of Akobo, the Pibor defines the western boundary of the salient. When it meets the Baro to produce the Sobat River, the Pibor delivers only 17 percent of the resulting flow; the Baro does the rest. The Baro River's watershed is the size of Denmark, only one-quarter of the Pibor plain to the south, but when the rain clouds from the south Atlantic rise above the Ethiopian highlands, the Baro cascades down the escarpment in surges. It discharges 8 billion cubic meters between June and October—10 percent of all the water to reach Aswan—and nothing thereafter. This massive spate, equivalent to the Semliki, cannot be contained on the Sobat plain. When it is tamed at the bottom of the escarpment, the Baro is navigable, but it cannot absorb the additional water from the Machar Marshes and the Khor Adura and Khor Jokau. These rivers descend in flood from the highlands, but unlike the sluggish waters from the Congo-Nile divide that disappear into the plains of the Bahr al-Ghazal and the Sudd, only half is lost. Four billion cubic meters of these Ethiopian waters, by the force of their flow down a precipitous slope, manage to reach the White Nile through the Sobat. The other 4 billion, 5 percent of the Nile waters that arrive at Aswan, evaporate into the atmosphere above the Machar Marshes.

The Machar Marshes lie in a depression between the Ethiopian escarpment and the Nile north of the Sobat, annually absorbing half the water from the Baro that the Sobat cannot carry to the Nile. It is off the beaten track of tribesmen, traders, and imperialists, a place where no one lives or wishes to except crocodiles and water birds. Even fugitives and southern Sudanese insurgents do not go into the marshes. The imperialists—Turks, Arabs, British, Sudanese—were not interested in a marsh on the periphery of their passage south through the Sudd to Africa. The U.S. Air Force was the first to survey Machar, in 1945. Others followed on the ground, but they were few, and their measurements were insufficient to understand Machar hydraulics except to confirm that the marsh absorbs the overflow from the Baro and the runoff from Ethiopian torrents. Even today the swamp remains all but unknown.

Hydrologists in the twentieth century have used the limited readings to promote their schemes for Nile control, for the loss of Ethiopian water in the marsh is more straightforward than Sudd hydraulics. Like the Sudd, evaporation claims half its waters. But it is a modest swamp that expands directly with the amount of rainfall and covers 2,500 to 5,000 square miles, roughly the size of Connecticut, without the lagoons and lakes that regulate Sudd waters. The marsh is not an obstacle to government, for no one lives there. And unlike the Sudd the marsh is not an obstacle to navigation, except for the few who have come to calculate its consumption of water.

The diversion of Ethiopian water into the wilderness of the Machar Marshes cannot diminish the importance of the Sobat River. Geologically and historically it is a very young river. Only ten thousand years ago the Sobat received the waters of Lake Turkana and eastern Africa. Its importance for Nile control was realized only recently. Garstin and his successors, obsessed with the waters of the Lake Plateau, were inclined to ignore the Sobat until it sent high waters down to the White Nile in 1917 and 1918. In those years the contribution from the Sobat was one-quarter of the total Nile waters at Aswan. Hurst and his officials from the Egyptian Ministry of Public Works began to measure the Sobat methodically and with growing enthusiasm.

They discovered that the Sobat was a short river, two hundred miles, with defined banks, vigorous flow, and gradual curves making its way across a Nilotic plain that was treeless and unbroken, except for a peculiar hummock called Doleib Hill. Rising above the Sobat near its confluence with the White Nile, the hill is the former home of American Presbyterianism in the Sudan. As the only high ground for many miles, for a hundred years it has been the place to measure the Sobat, particularly from September to December when the Ethiopian waters are in full flood. Despite the losses on the Nilotic plain and in the Machar Marshes, the Sobat is a major source of the

Nile. During the twentieth century its average annual flow discharged 14 percent of the total Nile waters at Aswan, equal to the equatorial waters that struggle through the Sudd to the Sobat, and exceeded only by the flow of the Blue Nile at Khartoum.[6]

Surprisingly, no one lived at the confluence of the Sobat and the White Nile until 1870 when Sir Samuel Baker established a large post, Tawfiqiyah, as the base camp for the greatest of all Nile expeditions. Baker, seeking to incorporate the upper Nile and the Lake Plateau into the expanding empire of Khedive Ismail, occupied the upper Nile and Equatoria, but he lost in his confrontations with the powerful states surrounding the equatorial lakes. The Sobat contributed to his failure. At its confluence with the White Nile, the substantial discharge from the Sobat retards the flow of the Nile from Lake No. When the discharge is greater than average, which it appears to have been in 1870, sudd can no longer pass downstream. The islands of aquatic plants became formidable obstructions, and getting past them in 1870 and 1871 so exhausted the expedition that Baker no longer had the resources or energy to advance the Egyptian empire to the Lake Plateau. Others came after Baker—Gordon, Emin Pasha, Marno, Gessi—but Tawfiqiyah fell into ruin during the Mahdiya; the Ansar preferred to stop at Fashoda to make their preparations for jihad on the Nilotic plain and the Lake Plateau beyond the Sudd.

After the British had firmly removed the French from the Nile in their confrontation at Fashoda, they rebuilt Tawfiqiyah, and their steamers chugged up the river to Lake No, the Sudd, and the lands beyond the rivers. When 20 billion cubic meters surged down the Sobat in 1917 and 1918, Tawfiqiyah was destroyed, ending the British imperial presence at the confluence. The British relocated their bastion of empire to a high bank, ten miles to the north, called Malakal. Malakal is perched above the eastern bank of the Nile five hundred river miles south of Khartoum, having no reason for its construction other than to record the Nile flow on the frontier of Islam. Old Nile hands of every ethnicity say that Africa begins at Malakal. There you can smell the fertile continent of Africa that lies to the south beyond the desert, protected by its sentinels, doleib palms on the west bank and the great banyan trees on the east. They guard the gateway to Africa.

Malakal hangs between land and river, a pendant between two worlds. To the north lie the Sahel and the desert, Arab and Muslim. To the south sprawl the Sudd, the Nilotic plain, and the Lake Plateau of Africans with different cultures, languages, and religions. Like any border town, Malakal belongs to neither world, absorbing some of the best and most of the worst of each, its identity as artificial as its creation. Yet Malakal has its moments. Thousands of white egrets, their plumage aflame in the

The waterfront at Malakal, with Anuak people bringing charcoal from the Sobat on floating islands of sudd

rays of the setting sun, sweep across the Nile at dusk to roost in the banyan trees that rise along the riverfront. In equatorial Africa there is no twilight, and when the sun goes down darkness falls instantly on the market of Malakal, as the islands of sudd float silently downstream.

In Malakal the Africans—Dinka, Nuer, Shilluk—intermingle with the Arabs from the north, the Fur from the west, and Ethiopians from the east. They banter, shout, and argue on the waterfront around the steamers and barges rusting in the Nile far from the dangers of war upstream. Under the banyan trees the gamblers play Wit, a game of chance, in defiance of any authority, departing only when their stakes are lost or night arrives. Downtown Malakal consists of squares delineated by conservative colonial administrators converted to socialist urban planning. Commercial shops line the dusty streets, and beyond them are the government buildings, the mosque, the church, and the suburbs of tukls scattered along the high ground in tribal ghettos, interspersed with small shops and the cacophony of competing radio stations. Dominating the waterfront is the sprawling compound of the Egyptian Irrigation Department, whose diminished authority is symbolized by its sagging barbed wire fence.

In the beginning, the officials of what was then called the Egyptian Irrigation Service worked their way up the Nile through the northern Sudan to Khartoum and then the White Nile where, like the centurions of Emperor Nero two thousand years before, they confronted the Sudd. In 1915 the service was transferred to the Ministry of Public Works and elevated to departmental status under Hurst, the new director of the ministry's physical department, who was determined to bring order to the measurement of the Nile waters. The place to begin measuring was at the new administrative post at the end of all the tributaries of the upper Nile basin, at Malakal.

At the end of World War I, Egypt's need for more water was compromised by the needs of those upstream in the Sudan. In 1920 a seven-year program of studies and surveys was launched from Malakal, "for the execution of those major engineering works forming part of the general scheme for the further control of the Nile to complete the development of Egypt." Money has never been a problem for the Egyptians when it concerns their Nile waters. Elaborate facilities mushroomed at Malakal. Houses, generators, six steamers, power barges, oil storage tanks, and bureaucratic buildings were surrounded by a formidable fence that dominated the shabby six-room Mudiriyya, the office of the imperial government. At the end of the waterfront was the modest bungalow of the British governor, whose unprotected flower garden was regularly ravaged at night by hungry hippos.[7]

The total expenditure by the Egyptian Irrigation Department for this operation to measure the Nile at Malakal far exceeded the budget of the Anglo-Egyptian government for the administration and governance of the whole of the southern Sudan. Without realizing the implications of its arrival in Africa, the department established a well-financed, secure, and autonomous imperial outpost on the east bank of the White Nile. The senior administrators at Malakal were originally British; only after World War II did Egyptians occupy these posts. They were there to secure the water of the upper Nile for Egypt, not to conduct anthropological investigations, sociological studies, or economic surveys for the millions of Sudanese who lived in the land beyond the rivers. They were strangers in a strange land, and their autonomy at Malakal only reinforced perceptions of their historic cultural arrogance when their elaborate facilities became a symbol of Egyptian imperialism.

Along the reach of the White Nile between Malakal and Khartoum the land turns from green to brown. The lush vegetation of Africa gradually disappears. The land is now covered by short grass that turns to scrub amid sand and stone. Camels and horses come to the river, and with them men and women speaking many different languages—Cushitic, Sudanic, Arabic. Most are Muslims. Many are not. The river is broad and ponderous, dotted with clusters of the beautiful and incestuous water hyacinth that intermingles with the pedestrian papyrus that slowly sinks to the bottom of the river. The slope that the White Nile traverses is less than that of the Sudd, but there is little rain and no tributaries to produce lagoons or swamps. Its sluggish current is content to bifurcate around islands. The land on either bank stretches across the Bilad al-Sudan ("Land of the Blacks"), the name given by medieval Arab geographers to the great Sudanic plain south of the Sahara. The horizon remains an interminable line of nothingness broken by occasional jabals, isolated granite hills that twelve thousand years ago conspired with sand dunes to block the flow from the equatorial lakes.

After flowing through this landscape northward for three hundred miles from Malakal, the river reaches the town of Kosti. Two bridges span the Nile at Kosti, one rail, another road, linking the rich agricultural region of Gezira with the western re-

The White Nile with saturated sudd sinking to the river bottom

gions of the Sudan, Kordofan and Darfur. The bridges are the first to cross the Nile north of Juba, eight hundred miles upstream. Unlike Juba and Malakal, Kosti was not a British imperial outpost but a ramshackle store established by a Greek trader, Constantinis Kosti, who had followed Kitchener up the Nile. He set up shop at the Nile crossing historically used by the pilgrims and merchants from the western Sudan to reach the Red Sea, Arabia, and Mecca, and it became known as Kosti town. Here Africans and Arabs on the caravan routes from east and west met those going up and down the Nile from north and south. Today the waterfront is the principal port of the White Nile. Its steamers carry goods and people in times of peace, weapons and food for the victims in time of war.

North of Kosti the White Nile divides to pass Aba Island, where Muhammad Ahmad retreated in 1870 to a life of rigorous asceticism. In 1881 he proclaimed to the Sudanese that he was the Mahdi, a leader many Muslims had expected to appear and restore justice to the oppressed. Aba Island became a fortress of devotion defended by his spiritual power and the martial prowess of his followers, the Ansar, who destroyed every punitive expedition sent against them. In 1882 he organized the *hijra,* the flight of the faithful, and his Ansar left the island to begin the destruction of Turkish and Egyptian rule in the Sudan, in which they succeeded with the capture of Khartoum in 1885. After this stunning victory, his death six months later appeared to confirm his spirituality.

Beyond Aba Island the reach of the White Nile is no longer a shallow, wide river but a broad reservoir held back by the Jabal Auliya Dam, thirty miles south of Khartoum. An elongated concrete structure built on an arid plain in 1937, Jabal Auliya was to store the waters of equatorial Africa and then release it in January when the massive flood from the Blue Nile was spent. The hydrologists, being British and quaint, called this water Timely, for it ran down the sluices during the winter and spring, from January to June, when the Ethiopian rivers did not. The hydrologic elegance of using the waters from the Lake Plateau to compensate for the inadequacy of the Blue Nile after its flood was irresistible. In the first half of the twentieth century there was plenty of water. The loss of 2.5 billion cubic meters from evaporation, or 60 percent of the water stored in the reservoir, seemed a small price to pay for more timely winter water in Egypt.

Jabal Auliya has been a barrier to the spread of the ubiquitous water hyacinth to the Nile downstream from Khartoum. Its reservoir has made water easily accessible for lucrative pump schemes on the White Nile. The arid wastelands surrounding it have recently become the place to relocate unwanted southern Sudanese from their ghettos in the suburbs of Khartoum. None of these innovations, however, can disguise the redundancy of the cement dam languishing in the Sudan sun. Its vast reservoir provides over-year storage, which is no longer needed since the completion of the High Dam at Aswan in 1971.

Thirty miles below Jabal Auliya the waters of the White Nile join those of the Blue at Khartoum, Arabic for "the elephant trunk." The name is derived more from the shape of the geologic spit of alluvial deposits nearby than from the elephants that used to live there. They disappeared during the desiccation of Africa two thousand years before the arrival of the Turks in 1821. The Turks converted a fishing village into the capital for their new imperial conquests of the Sudan and the upper Nile. The point where the two great rivers of the Nile come together at Khartoum is called the Mogren—the meeting—by the Arabs, and today it is commemorated by a bridge, a shabby amusement park, and that bastion of Western imperialism, the Nile Hilton. These symbols of modernization cannot replace the monuments in the Antiquities Museum, a few hundred yards along the waterfront of the Blue Nile, or the gauges that measure the Nile flow at the coming together of Africa for Egypt.

5 *The Blue Nile*

*The Nile has two special features: one is the extent of its reach since we do not
know of any other river in the inhabited world that is longer, for its beginnings
are springs that well from the mountain of the Moon which is purported to
be 11° south of the Equator, two is its increase which takes place when other
rivers dry up for it begins to increase when the long days start to end and
reaches its maximum with the autumn equinox when the canals are
opened to flood the lands.*
—*Abdullatif el-Baghdadi, ca. 1200*

Waldecker's spring on the hill of Kikizi in Burundi was only one of the coy fountains
of the Nile. The other, unknown to Herodotus, bubbled from the sacred spring of
Sakala in the heart of the highland plateau of Ethiopia. At an elevation of nine thousand feet, the spring lies more than two thousand feet higher than the manicured
grass of Kikizi a thousand miles away. The ground surrounding Sakala is a quagmire
from the waters seeping out of the mountain of Gish, a mile to the west, and covered
with thick bush bedecked with heather and flowers. The air is filled with the birdsong
of the Ethiopian stonechat.

The journey of the Blue Nile begins here at Sakala. The great river's remotest
headwaters tumble from the spring as a stream and then a river called the Little Abbai,

Mount Gish overlooking the sacred spring of Sakala, the beginnings of the Blue Nile (Photograph, Paul B. Henze)

which plunges down from the plateau until it reaches the placid waters of Lake Tana. From the south end of the lake flows the Great Abbai, the Abay Wanz in Amharic—the Blue Nile—which takes a southeasterly course until it plunges over Tisisat Falls. After this spectacular drop of 150 feet, the river curves in a large arc to the south and then to the west. Three main tributaries—the Didessa, the Dabus, and the Beles rivers—join the Blue Nile before it leaves the highlands for the plains of the Sudan. Here the river is blocked by its first real obstruction, the Roseires Dam. As it continues north of the dam, the river waters the fertile plain of the Gezira on the west behind another obstacle, the Sennar Dam, and then receives its last tributaries, the Dinder and the Rahad rivers, from the east. After winding its way for nine hundred miles from Lake Tana, the Blue Nile meets the White Nile at the great confluence in Khartoum.

The Ethiopians have come to the source of the Blue Nile for centuries to derive spiritual sustenance from the beginnings of a great river whose course and end they did not know. Europeans arrived in the seventeenth century, when the emperors of

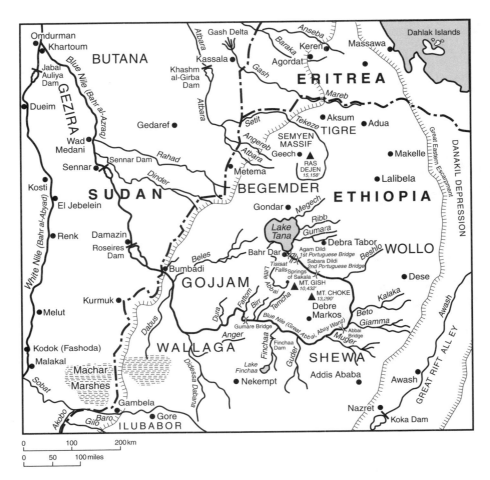

Ethiopia and the Blue Nile

Ethiopia consecrated the Church of Saint Michael and Zarabruk on a ridge a half mile above the sacred spring. The priests of the church became the custodians of the holy waters, and the only ones permitted to draw the hallowed libations from its depths for the pilgrims, the curious, and the occasional tourist. In 1615 the Spanish Jesuit Pedro Páez accompanied the Ethiopian emperor Susenyos to the spring of Sakala. In return the Spaniard converted the emperor to Roman Catholicism, thus achieving the dubious distinction of precipitating a rebellion in Ethiopia between Coptic Christian and Catholic Christian religious beliefs. Páez left a description of the spring:

The source of the Nile is in the western part of the kingdom of Goyam [Gojjam], in the upper part of the valley, which resembles a large plain, surrounded on every side with ridges of hills. . . . When I was living in this kingdom along with the emperor and his army, I ascended this place, viewed everything diligently and found at first two round fountains there, both about four palms [two feet] in diameter. . . . We tried also the depth of the fountain and put a lance into the first, which, entering 11 palms, seemed to touch, as it were, roots of the neighbouring trees entangled with one another. The second fountain bears from the first about a stone's throw cast; laying the depth of this, by putting a lance of 12 palms, we found no bottom, but having tied two lances together, in length 20 palms, we tried the thing again; but not even then could we find the bottom and the inhabitants say that the whole mountain is full of water.[1]

The Scottish laird James Bruce set out from Algiers in 1768 to seek the source of the Nile. Two years later he arrived at the sacred springs of Gish, where the Emperor Tekla Haymanot II appointed him governor of Sakala. To the relief of the Ethiopians, Bruce hated papists, but he did not linger to enjoy his satrapy and instead made his leisurely way home through the Sudan, Egypt, and Europe. Upon returning to London in 1774 his account of adventures in Ethiopia and the discovery of the source of the Nile was received with ridicule. His descriptions of the Nile source were no more believed by the sophisticated wits in the salons or the media of London than the accounts of the Spanish and Portuguese Jesuits. Bruce may have been mocked, but he was not ignored. His eight volumes, *Travels to Discover the Source of the Nile,* were avidly read by those who came after him to seek the source of the great river.

The stream gurgling out from the spring is the Little Abbai, sometimes called the Wetet, or Milk Abbai, because of the foam of its rapids as it rushes down from the highlands. The Little Abbai's ravine is protected by tall trees and thick undergrowth, and few Ethiopians are found there. They live on the plateau above the river that stretches to the Amadamit hills and the towering peaks of the Choke massif in the east. The Little Abbai is called the Gihon in the Bible, where it is described as one of the four rivers that flowed from the Garden of Eden, which was located in Ethiopia.

Like every mountain river, the drop of the Little Abbai is greatest at the beginning, where it runs through a steep valley of cedar forest surrounded by crags, craters, and extinct volcanoes. It falls over cataracts at a rate of seventy-eight feet per mile. After thirty-five miles the gradient lessens and the Little Abbai becomes broad and navigable, a tranquil, muddy river flowing across a plain of grass. Over the course of its seventy miles, the Little Abbai falls a total of thirty-five hundred feet. At its end, the river reaches the southeastern shore of Lake Tana, where it deposits its heavy sediment from the mountains at an expansive estuary protected by two spits of silt.

Lake Tana is a shallow lake, fourteen hundred square miles in area and only about thirty feet deep. To the east the plateau rises gradually into the highlands. Sluggish perennial rivers—the Megech, the Ribb, and the Gumara—run down into Tana's basin, contributing little water but providing a luxurious habitat for the crowned crane and the yellow-billed duck. West of the lake, only six miles from the shore, are cliffs that prevent any substantial contribution of water from their towering walls. But when the south Atlantic monsoon assaults this escarpment, enormous quantities are produced for the Sudan and Egypt on the western side of the watershed. These waters tumble into the canyon of the Blue Nile through mighty perennial rivers—the Beles, the Didessa, and the Dabus—and powerful intermittent tributaries flowing directly into the Sudan, including the Dinder, the Rahad, and the Atbara. Surrounded by precipitous landforms, Lake Tana contributes less than 7 percent of the total flow of the Blue Nile.

The lake is dotted with a hundred holy sites on its islands and shores. These were built for worship and contemplation by monks and emperors who were inspired by the isolation and sanctuary of its somnolent waters and rocky heights. The churches, monasteries, and imperial tombs of Lake Tana are rich repositories of the Ethiopian past in a remote and holy place. The first emperor, Menelik I, according to legend the son of Solomon and the queen of Sheba, arrived on the shore with the sacred ark from the Temple in Jerusalem. The Virgin Mary is said to have rested on the island of Tana Cherqos during her flight from the Holy Land to Egypt. Vestiges of Jewish and southern Arabian practices, reminiscent of pagan cults that have survived the imposition of Hebraic, Christian, and Muslim religious practices, persist among the people surrounding the lake.

By the fourteenth century Christianity had settled in churches and monasteries around Lake Tana, and its islands are dotted with churches built in medieval times. The monastery of Saint Stephen on the island of Daga was built amid lava outcrops, red loam, and *warka* fig trees. The more imposing monastery of Debre Mariam, on an island near Bahr Dar, was the work of Saint Thadewos, who was said to have power to part the waters and forbid crocodiles to enter the lake. Kebran Island became a favorite burial ground for the emperors after Amda Seyon built the Church of Saint Gabriel in the fourteenth century, with its rich wall paintings and large library of illuminated manuscripts. Other islands—Bet Manzo, Rima, Misilai, Tana Chargos—were all surmounted by shrines. Debre Sinai, the Church of Mount Sinai, was built on a promontory near the Dirma River.

North of the lake, the traditional route from the interior of Ethiopia to the Sudan and Egypt traversed the shore, north to Gondar and through the escarpment to Gallabat, the frontier town on the border between two worlds that neither Christian Ethiopians nor Muslim Sudanese have ever controlled. Churches and mosques on either side of this religious divide have been desecrated throughout the centuries. The power of religion on a volatile frontier, however, has seldom inhibited the flow of commerce. Throughout history a vigorous trade has passed through the northern lake ports and the Tana corridor to the Sudan and Egypt. There was coffee from the highlands of Ethiopia, for which the Sudanese and the Egyptians would pay any price. There were blocks of salt from the Danakil desert in the eastern Rift, which brought higher prices than Ethiopian concubines. The few ports of call on the lake were for moving the goods of the plateau down the Nile, for most people chose not to linger on its shore, which had few amenities and plenty of malaria.

Bahr Dar is a promontory of scoriaceous blocks of lava on the southern shore of Lake Tana, with a basalt dam that contains the lake at its outlet into the Blue Nile gorge. For centuries a small village and its Church of Saint George have overlooked the harbor guarded by towering figs and the roosting black-headed heron. During the 1950s development studies by British and German consulting firms concluded that Bahr Dar could become an industrial city, and perhaps the future capital of Ethiopia, if hydroelectric power from the Blue Nile were to be captured. This enthusiasm for progress appeared confirmed in 1963 with the completion of the Tis Abbai hydroelectric power station, built on the western bank, in the province of Gojjam, below Tisisat Falls, with assistance from Yugoslavia. Soviet planners arrived in the 1970s, and electrical and political power enabled them to transform Bahr Dar into a city of light industry, powerboats, airports, and rectangular residential districts.

The Blue Nile begins here at Bahr Dar. The Amhara people who command the river's heights both east and west call it the Tis Abbai because from December to July its waters are a rich blue-gray color, which in Amharic is described by the word *tis,* meaning smoke. In its flood, from August to November, the water turns tan-brown. Soon after leaving Lake Tana, the river's first rapids appear, at Chara Chara, an ancient ford for merchants and political officials who crossed the Abbai for trade and administration between Gojjam in the west and Addis Ababa in the east. A concrete bridge at Bahr Dar has supplanted the ford as a crossing point. In 1967, Emperor Haile Selassie built his last imperial palace on a hilltop below and east of the ford. Here he could gaze through glass doors, enveloped in bronze and defended by stone lions, on the waters of Lake Tana and the Blue Nile, taking great satisfaction from the bridge that had helped consolidate his empire beyond the lake and the river.

As the river makes its way from Lake Tana to the plains of the Bilad al-Sudan, it drops 4,600 feet in 450 miles, an average of 10 feet per mile. The average is deceiving, for the descent of the Blue Nile is not a smooth and steady affair. Instead it is interrupted by geologic and hydrologic obstructions, plunging suddenly over rapids and falls produced by lava dikes. These are formed by molten rock from the core of the earth that arrives infrequently and is tempered by cool water into a resistant mass. Farther downstream, tributaries in awesome spate carve massive quantities of sedimentary rock from the plateau, and then deposit them downstream where they block the flow of the river. These sedimentary rocks do not have the strength of lava, but they are reinforced annually during the rains when the tributaries add stone to what the river has worn away during the year.

All cataracts try to beguile the unwary with their Siren song of quiet water before the brink. After cascading over the rocks for eighteen miles from Lake Tana, the Blue Nile suddenly sweeps onto a serene expanse that insidiously appears protective, even somnolent. Just beyond this stretch, however, the river disappears over the lip of the great lava dam at Tisisat Falls, plunging vertically for 150 feet. During the rainy season it becomes a massive cascade, earning the name the Ethiopians use to describe the mists rising from the falling water, the Smoke that Thunders. In winter, the torrent separates into four falls surrounded by luxuriant flowers and butterflies left from the summer rains.

Below the falls the Abbai descends into an inner gorge with precipitous walls that constrict the river into a millrace 10 feet across in low water and 150 in flood. Here is where Emperor Fasiladas built the first Blue Nile bridge, Agam Dildi, in the seventeenth century. It was a single stone arch 30 feet wide with masonry side structures to keep the crossing above high water. Local folklore attributes the bridge to Portuguese stonemasons who remained in Ethiopia after the expulsion of the Jesuit priests, although it is possible that it was built by masons from India, where Iberian construction techniques were known. The identity of the builders has disappeared, but the memory of the Portuguese remains in the structure's name, for it is commonly called the Portuguese Bridge. It became a main artery of commerce and the means for Ethiopian imperial control between the eastern and western provinces that were divided by a great canyon.

Agam Dildi, the first Portuguese Bridge over the Blue Nile below Tisisat Falls (Photograph, Paul B. Henze)

Beyond the Portuguese Bridge the Abbai has cut through a great field of lava. The defile is dark, forbidding, malarial, and uninhabited except for the dense bush and trees that spring from the rocks beside the rapids. The canyon rises above this inner gorge a mile high and many miles wide. The Blue Nile's geology and hydrology are no different from other great chasms that have been shaped by their tributaries. Its streams, rivulets, and rivers are aqueducts for the deluge from the south Atlantic that is flushed into the canyon by the steep gradient from towering highlands. The ferocity and power of this massive movement of water cannot be imagined or predicted, but there are differences in the geologic formations of these ravines that control how much of this water reaches the mainstream and when. North of the canyon the rivers that tumble from the uplands of Gojjam are short and perennial. Their contributions are not generous, but they come at the right time to sustain the flow of the Blue Nile after its annual flood has passed to the Sudan and Egypt. Longer are the canyons of Shewa, which are fed by thousands of rivers large and small that drain an immense plateau south of the Abbai. These waters carry millions of tons of Ethiopian nutrients, and far down the river these have sustained the Egyptians for thousands of years.

The Blue Nile gorge below Tisisat Falls (Photograph, Paul B. Henze)

The gorge in this part of the Blue Nile is convulsed by rocks and boulders that are tossed in from the steep canyons perforating the river on either side. These side canyons prevent any track along the river, but each one has a trail down from the hamlets huddled above on the plateau. These paths descend through treeless lava cliffs that rise a thousand feet above the Abbai. Thirty miles beyond Agam Dildi is a second and more substantial bridge, the Sabara Dildi, or the Broken Bridge. This is also sometimes known as the Portuguese Bridge, for its masons, too, are remembered in oral traditions. The bridge spans the Blue Nile in two large arches eight feet wide, each supported by a stone pier in the middle of the river; three smaller, broken arches are needed to span the river in flood. Until the twentieth century it was the crossing for armies, merchants, and officials sent to assert the authority of the emperor in Addis Ababa over Gojjam in the west.

Beyond the Broken Bridge the Abbai has carved a hard passage through the lava plateau of Gojjam and reached the underlying soft sandstone. Tributaries enter from left and right through precipitous ravines, vibrant after the rains with the brilliant red globes of Ethiopian lilies. From the highlands of Gojjam the Tammai, the Ganj, the Chay, and the Gad rivers drop into the Blue Nile through side canyons fifteen hundred feet deep. These streams are torrents during the summer rains, dry beds in winter. On the left bank the canyons of the Beshlo and the Kalaka rivers are longer and not as steep, and they contribute more water than the tributaries from Gojjam. Here scrub forest and the thirsty tamarisk flourish from the limitless water and rich nutrients amid patches of teff, the millet native to Ethiopia, whose yields justify the arduous descent to the river by Amhara cultivators from the temperate but less fertile plateau.

The river cuts easily through the soft sandstone, falling a thousand feet in 150 miles before reaching Shafartak Ford, now spanned by the Abbai Bridge. Even after masonry bridges were built over the gorge in the seventeenth century, most Ethiopians waded, floated, or swam with their possessions across the Blue Nile at its many fords. Two hundred miles downriver from Lake Tana, Shafartak was the preferred crossing, for it was the most direct route from Addis Ababa to Debre Markos, the capital of Gojjam. It is a steep descent to the ford, nearly a mile from plateau to river through red sandstone, but there were springs halfway on either side of the canyon where caravans could prepare for the crossing. When the water was low, men and mules would wade. During flood, men, women, and their goods were carried on rafts of inflated skins, *jendies,* while the mules swam. At Shafartak the governors of Gojjam defended their autonomy from the authority of the central government in Addis Ababa. Control of the ford not only contained the imperial ambitions of emperors but enriched the provincial treasury of Gojjam through stiff tariffs, until the twentieth century when a paved motor road replaced the narrow caravan track. In 1948 a curvilinear bridge was built across the ford, symbolizing the determination of Haile Selassie to bind the western provinces to his central government.

The Ethiopian highlands and the Blue Nile (Photograph © Kazuyoshi Nomachi/Pacific Press Service)

Below Shafartak the Blue Nile flows majestically to the west through an expanding canyon patrolled by the Martial eagles that sail on the updrafts from its cliffs. Its northern walls on the right bank are lacerated by deep ravines from Gojjam. Its southern palisades are wide portals of extended canyons from Shewa and Wallaga. The rivers from Gojjam—the Wabas, Temcha, and Birr—are short. Their perennial flow, however, maintains the level of the Blue Nile after the flood like the timely water from the White Nile. The rivers from Shewa—the Giamma, Muger, Guder, and Finchaa—are long and seasonal. They have a massive flood in spate that has carved great side canyons into the southern highlands of the Blue Nile.

The floodplain of the gorge begins to expand, with the river cutting through the sandstone and leaving cones of basalt on its banks from strata high on its cliffs. There is rich soil here, but canyon claustrophobia keeps the Amhara huddled on the plateau above in the sunlight of their villages and churches, free from river malaria. They make the deep descent into the Abbai either to cultivate its shores or to cross the river. The peasants from the villages are rewarded with abundant yields of teff, chickpea *(shimbra),* and pepper *(simsim).* The traders and travelers must choose a path that leads to one of the Blue Nile fords—Balatai, Yekatel, Satana, Wamet, Jambir, Mabil, Guter, and Zakas. These fords are commercial and personal. Armies and officials were traditionally reluctant to commit themselves to the river crossing, but merchants regarded them as a reasonable commercial risk in low water after the harvest. Each of the fords had its clientele. The Mabil Ford below the Fatam was the historic crossing for the caravans of slaves being driven to be sold in the markets of northern Ethiopia. Forty miles downstream, the Zakas Ford marked the geologic, provincial, and ethnic frontier of western Ethiopia.

The Zakas crossing is at a sharp right angle in the Abbai, which at this point has dropped

The Blue Nile gorge (Photograph © Kazuyoshi Nomachi/Pacific Press Service)

twelve hundred feet in two hundred miles (six feet per mile) from Shafartak. The hippopotamuses are the only permanent residents, for no one lingers at the ford below the intermittent Dim River at the base of the towering Gum Yasus ridge. This immense spur, descending from the Ginda Cliffs of the western escarpment, drops from the Church of Gum Yasus on its promontory three thousand feet in seven miles through spectacular vistas to the Abbai. At the Zakas Ford the Blue Nile once again turns southwest. No longer confined by the perpendicular channels between Tisisat and Shafartak, it flows through a broad floodplain of depressed basins and major tributaries as it approaches the Bilad al-Sudan. There are no more rapids, only the thick humidity of malarial forests, and tributaries that contribute the most water to the Blue Nile from the high plateau—the Didessa, the Dabus, and the Beles rivers.

These three great tributaries are the hydrologic trinity of the Abbai. The Didessa provides 13 billion cubic meters of water, one-quarter of the total volume of the Blue Nile. The Didessa begins in mountain streams that become rivulets on the slopes of the Vennio and Wache ranges, which command Wallaga province south of the Abbai, much as Mount Choke dominates Gojjam above the gorge. Once formed, the Didessa flows east for fifty miles before turning north where it cuts a canyon for another hundred miles. Its basin covers thirteen thousand square miles, and during the summer rains its major tributaries—the Wama and the Anger from the east, the Dabana from the west—add to its powerful flood.

The Dabus is a very different river from the Didessa, despite similar beginnings. It rises in the mountains and their impenetrable bamboo forests around Asosa in southwest Wallaga. Its basin is approximately the same size as that of the Didessa, but it has more annual rainfall over more months. The canyon of the Didessa is comfortably carved in a majestic trough through a plateau, whereas the Dabus flows through the disintegrating escarpment of the Ethiopian highlands, assaulted by the torrential rains from the south Atlantic. Its narrow canyons are punctuated by flat basins that collect the enormous quantities of water that fall on the borderlands. The largest of these is the Dabus swamp, 350 square miles of stagnant water. It is a diminutive imitation of the great swamps of the Sudd, but it performs the same functions. The swamp is a regulator that controls the flow of the river, and water is devoured there by aquatic plants and evaporation from the surface. Unlike the Sudd, the Dabus swamp is confined by a narrow canyon. The water that escapes it contributes 4 billion cubic meters at its confluence with the Abbai.

The Beles is the most beguiling tributary of the trinity on the lower Abbai. It rises near Lake Tana, close to where the Blue Nile itself begins, but on the other side of the watershed west of the lake. The two rivers do not meet until the Blue Nile has finished its circuitous passage of five hundred miles around greater Gojjam. The Beles, meanwhile, takes a much more direct course, slicing down eight hundred feet in 120 miles to the Bilad al-Sudan, where it pours a billion cubic meters into the Blue Nile. Its dramatic geologic configuration has excited engineers of many nationalities with its potential for hydroelectric power. The U.S. Bureau of Reclamation estimated in 1946 that the river could produce a billion kilowatts of hydroelectric energy—more power than Ethiopia could absorb at least until the twenty-first century. In 1956 the giant German electronics company Siemens provided engineering details for a power station. Today, Italy has been assisting the Ethiopians to construct a modest project on the upper Beles.[2]

The Beles joins the Blue Nile near the Ethiopian-Sudanese border, an ungovernable frontier that governments of neither the Sudan nor Ethiopia have ever controlled, let alone administered. On the heights of the western escarpment live the Oromo people, whom the surrounding Amhara, Muslims, and Europeans have pejoratively called the Galla. The Oromo speak an eastern Cushitic language from the plains of Sidamo in southwestern Ethiopia. Their linguistic cousins are the western Cushites, who moved down the great Rift valleys of East Africa long before the arrival of the Bantu during the first millennium C.E.

The Oromo were a pastoral people who practiced some mixed farming on the plains. They were modest in number, and in the fourteenth century the expanding Amhara Christian empire overwhelmed and absorbed them. In the sixteenth century Muslims under the leadership of the charismatic imam of Harar, Ahmad ibn Ibrahim al-Ghazi, known as Ahmad Grañ (the Left-Handed), invaded the Ethiopian plateau. These warriors destroyed churches and monasteries, slaughtered priests and monks, and ransacked the palace of the emperor, demolishing the authority of the Christian Amhara in the western highlands, which the Oromo soon occupied. The hill country was no place for the pastoral life of the plains, but the Oromo brought with them a more prized commodity than scruffy sheep and emaciated cattle—arabica coffee, which flourished in the cool and well-watered soils of the highlands. Converted to agriculture, a disagreeable profession for former pastoralists, the Oromo worked the coffee using Shangalla slaves from the malarial lowlands and swamps of the lower Abbai. During the revival of the empire under Menelik II at the end of the nineteenth century, the Oromo were once again officially incorporated into the Amhara Christian state. At the beginning of the twenty-first century, the Oromo are once again seeking their cultural and political independence from the orbit of Addis Ababa.

The area surrounding this frontier is full of marshes punctuated by basalt outcrops and forested rolling hills. Few outsiders have come this far by water. In June 1903 a wealthy American interested in geography and sport, W. N. McMillan, tried to go downriver from the mouth of the Muger, but he soon wrapped his three steel boats around boulders in the rapids and had to hike back out to Addis Ababa. In the 1950s and 1960s there were several attempts by Germans, French, and Swiss. Arin Rubin, a Swede, canoed for nine days during high water from the Shafartak bridge to Khartoum—an extraordinary feat that he carried off with, understandably, more concern for crocodiles than for hydrology. In 1968, the first expedition to complete the passage of the canyon of the Blue Nile was led by Captain John ("Blashers") Blashford-Snell, with thirty-two recruits from elite units of the British army and selected civilians, elaborately equipped and trained at the Royal Military College of Science. After reconnaissance in July and August, they made their way down the river during full flood in September 1968, fighting off bandits, devious crocodiles, and the river, and surviving mainly on courage.

About thirty miles past its confluence with the Beles, the Blue Nile enters the Sudan at the Bumbadi River, about halfway between Lake Tana and Khartoum. It has fallen nearly a mile (4,510 feet) in 560 miles from Lake Tana, with wild fluctuations. From January to June the tributaries are dry or diminished and easy to cross, as only a billion cubic meters pass the fords of the Abbai during this time. The summer rains from the south Atlantic dramatically change the Blue Nile. By August the river in flood is carrying 16 billion cubic meters, which gradually dwindles as the rains stop until it is only 2 billion in December.

At the border of the Sudan the Blue Nile is checked, for it comes to an end as a free-flowing river where it enters the large reservoir formed by the Roseires Dam. The Roseires Dam was built at Damazin, four hundred miles upstream from Khartoum, in 1966. Provision for the dam in the Nile Waters Agreement of 1959 was intended as partial payment to the Sudan for its acceptance of the Aswan High Dam in Egypt. It was designed to retain a modest amount of the Abbai in its reservoir, 2.6 billion cubic meters, for hydropower and irrigation. The Blue Nile has exacted its own price from the dam for this confinement. As the first obstacle on a mighty river, the dam collects the debris and soil gathered from all the rivers of the Ethiopian highlands. Within ten years of its completion, the reservoir had lost three-quarters of its capacity thanks to the millions of tons of silt deposited there by the river.

Once released from Roseires, the Blue Nile flows broad and majestic across the Sudanic plain for another two hundred miles to Sennar. The plain tilts imperceptibly to

The lower Blue Nile gorge

the north, and on either side of the river the land is flat and covered with thorny bush and small heglig trees punctuated by arid grass pastures. Flowers blossom in the rains among the weeds in the meadows. From Sennar to Khartoum, the course of the Blue Nile is roughly parallel to the White Nile moving north with similar solemnity a hundred miles to the west toward their grand confluence. In the heartland of the Sudan, these two great rivers define an area a hundred miles wide and two hundred miles long, the Gezira, Arabic for "island." Until the completion of the Sennar Dam in 1925 the productivity of this Sahelian island plain was governed by the rains from the south Atlantic, not the waters of the Blue Nile. In good years, when the rain fell, the living was easy on both banks. The thunder would roll, the rain would fall, and the land would erupt in carpets of twining white and pink convolvulus and endless fields of sorghum, making it the granary of the Sudan. When the rains did not surge out of the southwest, the island between the rivers became a mirage, a land of harsh abstinence and unremitting heat.

The Sennar Dam transformed the Gezira plain from a place dependent on the vagaries of rainfall to one of rich fertility, sustained by irrigated agriculture. The dam was built at the site of the former capital of the storied Funj people, whose mighty kingdom flourished at Sennar and controlled the Gezira plain in the seventeenth and eighteenth centuries, until they were defeated by Muhammad Ali's forces in 1821 and relegated to the limbo of history. British engineers led by Sir Murdoch MacDonald, the irrigation adviser to the Egyptian Ministry of Public Works from 1912 to 1921, planned the Sennar Dam as a source of dependable water for reliable agriculture on the Gezira plain, thinking principally of cotton for British textile mills. The dam would store half a billion cubic meters of water to irrigate the Gezira during the crucial months of germination from January to April. Years of plenty would provide sufficient water for both the Sudan and Egypt, but the Egyptians feared that in years of drought there wouldn't be enough for them, which resulted in a storm of controversy. The dam was completed in July 1925 after numerous fiscal and construction crises, and since then it has provided a solid foundation for the Sudan's formerly nomadic and fragile agricultural economy. Today the site is a quiet place except for the roar of the Blue Nile when it is released through the two-mile dam's eighty gates after its confinement in a peaceful fifty-mile reservoir.

The Sennar Dam, 1926 (Reproduced by permission of Durham University Library)

Below Sennar the Dinder and the Rahad rivers join the Blue Nile. These begin in the rough hill country of the western Ethiopian escarpment and abruptly descend to the vast Sudanic plain of gray soils and brown sandstone. They are spate rivers, pouring copiously from June to September following the rains but then shrinking to pools and sandy riverbeds the rest of the year. They occupy a vast and neglected sub-basin covering eight thousand square miles, and in spite of their irregularity these rivers are major contributors to the Blue Nile. In the few months before they die the Dinder and the Rahad together deposit 4 billion cubic meters of water, 10 percent of the total Blue Nile flow, and millions of tons of nutritious soil. The drama occurs in August, when the Dinder disgorges nearly a billion cubic meters of water within five days. The Rahad collects its water from a basin one-third the size of the Dinder's, but in flood it supplies half as much as its southern neighbor.[3]

Below these tributaries, at the northern end of the Gezira, lies Khartoum, built at the great confluence of the Blue and White Niles. On most great rivers, the place of convergence with a powerful tributary becomes a hub of commerce, a focus of military and political strategy, a place to demarcate boundaries, a crossing for those arriving from somewhere else. These are meeting places of cultures, religions, and peoples of different color. In spite of the drama of two great rivers coming together to bind the longest and most ancient river of the world, until the nineteenth century Khartoum was neither a meeting place nor a center of any demonstrable activity except fishing. Geologically it was a sandy spit, invested with malaria and surrounded by a forest of thorny haraz trees. "Khartoum had no attractions in itself, no industries, and no inherent source of wealth," wrote one commentator. When the Turks arrived at the confluence in May 1821, Ismail, son of Muhammad Ali and commander of his expeditionary force, camped at the village of Omdurman on the west bank rather than cross the Nile to three mud huts and the crumbling remains of a forgotten cemetery.[4]

The following year the Turks established a more permanent camp of straw huts and a few more substantial tukls of mud brick, but the new rulers concentrated their control at Wad Medani, roughly halfway between Sennar and Khartoum. Ali Khurshid Agha arrived at Omdurman in May 1826 as the governor of Muhammad Ali's colony of Sennar, and he recognized the importance of the confluence of the two great rivers. He established a unified administration in the Sudan for his viceroy in Cairo, placing its capital at Khartoum, and in the process becoming one of the great imperial proconsuls of any nationality on the Nile. By the time he left in 1838, Khartoum was home to barracks, a hospital, a new mosque, a thriving bazaar, four hundred permanent houses, and thirty thousand inhabitants.

Since then Khartoum has never looked back. Pretentious houses were built east of the governor-general's palace on the banks of the Blue Nile. In the nineteenth century a few were grand establishments that gave Khartoum the panache of an African frontier town. In 1876 Dr. Wilhelm Junker, the German-Russian naturalist returning from his explorations on the Congo-Nile watershed, dined with Muhammad Ahmad al-Aqqad, the successful agent from the House of Aqqad at Aswan, in his well-appointed establishment on the Blue Nile embankment. Muhammad was the most powerful trader in ivory and slaves from the Bahr al-Jabal to the Victoria Nile. He employed the governor-general's band to entertain Dr. Junker, with a certain amount of dissonance, with waltzes from Strauss and excerpts from *Aïda*. Little had changed on the Nile since Rhadames, in love with Aïda, betrayed the plans for the Egyptian invasion of Ethiopia.

6 *From Khartoum to Kush*

The Ethiopians [Nubian soldiers of Kush] were clothed in panthers' and lions'
skins, and carried long bows, not less than four cubits in length, made from
branches of palm trees, and on them they placed short arrows made of cane;
instead of iron they were tipped with a stone, which was made sharp.
—Herodotus, fifth century B.C.E.

The Nile becomes complete at Khartoum, where it begins a new passage through the
Nubian swell, a geologic uplift that separates the plains of the Sahel from the Egyptian Nile. Over the thousand miles from Khartoum to Aswan, the Nile falls more
steeply than on the plains, measured here in feet per mile rather than inches. The geology of the Nubian swell alternates between hard granite and soft sandstone. The
power of moving water over time has worn down the sediments but not the more resistant granite, and the remaining hard rock has produced the famous rapids known
as the six cataracts. The northernmost, at Aswan, is called the first cataract, and from
there the others proceed upstream at regular intervals to the sixth at Sabaluqa, fifty
miles north of Khartoum. The cataracts are modest rapids, navigable in high water,
that cannot compare to the majesty of Kabarega Falls on the Victoria Nile or Tisisat
Falls on the Blue Nile. But they have helped define the history of this vast region,
known to those who come from the north as the Corridor to Africa.

For those who come out of Africa, the Nile begins at the Sabaluqa gorge, the gateway to Nubia and the ruins of the ancient kingdom of Kush. Sabaluqa is the first
gorge cut by the waters coming down the river through the granite of the Nubian

The great confluence of the Blue and White Niles at Khartoum (Photograph by J. F. E. Bloss, reproduced by permission of Mrs. C. M. L. Bloss and Durham University Library)

swell. Its walls rise more than three hundred feet high for eight miles, forming a natural defensive position that surprisingly has been ignored by those who have failed to control the heartland of the Sudan. Flowing out of Sabaluqa into the placid waters of the Shendi Reach, the Nile surrounds the islands and overflows onto the verdant fields beyond the river. This is the great oasis of the Bilad al-Sudan for the nomads who pass through Sahelian grass, thorn trees, and acacias to pitch their camps in the sand. These nomads, non-Arabs known as the Beja, come from the Red Sea Hills and the Butana Plain in the east with their herds of camels. They are an ancient people, descendants of the Medjay raiders from the eastern Sudan, who harassed the dynastic Egyptians, and the Blemmyes, whose predatory instincts disconcerted the Romans.

These are lands of great antiquity that do not belong to either Egypt or Africa. Herodotus knew there was a city called Meroe, the later capital of Kush, on the Nile south of Egypt somewhere in Africa. The ruins of Meroe, its cities and temples, remain on the eastern bank of the Nile shortly before it meets its last major tributary, the Atbara River. South of the ruins, in the large area between the Nile and the Atbara lies the Butana Plain, sometimes called the Island of Meroe. After two thousand years of unremitting desiccation and the environmental avarice of its inhabitants, this island is today an arid hinterland. It was not always a Sahelian steppe. For nearly a thousand years (from around 500 B.C.E. to 300 C.E.) after the capital of Kush was relocated to Meroe from Napata, the Island of Meroe was parkland. There were forests for fuel to smelt iron and forage for elephants, which were the center of a cult at the great temple complex of Musawwarat es-Sufra, southeast of the capital. At Meroe an intermittent stream, the Wadi Hawad, would sometimes disgorge the runoff of rain from the Butana Plain, but its annual dry bed was historically the high road for trade and invasion across the steppe to the Atbara and the ancient kingdom of Aksum in the Ethiopian highlands.

At the end of the seventeenth century, the Shilluk could no longer dominate the region around the confluence of the White and Blue Niles against the expanding power of the Fur kingdom from Darfur in the west and the Funj kingdom at Sennar in the east. Merchants and pilgrims from the western Bilad al-Sudan, seeking to avoid the interminable conflicts on the direct route between the two, went north of the great confluence, past the sixth cataract at Sabaluqa, to cross the Nile at Shendi. This village became a bustling emporium for another two hundred years at the intersection of two great perpendicular trade routes. From the west came trans-Sahelian caravans to exchange goods, gossip, people, and ideas before taking the way east to Quz Rajab

Pyramids of the kings and queens of the kingdom of Kush at Meroe (Reproduced by permission of Durham University Library)

on the Atbara, and eventually to the Red Sea. From the south came traders with their goods, mostly ivory and slaves, and unfamiliar customs and news before going north across the Bayuda or Nubian deserts to the Nile and then down the river.

Shendi was ruled by *makks* (petty kings) of the Ja'aliyyin nomads. These were the descendants of rustic immigrants from Arabia, the unruly Bedouins of upper Egypt during the Middle Ages. Always in search of greener pastures and loot, the Ja'aliyyin first went south into the Red Sea Hills, where they were joined by other Arabs who for centuries had crossed the Red Sea from Arabia and moved west to the Nile. Their progress over generations gave their ravenous camels, goats, and sheep ample opportunity to accelerate the desiccation of the Island of Meroe. The Ja'aliyyin brought Islam and Arabic to the Sudan, but over time they were assimilated through marriage with the Beja of the Red Sea Hills, the Nubians of the Nile, and other Africans from south of the confluence.

The Ja'aliyyin who came to the Nile, like every refugee from desertification in the past five thousand years, sought to settle on well-watered land. Their relations with pastoral kin who remained in the hinterland were ancestral and symbiotic. This closeness began to dissolve when both became Muslims, speaking Arabic, with Nubian and Arab wives and African concubines, manufacturing Arab genealogies in search of legitimacy. Their makks were warlords, powerful personalities. The most remembered is Makk Nimr, a rascal known as the Leopard, who as the Ja'ali city boss of Shendi from around 1785 to 1846 heroically defied Muhammad Ali and his Turks. Shendi's caravan trade was disrupted during the Mahdiya at the end of the nineteenth century, and again by the construction of the railway to Khartoum in the twentieth, and the town has never recovered. Today it is a forgotten river outpost that the Nile passes by on its way to the Atbara.

The Atbara River, the Bahr al-Aswad, provides the last water for the Nile during its fifteen-hundred-mile passage through the Nubian and Egyptian deserts. The Atbara is a major contributor to the Nile, carrying a volume equal to that of the Sobat. As at Khartoum, however, its confluence has been of no historic consequence in antiquity or modernity. No one had ever settled there until the twentieth century, when the imperial British in Sudan required the dependability of a railway rather than the difficulty of navigating the Nile. They established the headquarters of Sudan Railways at the town of Atbara, and from here their locomotives soon reached across the Butana to Port Sudan, the Red Sea, and the world.

The Atbara begins in the Semyen Mountains of Gondar in northern Ethiopia, where the volcanic summits are as high as the granite peaks of the Colorado Rockies

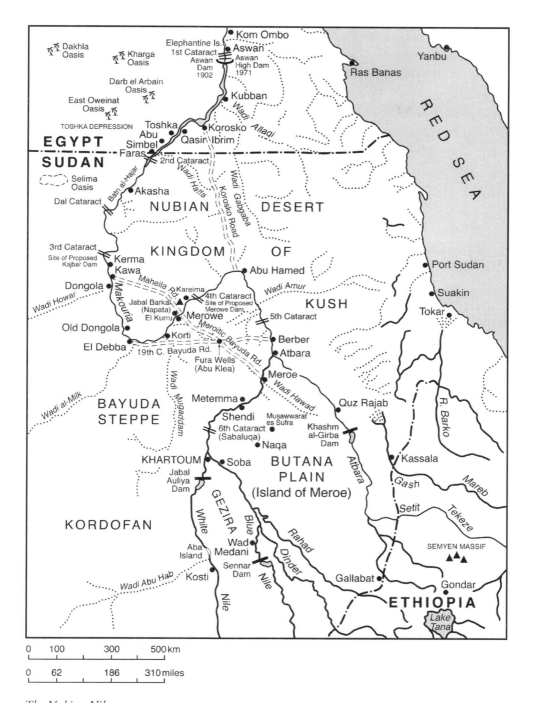

The Nubian Nile

and deep ravines imprison the steep gradients of their waters. The Atbara has no lakes for its sources, only thousands of mountain streams swollen by the annual rains from July to October. These torrents become the rivers Angereb and Tekeze (known in its lower reaches as the Setit), and they meet below the Ethiopian escarpment on the plains of the Sudan to form the Atbara. During the months of flood the Atbara contributes an estimated 13 percent of the Nile's water and 12 percent of the soil that ends up in Egypt. The water received by the Egyptians from the Atbara has been measured more accurately in the twentieth century at 10.6 billion cubic meters. The flood becomes a trickle from November to January, and from March to May the river is just a dry bed.

For thousands and thousands of years, as summer approached and the river dried away, it would leave pools where the gazelles and hyenas from the Sahel came to drink with the multitude of birds flaunting their plumage as the African sun dropped like a fireball into the Bilad al-Sudan. The Nile perch, crocodiles, and turtles would sink deeper into the shrinking pools. Suddenly, a rumble like thunder in a cloudless sky would fill the air, and the torrent appeared, the spate of the Atbara released from the Ethiopian highlands, a wall of water annually sweeping down the dry riverbed. Sir Samuel Baker described the scene he witnessed on the night of 23 June 1861: "The river was coming down. . . . All was darkness and confusion," as the Sudanese camping by the pools raced to high ground shouting their warning, "El Bahr! [The river!] El Bahr!" The next morning, standing safely on the banks of the Atbara with his wife, Florence, Baker wrote: "The wonder of the desert! yesterday there was a barren sheet of glaring sand. . . . In one night there was a mysterious change—wonders of the mighty Nile!—an army of water was hastening to the wasted river . . . to-day a magnificent stream some 500 yards in width and from fifteen to twenty feet in depth, flowed through the dreary desert! . . . The rains were pouring in Abyssinia!"[1]

The shouts of warning are no longer needed. In 1966 a dam on the Atbara was completed at Khashm al-Girba on the Butana Plain below the Ethiopian escarpment. The Khashm al-Girba Dam removed the threat of the annual Atbara spate, and provides irrigation, but it has resolved little else. Construction of the Aswan High Dam in the 1960s, accompanied by the rising waters of Lake Nasser, forced the displacement of fifty thousand Sudanese Nubians, the Halfawis, who lost their land and their beloved date palms. They were resettled against their will at Khashm al-Girba, despite acceptable alternatives closer to their homeland and kin. The Halfawis were farmers, but the Sudanese government relocated them on the pastures of herders, the Shukriyya. No government in history, no matter how enlightened or committed to progress, has ever successfully mediated a range war, and the competing claims of the Nubian sod-busters and the Shukriyya pastoralists are no exception. In addition, the reservoir formed by the Khashm al-Girba Dam has lost 40 percent of its capacity due to siltation. The dam cannot stop the Angereb and Tekeze rivers from carrying away the soil of the Ethiopian highlands, but it does prevent this sediment, rich in nutrients, from reaching the Nile at the Atbara confluence.[2]

Between the Atbara and Abu Hamed, a hundred miles downstream, the Nile drops 180 feet over the fifth cataract, north of Berber. This fall, over one and a half feet per mile, creates a current made strong as much by its acceleration as by its volume, and it defines another singular reach of the Nubian Nile. The Meroitic, or Berber, Reach was never a river of commerce or communication. The kingdom of Kush, the Christian states, and the Nubian Arab tribal principalities of the modern millennium were totally dependent on the waters of the Nile, but their political, commercial, and religious life was determined more by the speed of the overland desert crossings than a sluggish or tumultuous Nile.

The way to Egypt in ancient times lay up the Bayuda Road, which traveled northwest from Meroe across the Bayuda desert to Jabal Barkal on the Nile, and continued from there up the Maheila Road to Kawa. In the nineteenth century, the route of the Bayuda Road shifted, leaving the Nile at Berber, downstream from Meroe, and heading west to El Debba at the bottom of the river's great S-bend. Sir Garnet Wolseley, on a mission to rescue Chinese Gordon at Khartoum in 1885, chose El Debba as his place of entry to the Sudan. At the Fura wells, known today as Abu Klea, his flying column of 1,600 men and 2,500 camels was nearly broken by the Ansar of the Mahdi. It was a dubious victory for the British and Wolseley, who failed to reach Gordon in time. Thirteen years later, Horatio Kitchener knew better. He was an engineer fluent in Arabic, with experience on the Sudanese frontier. He decided on a bold strategy to invade the Sudan with a railway on the sands of the historic route across the Nubian Desert, leaving the ruins of Jabal Barkal, Napata, and El Debba to the archaeologists and the goats.

This track from the Sudan to Egypt began at Abu Hamed. It was the unforgiving Korosko Road that crossed one of the world's great deserts of sand and stone. During the many centuries of dynastic Egypt, particularly during the New Kingdom, the route passed through the gold mines and quarries of the Wadi Gabgaba and the Wadi Allaqi to the Nile at Kubban, the port of entry and traffic control seventy-five miles south of Aswan. When the mines became exhausted and trade shifted to ivory and slaves, the more direct route from Abu Hamed was taken, following the Wadi Korosko to the Nile. Halfway between the second cataract and Aswan, Korosko and its road had great risks. There were few wells, and they frequently disappeared in the great *habubs* (sandstorms) of the Sudan; every traveler, ancient and modern, has recorded the fear of losing his way in the sand. But the risk has often been deemed worth the benefit of avoiding the great S-bend of the Nile, with its three cataracts as well as the formidable rock garden of the Batn al-Hajar, the Belly of the Rocks. The hazardous overland trails were disagreeable in the best of times, the winter, and intolerable in the worst, the summer, but most everyone has avoided the Abu Hamed Reach of the Nile.

The town of Abu Hamed represents the poverty of its reach. Here the river turns to the southwest, and consequently it flows in the same direction as the prevailing winds. From El Debba to Abu Hamed, it is all but impossible to sail upstream, the usual method of ascending the river. In antiquity the Kushites shunned Abu Hamed. The kings of Christian Nubia ignored it. For the past millennium no one but nomads and Nile villagers inhabited the site until Kitchener, invading the Sudan in 1897, required a terminal on the Nile for his desert railway. Abu Hamed's water tower replenished thirsty locomotives and passengers after they had crossed two hundred miles of the Nubian Desert from Wadi Halfa down the old Korosko Road. Today it is a run-down rail and river town with a hydrologic station, not far from the railroad tracks, where officials from the Egyptian Ministry of Public Works record the river's flow, for at Abu Hamed the Nile makes its dramatic turn at the peak of the S-bend to flow southwest to Egypt.[3]

Unlike the kings of Kush, medieval Christian patriarchs of Makouria, or the Shayqiyya chieftains of the nineteenth century, the British and Egyptian hydrologists of the twentieth century had good reason to measure the Nile at the top of the Abu Hamed Reach. Sixty miles to the southwest, the Nile descends through its steepest gradient since the Ethiopian highlands. Just above the first capital of the kingdom of Kush, Napata, at Jabal Barkal, the fourth cataract begins to fall three feet per mile over boulders and around islands. The drop, despite the absence of a gorge, attracted the attention of the British dam builders during the first half of the twentieth century, and they included the site in their plans for Nile control. The completion of the High Dam at Aswan in 1971 ended Nile planning south of Aswan. There was no longer any need for a dam at the fourth cataract to store water, except in the minds of Sudanese nationalists seeking to assert their hydrologic independence from Egypt and their resentment at the displacements of the Halfawis to Khashm al-Girba. The Sudanese government's determination to proceed with the Merowe hydroelectric dam here with loans from the United Arab Emirates is yet another example of the political and economic impoverishment of the Nile Valley states, which have yet to find a consensus or the resources for the conservation of the waters of their river.

The Abu Hamed Reach is the home of the Shayqiyya, who have maintained their character and customs distinct from the Ja'aliyyin upstream and the Nubians downriver. Their origins are obscure, but their traditions as disciplined warriors are well known. The Shayqiyya are an Arabic people, although the history of their warlords is reminiscent of the warrior pharaohs of Kush at Napata two millennia before their arrival from Arabia and upper Egypt. They were the only Sudanese to mobilize against the invading army of Muhammad Ali in 1821. Their crocodile shields and spears were no match for the firearms of the Turks, but discipline has provided their descendants employment as irregular troops and policemen for every Sudanese government in the twentieth century.

The granite of the Abu Hamed Reach has long defied the power of moving Nile water at the fourth cataract. Below the cataract, the vertical cliffs of Jabal Barkal rise three hundred feet above the river and the plain. This isolated butte is a spiritual sanctuary for the Nubians, and at its base was born the kingdom of Kush from its Egyptian antecedents. The dynastic Egyptians came south of Aswan only when they were strong, and beyond the first cataract was the second and the Batn al-Hajar, buttressed on either bank by implacable desert. Only the most powerful pharaohs dared to establish Egyptian imperial authority at trading forts and temples on the Nubian Nile, despite the insatiable demand throughout dynastic Egypt for the gold, gems, diorite, granite, ivory, and slaves of Nubia. When Egypt was strong and united, its armies sought to control this trade by occupation. When Egypt was weak and divided, the pharaohs abandoned their imperial control beyond Aswan. During the Middle Kingdom (circa 1938–1786 B.C.E.), the pharaohs extended the frontier to the second cataract with massive fortified posts to control the trade and protect the temples, but they left governance between the forts and the hinterland to Nubian surrogates.

A succession of low Niles and the invasion of the Hyksos from Asia led to the disintegration of the centralized Egyptian state. The Middle Kingdom was followed by the dark age of the Second Intermediate Period (circa 1750–1650 B.C.E.), precipitating the Egyptian withdrawal from Nubia to Elephantine Island at Aswan, the historic gate to the south, the bastion that has defended Egypt on its southern frontier for five thousand years. Dynastic Egypt recovered with the reign of Amosis (1570–1546 B.C.E.), who defeated the Hyksos and reunified the land under the New Kingdom. His successors advanced up the Nile, restored their abandoned forts, and marched all the way to the fifth cataract at Berber. Not surprisingly, they established the center of their Nubian colony at Jabal Barkal. Here at the base of the cliffs the most powerful and long-lived pharaoh of the New Kingdom, Ramses II, who reigned from 1290 to 1224 B.C.E., completed the Temple of Amun. It was the Karnak of Kush, the center of a large complex of religious and secular structures known as Napata.

Two hundred years after Ramses II and another succession of low Niles, political and religious unrest in Egypt plunged the New Kingdom into decline and another dark age, the Third Intermediate Period, during the eleventh and tenth centuries B.C.E. By the ninth century the imperial and colonial presence of Egypt in Nubia had disappeared except for the monuments. The kingdom of Kush rose from the Egyptian ruins. The unknown kings of Kush who ruled following the Egyptian withdrawal are

The ruins of the Temple of Amun at the base of Jabal Barkal at Napata, a capital of the kingdom of Kush (Photograph, Royal Air Force, Crown copyright, reproduced by permission of Durham University Library)

buried in royal tombs at El Kurru, seven miles downstream from Napata, and Nuri, seven miles upstream on the opposite bank. Later kings of Kush mobilized the Nubians, the soldiers of Kush, to march from Jabal Barkal to Thebes and beyond. They conquered Egypt. They were the Lords of the Two Lands, the pharaohs of the Twenty-fifth Dynasty (circa 747–656 B.C.E.), and they consolidated an empire from the fifth cataract of the Nile to Jerusalem, a feat unequaled in history until the conquests of Muhammad Ali in the nineteenth century.

Their rule was a dramatic but flickering flame, lasting less than a hundred years, in the long history of dynastic Egypt. Kashta, Shabaqo, Taharqo, and Tanwetami were successful rulers who proved unable to sustain their dynasty against the repeated incursions of the Assyrians with their superior weaponry. In 654 B.C.E. the Egyptian vassals of the Assyrians reclaimed control of Thebes. The kings of Kush retired in defeat to their sanctuary at Napata, and the inscribed names of their pharaohs and officials of the Twenty-fifth Dynasty were methodically removed from the monuments in Egypt. The imperial ambitions of their successors were confined to defending against the invasions launched from Aswan for a thousand years by Egyptians, Persians, Greeks, and Romans. These incursions, or *razzias,* were meant to capture loot, military glory, or punishment for Kushite assaults on the frontier at Aswan. The raiders had no intention of reviving the colonial occupation of the Middle and New Kingdoms. The Nile cataracts, the Batn al-Hajar, and the desert were a better defense than armies, for Kush had become increasingly isolated in a changing world. The Corridor to Africa was no longer a passage for international relations and trade, which had shifted from India, the Persian Gulf, and the Red Sea, the Sabaean Lane, to the northern shores of the Mediterranean Sea.

Napata slowly succumbed. A somnolent backwater on the Nile, it has not changed in close to two thousand years, since the final demise of the kingdom of Kush in 350 C.E. at the hands of the the Ethiopian king of Aksum, Ezana. The gold mines were exhausted. The granite and blocks of diorite were not needed for an Egypt that no longer built monuments. Slaves and ivory were always in demand, but they were more readily obtained from the Island of Meroe and its parklands across the Bayuda. Meroe became the capital of Kush for nearly a thousand years beginning in the fourth century B.C.E. Since at least that time, the stretch of river downstream from Napata, the Dongola Reach, has been another forgotten eddy in the Nile. It forms the final section of the great S-bend, and is conveniently cut off by the shorter overland route up the Maheila Road roughly from the fourth to the third cataract. This route has not changed in four thousand years. The reach begins at Kareima, several miles upstream from Jabal Barkal, and runs two hundred miles downstream to the ruins of Kerma, north of Kawa.

The Dongola Reach is named for its recent inhabitants, the Danaqla, Men of Dongola, who claim to be Ja'aliyyin Arabs like their southern brethren from Shendi, but in fact they are very conscious of their non-Arab, Nubian origins, which have made them a distinctive group in the modern Sudan. Their Nilo-Saharan language and Nubian background remain the foundation of their heritage even after half a millennium of Arab immigration to their banks of the Nile. Between the granite of the fourth and third cataracts the Nile delivers its water and its Ethiopian nutrients on an alluvial plain of sandstone. There are no jabals and no cliffs to obstruct the horizon. The only definition in this featureless landscape is the precise line drawn in the sand between cultivation and desert. There is little rain—one inch annually at Dongola. It is sufficient to support plants and animals that tolerate desiccation, but it is not enough for people. The water of the Nile has sustained civilization on the Dongola Reach and the thin green line of abundant cultivation that supported the Christian kingdom of Makouria at Old Dongola.

There are two Dongolas on the reach, old and new. The ruins of Old Dongola remain bleached by the sun ten miles north of El Debba on the east bank of the Nile. It was a place of no interest to pharaohs or the kings of Kush, but its location on higher ground upstream from the Letti basin and irrigated fields provided the agricultural resources for the kingdom of Makouria after its conversion to Christianity in the sixth century C.E. Abd Allah ibn Salim al-Aswani, the Fatimid ambassador to Makouria, reported in 969 the "beautiful buildings, churches, monasteries, and many palm trees, vines, gardens, fields and large pastures in which graze handsome and well-bred camels. Their Chief visits here frequently, because on the south it borders on their capital city of Dongola." Old Dongola was the center of Nubian Christianity, and its powerful bishops carried on the struggle between church and state from a cathedral that was increasingly falling under the shadow of the Arabs and Islam.[4]

Within the decade following the death of the prophet Muhammad, the Arabs had conquered Egypt, in 641. Ten years later the Arab governor of Egypt, Abd Allah ibn Sad Abu Sarh, invaded Nubia, only to encounter the most determined resistance the Arabs ever faced during the first century of their conquests from the Indus to Spain. When the Arab horsemen laid siege to Dongola, they were decimated by the kingdom of Makouria's Nubian archers, known as the pupil-smiters, the legendary bowmen of the pharaohs and the kings of Kush. The Arabs launched their cavalry and catapults against the walls of Dongola in a titanic battle, described by an Arab poet: "My eyes

The Ruwenzori, the fabled Mountains of the Moon, with their glaciers, snows, and streams (Photograph © Kazuyoshi Nomachi/Pacific Press Service)

The Senecio rain forest flourishes at 12,500 to 15,000 feet, just below the Ruwenzori glaciers, in one of the wettest regions in the world. The name Senecio derives from Latin and refers to the hoary appearance of the leaves. (Photograph © Kazuyoshi Nomachi/Pacific Press Service)

Lake Victoria (Photograph © Robert Caputo/Aurora)

The Sudd (Photograph © Kazuyoshi Nomachi/Pacific Press Service)

The Nile crocodile, which the ancient Egyptians revered in the form of Sobek, the crocodile god. Hunting and the construction of the first Aswan Dam in 1902 eliminated the crocodiles from the Egyptian Nile, but they are still found in Lake Nasser behind the High Dam. (Photograph © Kazuyoshi Nomachi/Pacific Press Service)

The Sobat River at its confluence with the White Nile

The White Nile at sunset

Tankwas, or reed rafts, on Lake Tana bringing firewood to Bahr Dar, the outlet from the lake into the gorge of the Blue Nile (Photograph © Kazuyoshi Nomachi/Pacific Press Service)

Tisisat Falls

*A town in the Gezira Plain on the Blue Nile near Sennar, the Sudan (Photograph ©
Kazuyoshi Nomachi/Pacific Press Service)*

*The kiosk at the temple complex of Naqa in the kingdom of Kush (Photograph, D. A.
Welsby/British Museum Press)*

Temple ruins, guarded by stone elephants, at Musawwarat es-Sufra (Photograph, D. A. Welsby/British Museum Press)

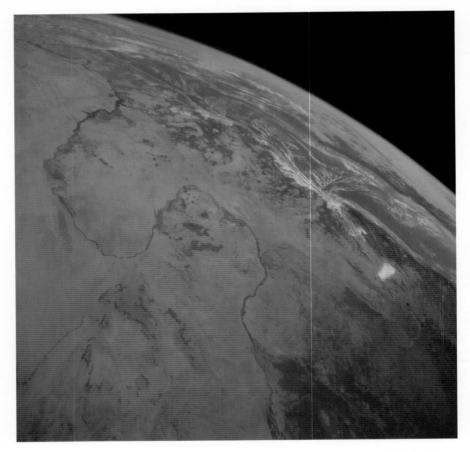

The great S-bend of the Nile, seen from space (Astronaut photo courtesy of NASA, Johnson Space Center, Earth Science and Image Analysis Laboratory)

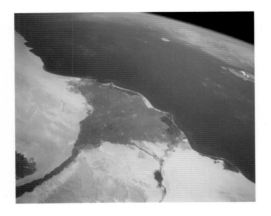

The Nile Delta from space (Astronaut photo courtesy of NASA, Johnson Space Center, Earth Science and Image Analysis Laboratory)

ne'er saw another fight like Dongola, with rushing horses loaded down with coats of mail." The battle ended inconclusively, but surprisingly there were only winners. In one of those few sensible moments in history, the humbled adversaries agreed to a negotiated written agreement, the *Baqt,* by which each party agreed to leave the other alone and to keep peace on the frontier south of Aswan. The Baqt is one of the most fa-

Old Dongola (Photograph by Stuart Tyson Smith)

mous documents of medieval times, whether Christian or Islamic, and it defined the terms of peace for six hundred years (652–1257 C.E.) on the frontier between Christian Nubia and the Islamic world. Its longevity remains to this day a record in the history of international relations among nation-states. Originally regarded as a truce, not a treaty, its terms were more the result of reality and benefits than any immutable covenant of ambiguous diplomatic jurisprudence.[5]

The Arabs and their successors departed from Nubia for six hundred years, but it became a peace of intellectual, religious, and commercial poverty for the Nubians. Surrounded by Islamic Arabs and Turks, their political ideology, spiritual inspiration, and trade withered on the banks of the Nubian Nile. The age of the archers was over. The Nubians lacked the economic and spiritual resources to withstand the arrival of the Arab Bedouins from the thirteenth to the sixteenth centuries. The Bedouins were Ja'aliyyin nomads from upper Egypt and Arabia with sheep, goats, and camels, and they ate up the land, the secular and spiritual authority of Makouria, and the Christian kingdom of Alwa to the south. Christianity and its kingdoms disappeared, not in any conflagration. They just faded away. Old Dongola crumbled into ruins. The Nubians became Muslims, although they retain their language and cultural traditions.

North of Old Dongola, at the third cataract, lies Kerma. This strategic location has assured the town's survival for five thousand years, for it controlled the end of the ancient trade routes across the eastern desert from the Red Sea to the Nile and the African goods that came up the Maheila Road from Jabal Barkal to Kawa. The fortunes of its Nubian residents have fluctuated throughout these many millennia with the power of the pharaohs at Aswan, the kings of Kush from Jabal Barkal, Ballana chieftains in lower Nubia, Christian kings upstream, and the makks of the Ja'aliyyin Arabs in modern times. The Nubian chiefs asserted their independence when the pharaohs to the north and the kings to the south no longer had the resources to claim their allegiance.

The third cataract was the great cataract. The granite that had disappeared beneath the sandstone of the Dongola Reach returns here, as can be seen in the stone quarries at Tumbus. The cataract was described by Ibn Salim al-Aswani, the tenth-century ambassador of the Muslim Fatimid governor of Cairo to the Christian king of Makouria, the Lord of the Mountain. Ambassador Aswani sensibly came up the Nile in the cool of winter, when the Nile is low with wide banks and rocks dangerously exposed. During the annual Nile flood in summer the boulders of the great cataract are covered and navigable both up and downstream. From the third to the second cataract, at Wadi Halfa, the Nile falls two feet per mile for 125 miles. On the west bank the yellow sand dunes disappear into the setting sun of the Libyan Desert. On the east there was a rich but narrow alluvial floodplain for fifty miles between isolated granite jabals rising a thousand feet above the river. The land has been intensively cultivated for thousands of years, thanks to the contribution of nutrients from the soils of Ethiopia. Below the Dal Cataract, Lake Nasser (known as Lake Nubia in the Sudan) has swallowed the rocks of the Batn al-Hajar and the monuments and ruins of lower Nubia, all of which are now only a memory.[6]

The Batn al-Hajar was seventy-five miles of rocks, granite islands, and rapids, from the Dal Cataract to Wadi Halfa. Few tried to go up the rapids except in flood. The sensible went overland. The Batn al-Hajar was the granite curtain for the Corridor to Africa. Ten major rapids discouraged the imperial ambitions of every conqueror who sought to pass south of Aswan for five thousand years. Experienced boatmen going downstream can run many of the most formidable rapids that obstruct the rivers of the world, but few can negotiate a rapid going upstream unless, as on the Nile, the flood is so great that the rapids disappear and the contest becomes one between the river and the strength of the oarsman, the paddle wheel, or the propeller. In low water the Batn al-Hajar was the Nubian shield that opposed, but never wholly prevented, Egyptian military adventures.

Throughout the Batn al-Hajar there were none of the alluvial plains of Dongola, only pockets of cultivation surrounded by granite outcrops on steep banks that made traditional irrigation impossible. Wind as well as rock shaped the landscape of this reach. The dry, cold northeast monsoon from the steppes of Central Asia prevails during the winter months. Throughout time its winds have stripped the yellow sands of Nubia from the rocks on the east bank. Checked by the Nile, flowing from the southwest into the wind, the coarse grains of Nubian sand tumble onto the west bank to fill the wadis and build elongated dunes from the nearest granite outcrop. The east bank is a barren cemetery of gravel and granitic debris that any experienced desert traveler would avoid for the supple sands on the west bank, the route of the caravans.

The Batn al-Hajar came to an end at the second cataract, whose rocks have disappeared beneath the waters of Lake Nasser. During the Middle Kingdom the pharaohs of the Twelfth Dynasty constructed ten massive forts forty miles above and below the second cataract and a slipway to drag their boats a mile and half around Kabuka, the most feared rapid at the second cataract. They were frontier posts to protect the flow of commerce through the cataract and the narrow channels of the Batn al-Hajar where Nubians and nomads on the banks could easily seize any vessel and its cargo that didn't have a military escort. Portage around the rapids in low water was particularly vulnerable to attack from desert nomads unless protected from the forts. The frontier between Egypt and the Sudan, as defined by the British in 1898, included an enclave below the cataract for the date palms of Wadi Halfa and the terminal of the desert railway to Abu Hamed that circumvented the S-bend of the Nile and the Maheila and Bayuda roads.

Before the completion of the High Dam the Nile had carved a trench through the sandstone of lower Nubia from the second cataract to the granite of the first at Aswan, the head of navigation eight hundred river miles from the Mediterranean. This was the inhospitable Aswan Reach, with no floodplain for cultivation. When the Nile dropped during the winter months the river was hardly visible below the stone outcrops on either bank. It has always been a desolate land despised by Egyptian cultivators, but its passage to Africa proved irresistible to pharaohs, pashas, and politicians ambitious to accumulate the wealth of lower Nubia—gold, gems, stone for monuments and temples, ivory, and, most important, slaves.

Slavery and slave trading are ancient practices in the Sudan. The first recorded account of the acquisition of slaves from the Sudan was inscribed on an outcrop near the second cataract during the reign of Pharaoh Djur (circa 2900 B.C.E.), during the First Dynasty. It shows a Nubian chief bound to the prow of an Egyptian ship with his followers being carried off into slavery. During the millennia that followed slaves were sent down the Nile as goods in commercial transactions. Most slaves, however, were captives seized during pharaonic military expeditions south of Aswan into Nubia when Egypt was an imperial power, from roughly 2900 to 332 B.C.E. As prisoners of the pharaohs, the slaves were used as mercenaries in the royal armies and as domestic servants and concubines for the Egyptian nobility, in return for services and loyalty. The economy of dynastic Egypt did not depend on slave labor except in the gold and diorite mines of Nubia. Pharaoh Sneferu (circa 2700 B.C.E.) of the Fourth Dynasty returned from Nubia with seven thousand slaves, he claimed, although this number was probably an exaggeration since it amounted to the estimated total population of lower Nubia.[7]

Throughout history slaves have usually been obtained by raiding, but gold, emeralds, diorite, and even ivory cannot be extracted by the razzia. Only a more permanent occupation, the colonization of lower Nubia, could obtain a steady flow of human and mineral resources. The mines in the desert were worked by Nubian slaves. To control their production and the passage of commerce on the Nile, the Egyptians built forts on the bluffs above the river. Popular sites were the deltas of the dry wadis that have sculpted the side canyons, which permitted cultivation by Egyptian colonists who were only too happy to return home when their terms of mandatory service to the pharaoh expired.

Dynastic Egyptian imperialism reached its zenith under the New Kingdom (circa 1550–1070 B.C.E.), during which time Egypt's population reached 3 million. Its pharaohs dominated the Nile Valley from the delta to Nubia, consolidating their authority as far south as the second cataract and across the Maheila Road to the fourth cataract at Jabal Barkal. The Nubian elites prospered from Egyptian schemes for economic exploitation, and they became deeply influenced by Egyptian culture and customs, but the Nubian serfs who labored on the tributary deltas and the Nubian slaves who worked the mines remained untouched by the Egyptian experience. Five hundred years after the Egyptian colonization of Nubia, the Twentieth Dynasty of the New Kingdom withdrew to Aswan in 1085 B.C.E. For another two thousand years the Nubians maintained their independence. The flow of commerce, culture, and religion between Egypt and Africa continued, but neither the Egyptians nor the Nubians lost their identity.

For five thousand years Nubia has been the link between Egypt and Africa, through economic interdependence, cultural borrowing, centuries of colonization from Egypt, triumphant conquests by the Nubian kings of Kush. During the first decade of the twentieth century the great Egyptologist George Andrew Riesner came to understand from his excavations the pivotal role of Kush in the history of Egypt and Africa. A half century later William Y. Adams described the Nubian Nile as the Corridor to Africa. His archaeological excavations in Nubia, undertaken before their ruins disappeared beneath the waters of the High Dam, demonstrated that Nubia, not just Kush, unlocks the door to the relationship between Africa and Egypt. Like the Ethiopians, the

Egyptians were in Africa but not of it. The Nubians, by language and culture, were of Africa. They brought the two together.

The relation between Africa and Egypt has been the subject of constant debate, characterized by ethnic arrogance, racial emotion, and intellectual manipulation, throughout the twentieth century. Afrocentrists insist that the roots of dynastic Egyptian civilization are to be found in the heart of Africa. Others have argued that these African origins of dynastic Egypt were responsible for the beginnings of civilization in the Mediterranean, Asia Minor, and Greece. But there are also those who refuse to accept the notion of Egypt's African roots at all, let alone the Mediterranean's. These sterile confrontations have largely ignored the Nile. All the protagonists have failed to understand that the Corridor to Africa, through which have passed for thousands of years the diverse societies living in the Nile basin, has been the bond between Africa and Egypt on the Nubian Reach of the Nile.

7 *The Egyptian Nile and Its Delta*

Thus do they, sir: they take the flow o' th' Nile
By certain scales i'th' pyramid; they know,
By the height, the lowness, or the mean, if dearth
Or foison follow: the higher Nilus swells,
The more it promises: as it ebbs, the seedsman
Upon the slime and ooze scatters the grain,
And shortly comes to harvest.
—*Shakespeare*, Antony and Cleopatra

The contemporary Egyptian Nile Valley and its delta are the result of eight thousand years of deposition of Ethiopian silt by the river overflowing its banks during the annual flood. From Aswan to the Mediterranean Sea, 682 miles, the alluvium abandoned on the land was mud. Exposure to air and sun turned the mud to soil and then earth, rich in nutrients that are the source of the extraordinarily fertile land of Egypt. The accumulation of Nile silt raised a cultivatable land mass along the river and in its delta of some 8,500 square miles, an area the size of New Jersey. When the rains in Africa were below average, the Nile did not possess the capacity to carry a normal load of Ethiopian soil, and consequently it deposited less. When the level of the Mediterranean Sea dropped, the Nile flowed with greater vigor, without stopping at Aswan, Cairo, or the delta to dump its earthly treasure. When the rain was abundant in the Ethiopian highlands, the Nile was deep and full, carrying huge quantities of alluvial sediment from powerful tributaries on the plateau. When the Mediterranean rose, it blocked the Nile estuaries at the delta, leaving the river no choice but to drop its silt in Egypt.

Far in the geologic past, the Nile carried heavy gravel and sand into the Mediterranean, extending the delta twelve miles into the sea. Eight thousand years ago, during the formation of the modern Nile (the Neonile), these coarse sediments were replaced by granules of Ethiopian silt. For the past two thousand years larger quantities of fine-grained Ethiopian mud were dropped into the valley and the delta, culminating in a massive deposition in the last half of the nineteenth century. From the first to the sixth centuries C.E. the rising waters of the Mediterranean Sea blocked the delta outlets of the Nile and inhibited its flow. The Mediterranean rose again from the fourteenth to the seventeenth centuries and once more in the mid nineteenth century, precipitating the rapid rise in the bed of the Nile Valley and its floodplain. During the past thousand years the Nile Valley in Egypt accumulated 65 percent of its contemporary soil. The average amount deposited was ten inches each century, rising to as much as fourteen inches during the periods of higher levels when the Mediterranean Sea rose approximately thirty-six feet. In geologic time, this change over a thousand years was a huge transformation that happened almost instantaneously.[1]

Egyptian civilizations from dynastic to modern have prospered for five thousand years thanks to the Nile waters, and especially to this Ethiopian silt. The dynastic Egyptians called it the black land, or *kmt,* which was also their name for Egypt in the Nile Valley. The first attempt to calculate the rate of accumulation in upper Egypt was not made until the 1920s. During that decade, it was estimated, 110 million tons of suspended silt passed through the first Aswan Dam annually. Of this amount, 58 million tons reached Cairo, leaving a total accumulation in upper Egypt of 52 million. Similar measurements taken near the mouth of the river found that 36 million tons were deposited annually in the perennially irrigated fields of the delta, which meant that 22 million tons reached the sea to be washed away by the strong eastward shore currents.[2]

When the Nile overflowed its banks during the annual flood, it naturally dropped the heavier sediments on the embankments, with the water that continued across the floodplain carrying the finer loam. Over time, the river built a ten-foot wall on both banks. These levees, high and dry above the flood, were obvious sites for settlements. Below the embankments, east and west of the river, were low-lying basins contained by the desert where the Nile water, rich with nutrients, saturated the land and produced the astonishing fertility of Egypt. The determination of the Egyptians, ancient

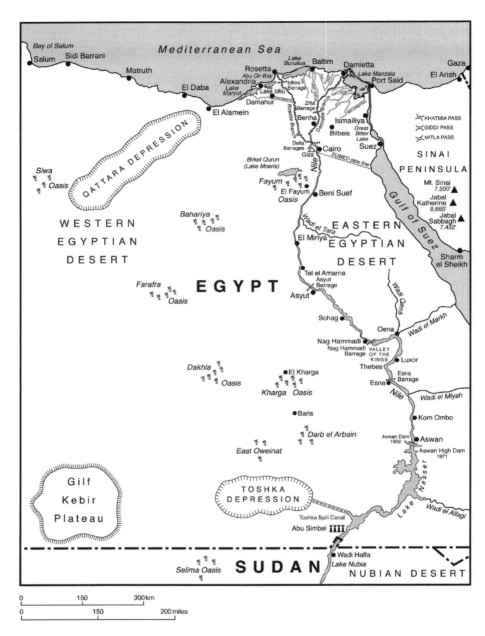

The Egyptian Nile and Its Delta

and modern, to defend their villages on the elevated levees was perpetually challenged by the river, whose natural flow constantly changed with time and whose bed steadily rose with the deposition of sediment. When the Nile in full flood was higher than the plain, it would break through the raised banks, in the process creating the islands of the modern Nile, oxbow lakes truncated from the main course of the river, and the numerous channels of a striated stream.

These wanderings of the Nile combined to produce a shift of the main channel from west to east by more than two miles over the past two thousand years. This eastern reconfiguration historically left islands in the river and hillocks, or *tels,* in the west that mark the village sites of an older Nile. There was a limestone ridge at Asyut that diverted the river into the Bahr Yussef, a major channel that meanders through middle Egypt parallel to and west of the Nile, joining the main stream south of Memphis. The combined flow did not disturb the steady eastward drift of the river until it arrived at Cairo. Here, at the gateway to the delta, the flow of the Egyptian Nile changed from its pattern upstream of shifting west to east and instead moved gradually east to west. Despite voluminous literature on the subject, the reason for this digression remains open to speculation, but the results were clear. The shift of the river channel to the west made possible the city of Cairo, ancient and modern, by leaving land on which it could be built between the river and the Mokattam hills. Canals, embankments, and regulators controlled the river further, allowing the expansion of the city.

The Arabs swept into Egypt from Arabia in 639, and in 642 the Byzantines surrendered to them at Alexandria. Amr ibn al-As, the commander of the western Arab army, founded a new capital, Fustat, on the east bank of the Nile near the site of the Roman administrative fortress of Babylon. Here he constructed his famous mosque, the first in Africa, before leading the Arab armies westward across North Africa to the Maghrib and the Atlantic. During the subsequent centuries the banks of the Nile in this area remained relatively well defined. On the west bank there was little but Nile water between river, pyramids, and sand. Fustat began as an army camp that became a city of communities, expanding to high ground east of the Nile under Abbasid and Tulunid rulers of the eighth and ninth centuries. In 969 the Fatimids conquered Egypt and occupied Fustat. Their brilliant general Jawhar "carried with him precise plans for the construction of a princely city," one that would rival Baghdad. This new capital was built on land that had been under water when Fustat was founded, two miles to the north, and it was called al-Qahira, "the Victorious"—Cairo. In the twelfth century Saladin extended the walls of Fatimid Cairo to the Mokattam hills in the east, where he constructed a citadel, and in the west to the old river port of El

Max on the Nile. Fustat eventually became part of Cairo, the district known today as Old Cairo.[3]

The stability of the Nile banks at Cairo was not to be found in its channel. During the period of low Niles that spanned the twelfth and thirteenth centuries, an island known as the Geziret al-Fil appeared, in 1174. It was regularly submerged by the annual flood, but increasing deposits during succeeding low Nile flows caused it to become connected to the mainland, in 1280. Today this area is home to Ramses Square and the districts of Shubra, Geziret Badran, and Sabtiya in the heart of Cairo. About 1300 a second island appeared, between Roda Island and Geziret al-Fil, and became known as Bulaq. A port was established at Bulaq, then at the southern extremity of the city, in 1313 to replace the old port of El Max, which had become high and dry. When it was founded in the fourteenth century Bulaq was more than a mile from the heart of Cairo, and when the French conquered Egypt in 1798 there were extensive cultivated fields between the port and the city. Bulaq today is part of the city, although it has remained an island, and is the location of the affluent districts of Zamalek and Gezira.[4]

These islands in the stream were, not surprisingly, soft with Ethiopian mud and surrounded by swampy ground between them and the city of Cairo a mile east on higher ground. As early as the fourteenth century an extension of the Khalig Canal drained the spongy soil east of the Geziret al-Fil. Another ditch, now Ramses Street, enabled the expansion of the city between the present Nile Hilton Hotel and the intersection with the Khalig Canal, now Port Said Street. Land reclamation east of the Nile by Mamluk and Ottoman rulers laid the foundations for modern Cairo during the centuries when the channel of the Nile was moving west. Alternating high and low floods in the fifteenth century were followed by generally average flows in the sixteenth, and then by two centuries of normal or low flows. Beginning with the flood of 1800, the nineteenth century was characterized by high floods, particularly those of 1818–1820. During the course of these five centuries, the Nile channel relentlessly carved its way westward, eating toward the pyramids at Giza until the British occupation in 1882 and the arrival of British engineers with years of experience irrigating India.

Under the leadership of Sir Colin Scott-Moncrieff, who arrived in 1883, and supported by the imperial authority of Lord Cromer, the engineers in the Egyptian Ministry of Public Works restored the crumbling irrigation infrastructure built by Muhammad Ali and raised the first dam at Aswan. They also brought the Nile under control at Cairo. To prevent further westward erosion by the river, they had massive stone levees constructed at the foot of the Roda and Geziret islands to divert the flow into the eastern arm of the Nile. They also built walls of stone along both banks to contain the river. The walls along Giza Street, on the western side, defended the plain beyond from flood and enabled the expansion of the city west of the river to the pyramids. These achievements have been frequently overlooked in the imperial and national literature.

Just north of Cairo the river splits into two main branches as it flows to the sea. The land watered by these and many smaller channels forms the great Nile Delta, a huge inverted triangle covering 8,500 square miles. The delta is particularly dramatic when seen in satellite photographs, which clearly show the two main channels flowing a hundred miles north from Cairo, northwest to Rosetta and northeast to Damietta, and between them an emerald green island surrounded by seas of bright blue water and solemn yellow sands. The base of the delta forms an arc that follows the coast of the Mediterranean Sea for 180 miles, from Alexandria in the west to Port Said, at the entrance to the Suez Canal, in the east. The slope of the land traversed by the two branches is gradual, four feet per mile, but it is still nearly twice that of the Nile from Aswan to Cairo, which drops at only two and a half feet per mile.[5]

In geologic time the delta of today, like the floodplain of the Nile upstream, is of recent vintage, dating only to some eight thousand years ago. Beneath the modern alluvial soil lie layers of coarse gravel and sand that were deposited from the eastern Egyptian desert by the earliest Nile, geologically known as the Eonile, roughly 6 million years ago. The canyon of the Eonile was invaded by the rising waters of the Mediterranean to transform the river in an eight-hundred-mile gulf to Aswan. When the sea fell the river returned as the Paleonile, carrying fine-grained sands that created a fan-shaped delta. Another layer was added by the Prenile some seven hundred thousand years ago. The Prenile was a river of great vigor that brought enormous quantities of heavy gravel out of Africa far into the Mediterranean, producing a delta four times the size of today's. Three hundred thousand years later the Prenile had permanently established the African beginnings of the Nile.

Climatic change brought about the Prenile's geologic successor, the Neonile, a much subdued river, which by comparison carried little sediment and consequently surrendered much of it to the sea. The surrender was not unconditional. The diminished flow of the modern Nile, beginning seven to eight thousand years ago, fixed its retreat along the arcuate shoreline seen on the delta today. Because the river no longer had the capacity to carry coarse sand and gravel, it conveyed Ethiopian mud instead. The Nile waters deposited this sediment over the delta, at a rate of about 35 million tons per year, forming the nutrient-rich alluvial soil of modern times. This sweet soil, resting on the solid and stable core of gravel and sand of the Eonile and the Prenile, made possible the bountiful human habitation in the delta. Unlike the other great river deltas of the world, these coarse deposits prevented the fine and fragile alluvium from subsiding below the sea and out of sight from those who wished to till it.

The evolution of the delta has been determined as much by the sea as by the river. The Mediterranean has been a millennial bathtub that goes up and down, depending on global climate. When the glacial ice began its retreat fifteen thousand years ago, the level of the Mediterranean was four hundred feet below the surface of the sea today. The global temperature increased about fifteen degrees Fahrenheit by around 5000 B.C.E., during which time the Mediterranean rose fifteen feet, eliminating the large delta of the Prenile and inundating the shoreline of the western delta. The sea continued to rise, until by 2000 B.C.E. it was only three feet below the surface of today. There the Mediterranean stabilized, until it began to move upward again during the first millennium C.E. It rose again during the fourteenth century. When the temperature fell during the next two centuries, a time known as the Little Ice Age, there was another retreat of the sea, pursued by an expanding Nile Delta. The Mediterranean gradually recovered beginning in the late seventeenth century. During the twentieth century the Mediterranean steadily rose, inundating the shorelines of the delta with a large influx of salt water, which ended any prospects for successful cultivation on its northern periphery.

The rise and fall of the sea became a regulator for the deposition of Nile alluvial sediment in the delta, while its centuries of irregular inundation created the brackish lagoons and lakes that today lie behind the barrier of coastal sand dunes. Until the late twentieth century this shoreline of sand and saline water was inhabited only by scattered villages of fishermen. The lakes include Maryut, which is south of Alexandria, Idku, Burullus, and Manzala at Port Said in the east. Behind them are swamps that have kept the coast isolated from the fertile and populous fields of the delta supplied by the freshwater of the Nile through an ancient and intricate system of canals and ditches. These rich lands had settlements before the dynasties of the pharaohs upstream. They occupied the mounds and sandbars of high ground that became villages and towns along the northern periphery of the delta in predynastic Egypt.

Another large lake formed in somewhat similar fashion, Birket Qarun, sits about sixty miles southwest of Cairo in a unique geologic monument, the Fayum depression. Located on a limestone plateau surrounded by cliffs and a ridge that separates it from the Nile Valley, the depression is in places as much as 160 feet below sea level. The violent high waters of the Prenile, 400,000 years ago, eroded through the ridge to form the Hawara Channel, which filled the depression with water 288 feet deep. The retreat of the Prenile severed the connection with the Nile, leaving the Hawara Channel a bed of gravel. Thereafter in high flood the Nile discharged its excess through the channel into the lake, and when it was low the connection between river and lake disappeared. Once imprisoned in the depression, the water could not return to the river. When Herodotus traveled to Egypt in 460 B.C.E., he described a great lake to the south, Lake Moeris, which he presumed was artificially made with water from the Nile. It was 450 miles in circumference and 324 feet deep, and into it the Nile flowed during the six months of its flood, only to flow out during the remainder of the year when the river fell below the level of the lake. This hydrologic relationship with the Nile remains controversial, but there is agreement that the brackish Birket Qarun is the remnant of the larger historic Lake Moeris.

Predynastic settlements in the Nile Valley were not confined to the perimeter of the Nile Delta. Small bands of hunter-gatherers congregated in semipermanent camps by the Nile, retreating in flood, returning when the river fell. They collected seeds, fruits, and tubers from the nut-grass and club-rush, and caught catfish and waterfowl during their southward migration in the autumn. These settlements continued to proliferate, and some became more permanent hamlets or villages as a result of the changes in global climate transforming the Sahara and the Nile Valley.

The most recent ice age ended some eighteen thousand years ago, and the retreat of the glaciers was complete about thirty-five hundred years later. This was followed by a period of relatively heavy rainfall called the Nabtian Wet Phase (circa 10,000–4000 B.C.E.), when clouds from the south Atlantic reached as far north as the Sahara. These were verdant millennia for Saharan Africa. The desert became savanna grass, steppe, and scattered forests in which elephants and giraffes devoured the vegetation and the leaves of tall trees. The vast plains supported gazelles, hartebeest, and zebras, which were stalked by lions and leopards. Hippopotamuses and fish snorted and swam in sluggish rivers and shallow lakes the size of inland seas, the last remnant of which is marshy Lake Chad. This bucolic image of life in the Sahara could not last. The rains had created the modern Nile, but the relentless desiccation of the great Sahara desert after 4000 B.C.E. transformed its valley.

Humans can live without food for ten or more days, but they cannot survive more than three without water. During the drying of the Sahara the hunters and gatherers came from barren riverbeds and shrunken lakes to drink and join those who had long roamed the banks of the Nile. As the days of hunting and gathering came to a close, these people settled in camps that became villages. Their increasing numbers could be sustained only by a dependable supply of food and the organization of society to deliver it. Those who came to the Nile had no choice but to adopt a sedentary way of life in limited space. Competition for territory was often violent, judging from the broken skulls and bones found in their cemeteries. People began to cultivate crops—wheat, barley, peas, and lentils—introduced from the fertile crescent of the Near East, where these varieties had been domesticated as early as 9000 B.C.E., some four thousand years before they were grown in the Nile Valley. By 3300 B.C.E. the cluster of hamlets at Nagada, fifteen miles north of Thebes, had become a walled town. Upstream, Nekhen (later Hierakonpolis), the city of the falcon, had thousands of inhabitants and kings whose remains are the lost beginnings of dynastic Egypt.[6]

By 3200 B.C.E. the combination of cultivation, the boundaries imposed by the desiccation of the desert, and the need to organize settlements produced a plethora of local chieftains along the banks of the Nile and in its delta. These warlords vied with one another for control of territory to organize agriculture, trade to provide capital, and religion to give inspiration, but from these obscure beginnings the dynastic tradition of Egypt was established. Thereafter, the pharaoh remained the imperial authority throughout the Nile Valley during the Old, the Middle, and the New Kingdoms, thirty-one dynasties in all, until the conquest by Alexander the Great and his Greek legions in 332 B.C.E.

The greatest challenge to the early pharaohs was the unification of two lands—upper and lower Egypt, the river and the delta. The cultural and economic differences between those who lived along the narrow sliver of land beside the river in upper Egypt and those who lived in the great fan of the delta in lower Egypt were contained only by the power of the state, beginning with the first dynasties of the Old Kingdom. Before the earliest known pharaohs, King Namer emerged from the shadows into the historical record by subjugating his enemies in the delta, but it was King Scorpion in 3100 B.C.E. who has the best claim to be the first ruler of a unified Egypt, symbolized by his capital at Thinis on the west bank, halfway between the first cataract at Aswan and the Nile Delta.

Unification could be sustained only through political stability, which has depended throughout the millennia on the highway of the Nile. In predynastic centuries the Egyptians were sailing up and down the river for trade, transport, and pleasure. The pharaohs of the Old Kingdom traveled in the grand imperial barge with pomp and circumstance from the southern frontier at Aswan to the delta, demonstrating the unification of upper and lower Egypt. Behind them came barges low in the water from the weight of great blocks of limestone to build their pyramids. Until the intro-

The Egyptian Nile

duction of the internal combustion engine in the twentieth century river traffic on the Nile waterway was dominated by fleets of feluccas, with their broad bottoms and giant lateen sails, designed to exploit the wind on the river. During the flood, from June to October, the Nile flows at a fulsome five miles an hour, which will carry a felucca five hundred miles from Thebes to Memphis in less than two weeks. There are no obstacles to navigation during high Nile, but as the river drops sandbanks appear. When the Nile is low, the north winds from Asia come to the rescue to blow the feluccas upstream against a diminished current.

Throughout the millennia Egypt has been characterized by an intuitive and inherited conservatism produced by desert and river. The deserts east and west were a formidable barrier that insulated upper Egypt from the outside world, and its inhabitants developed a deep devotion to a continuing way of living from one century to another, undisturbed by foreign intruders. The Nile reinforced this conservatism by demanding obedience to its rules. It governed the rhythm of life, from sowing to harvest, and from one year to the next, as well as the rituals of religion, trade, and politics, unaffected by unwelcome foreign people or ideas.

The names for the seasons of cultivation have changed over the years, thanks to cultural, linguistic, and religious differences, but the necessary activities have remained the same. The year begins when the river overflows its banks and spreads over the Nile floodplain. In dynastic Egypt the inundation was called *akhet*. It was commemorated in Cairo every year until recent times on 17 June, when the "herald of the Nile" stalked through the streets proclaiming the time for the flooding of the fields. *Peret* was the dynastic Egyptian name for the season of sowing that followed the inundation, marked by the celebration of an annual festival. Harvesting was in April and May. By this time the sun and heat of early summer began to dry out the soil, which soon hardened to a cementlike, cracked surface. The cracking was crucial, for it allowed aeration of the soil, without which the accumulation of salts would have destroyed the fertility of Egypt. This season of drought, known to the dynastic Egyptians as *shemu,* finally ended with the appearance of the next flood, which they marked with festivities called the *wen renpet* to welcome the beginning of the new annual cycle.

The crops grown according to this regimen dictated by the Nile were mainly cereal grains: half the arable land was devoted to them. The oldest was barley, which was grown in Neolithic settlements, predynastic Egypt, and the Old and Middle Kingdoms. During the New Kingdom a Eurasian wheat, emmer, became the principal source of food. Later, the ruling dynasty of the Greek Ptolemies (305–145 B.C.E.) undertook a program of agricultural expansion, and winter wheat became the dominant crop for consumption and export. The only cereal indigenous to Africa was dura *(Sorghum vulgare),* although there is no record of it in dynastic Egypt. It was probably introduced in Egypt sometime during the first millennium C.E., traveling down the Nile or across the established trans-Saharan caravan routes. Today it is the principal crop for the vast Sahel and savanna lands south of the Sahara.[7]

Large areas were also used for pasture, particularly after the Romans introduced *bersim* (Egyptian clover). As late as the eighteenth century bersim pastures occupied one-fourth of the delta and one-sixth of upper Egypt. Unlike other African or Middle Eastern pastures, however, those in Egypt were used to raise draft animals for cultivation rather than cattle, goats, or sheep for food and cash. Flax was also widely cultivated since predynastic times for the famous Egyptian linen industry. Beans, leeks, lentils, onions, and peas have always been the food of the common people. Lettuce was grown in household gardens and was considered an aphrodisiac. Oil for cooking, illumination, or medicinal ointments was squeezed from the castor plant and flax, but under the Ptolemies sesame became the most highly valued in the oil trade. Fruit trees and vines flourished on the tels, the islands of higher ground above the flood. The date palm was the most highly prized and profitable tree, but figs and pomegranates were also valuable sources of fruit. Grapes were given special attention in vineyards along the coastline of the delta. Winemakers produced five different varieties from the grapes, with red wine being preferred in the Old Kingdom and white during the New.[8]

Even as early as the predynastic period, the inundation of the Egyptian floodplain was not a haphazard affair except during years of uncontrollable floods. Techniques for irrigation were first used in upper Egypt and spread downstream to the delta. Over the years the Egyptians developed an intricate system of canals and regulators to distribute water from the river evenly to each basin. The depth of this water depended on the volume in the Nile, but in the nineteenth century the average was four feet in upper Egypt, less in the delta. The water historically remained in the fields for forty to sixty days, after which it was returned to the river. In times of dearth the water in one basin would be drained into another, with little if anything left for the river. Times of very high Nile were equally disastrous as those of dearth, but in the twentieth century B.C.E. Pharaoh Amenemhet I devised a way to divert the excess into the Fayum depression, where his successors of the Twelfth Dynasty reclaimed a large amount of acreage.

Basin irrigation, however, was a one-crop system, "an advanced stage of subsistence agriculture" that produced a plentiful crop once a year, sufficient to feed the people and provide a surplus for the pharaoh. It could not sustain large population increases. Even in dynastic Egypt there were attempts to grow a second crop in summer on higher ground, but this required lifting the water from the basins below. In Middle Egypt there was ample subsoil water from wells at Abydos, Memphis, and Thebes, but only the waters of the Nile could provide the necessary quantity. During the Old and Middle Kingdoms water was carried in pots, hardly sufficient to irrigate fields. In the New Kingdom the shaduf was invented. This was a pole balanced on a fulcrum, with a bucket hanging at one end and a stone counterweight at the other. It was labor intensive, requiring two men—one to fill the bucket, the other to lean on the counterweight to raise the water and dump it into an irrigation ditch—and its capacity was never enough to irrigate more than gardens or small plots.[9]

The Ptolemies were determined to expand and modernize the agriculture of dynastic Egypt. To further their ambitious schemes they employed a water-lifting device invented by the Greek mathematician Archimedes. The Archimedean screw was a large corkscrew encased in a watertight tube; when the bottom was lowered into the river and the screw turned with vigor, water was entrapped and raised to spill from the top into a ditch in the thirsty soil. It was not a great success. More effective was the saqia, a large wheel with pots attached around the circumference. The wheel was

Using a shaduf to lift water from the Nile (Photograph © Kazuyoshi Nomachi/Pacific Press Service)

mounted upright on a horizontal shaft, which was driven by a gear that was turned by oxen, over whom a lethargic teenager or an old pensioner would apply the whip. Oxen were worked in two-hour shifts, and the wheel could lift water as much as thirteen feet, irrigating twelve acres during the summer season for a second crop. The saqia raised water with modest efficiency, but it was a long-lasting technological revolution: it was not replaced until the last half of the twentieth century, by the gasoline-powered pump. Waterwheels enabled the Ptolemies to reclaim the Fayum, adding 325,000 acres of fertile land. All together, proliferation of the saqia along the river and in the delta expanded agricultural acreage of Egypt by 10 to 15 percent.[10]

The amount of land under cultivation or pasture in dynastic Egypt has been estimated at three and a half million feddans (1 feddan equals 1.038 acres). This total is a rough average that does not accurately reflect the years of huge reductions in acreage due to drastically high or low Niles, nor the remarkable expansion of agriculture in Hellenic and Roman times. But it is an important benchmark in one way, because the amount of land producing food determined the number of people that could live by the Egyptian Nile. The correlation between the amount of land under cultivation and the number of people it could sustain remains controversial, but it is the most judicious, if not the only, means of estimating the population of Egypt throughout the ages until 1801. Classical writers have always had a tendency to exaggerate. Contemporary theorists measure protein consumption, using numbers that fail to take into account such irritable practicalities as waste or the consistent export of Egyptian grain. There can be no definitive conclusions, but using imprecise demographic patterns tied to the number of feddans under cultivation at least provides a reasonable estimate.

In the beginnings of dynastic Egypt there were fewer than a million inhabitants in the Egyptian Nile Valley. The expansion of cultivation in the delta during the New

A saqia in operation on the Nile (Photograph © Kazuyoshi Nomachi/Pacific Press Service)

Kingdom resulted in a steady increase, to more than 3 million Egyptians by the end of ancient Egypt. The arrival of Alexander the Great and his successors, the Greek Ptolemies, brought new technology and the reclamation of the Fayum and the delta, and the result was a population that reached 5 million at the height of Ptolemaic rule. Under the Romans, however, the population of Egypt steadily declined. Unlike the Ptolemies, who were Greeks that had become Egyptians, imperial Rome came to exploit the land, and its method was harsh taxation in grain that Rome desperately needed. Farmers responded as they have from time immemorial. By the third century C.E., land under cultivation in Egypt had been reduced by half, as the impoverished peasants either left or refused to cultivate for the tax collector.[11]

The rulers of Byzantium did not employ the tough tactics of imperial Rome, but natural causes beyond their control further decimated the Egyptians. From 542 to 600 C.E. the plague swept through the Nile Valley with devastating effect. It was accompanied by extremely low Nile floods and the reduction of arable land in the northeastern delta through submergence in the cruel sea. The loss was staggering. By the seventh century the population of Byzantine Egypt had been reduced to fewer than 4 million, the population of the New Kingdom two thousand years in the distant past.

The arrival of the Arabs in 639 may have ended Byzantine administrative incompetence, but from the eighth to the eleventh centuries the land under cultivation continued to decline, and with it the fecundity of the Egyptians. After six hundred years of Arab rule, when the Mamluks eliminated the last Ayyubid sultan in 1250, the population of Egypt was no greater than when the Arabs had arrived in the seventh century.

The Mamluks were originally white slaves of Turkish ethnicity from Kipacak on the Black Sea. They were brought to Alexandria by Genoese traders to be trained as Muslim slave soldiers for the Arabs. The first regiments in Egypt were organized in 1240 and quartered near the nilometer on the Island of Roda opposite the marsh and fields that separated it from the city of medieval Cairo. As a military caste they soon established control of the state by force of arms and the legitimacy to rule by their defense of Islam against Christian, Mongol, and Turcoman (Ottoman) invaders. Under able and strong commanders, who assumed the title of sultan, the Mamluk dynasty prospered from the Indian Ocean trade and far-flung diplomatic and mercantile relations with the western Sudan and the Christian states of the Mediterranean. The Mamluks succeeded in ruling Egypt for more than 250 years, until they were defeated by the Ottoman Turks, at the Battle of Mardj Dabik, in 1516.

Their defeat did not result in the end of Mamluk authority. The Ottoman Turks were now the titular rulers, but the Mamluks controlled the land through intricate family ties, established over generations of intermarriage within the military caste. As landlords they were more concerned with personal aggrandizement than the development of their land or its peasant cultivators, and they ruthlessly exploited the fellahin who for three centuries had provided the resources for their armies, mosques, and monuments. The Mamluks were, however, no more immune than their serfs to the fifty plagues and epidemics that swept through Egypt between the fourteenth and eighteenth centuries, on average one every eleven years, as the grim agents of population control. By the end of the eighteenth century, the population of Egypt had not increased in thirteen hundred years and still stood at a little less than 4 million.

This bucolic existence was suddenly shattered on 1 July 1798, when a French expeditionary force under the command of Napoléon Bonaparte disembarked at Alexandria. Unable to strike at Great Britain across the English Channel, Napoléon dusted off a plan for the conquest of Egypt prepared a hundred years earlier for Louis XIV, by which he sought to inflict a mortal blow to the British empire in Asia, India, and the Orient. The invasion was the most determined European intervention in Egypt since the unsuccessful crusade of the French under King Louis IX in the thirteenth century, and a turning point in the historical relations between western Europe and the Middle East. Napoléon advanced on Cairo, where his cannons blew away the courageous but medieval Mamluk warriors at the Battle of the Pyramids on 21 July.

His romantic invasion of the East soon turned to disaster. Lord Horatio Nelson and the British fleet annihilated the French squadron at Abu Qir, on 1 August, in the Battle of the Nile. Thereafter, isolated in Egypt, Napoléon and his battalions had to suppress, with ill-disguised brutality, a rebellion by the citizens of Cairo in October, while his troops were dying from the plague and resistance in Ottoman Palestine. After little more than a year he slipped off in the dead of night, in August 1799, eluding British naval patrols in the Mediterranean and returning to France to revive his meteoric career on the more familiar battlefields of Europe. He left behind, as he usually did, a legacy from his abortive adventure.

Some 150 scholars and scientists had accompanied the French army. They investigated every aspect of Egyptian life, particularly the monuments and ruins of dynastic Egypt. They discovered the Rosetta Stone, which unlocked the mysteries of Egyptian hieroglyphics, and they laid the foundation for the study of Egyptology, then and today, in the monumental twenty-six volumes of the *Description de l'Egypte*. Napoléon may have shaken Egypt from its centuries of lethargy, but the departure of the French created a political vacuum and the opportunity for one man, Muhammad Ali, to emerge from the chaos by 1811 to make himself master of Egypt and launch its modernization.

Muhammad Ali was a Rumelian Turk born in Kavalla in Macedonian Greece in 1769, the son of a minor Ottoman government official. He arrived in Egypt in 1799 in command of a Macedonian detachment of the Ottoman army to fight the French. A man of ability and charm, and utterly ruthless, he organized and commanded the loyalty of the unemployed mercenaries from the Ottoman armies after the departure of the French. Thereafter he played, with skill and to his great personal satisfaction, Turk against Mamluk. In 1805 he eliminated the Turkish governor of Cairo, and was recognized as the governor's successor in the Citadel by the Ottoman Sublime Porte in Constantinople. That took care of the Turks.

The Mamluks were more dangerous, in Muhammad Ali's mind, so if he was to consolidate his control of Egypt they had to be destroyed. In his methodical way he bided his time, building his strength. On the night of 1 March 1811, he invited all the Mamluk elite to a grand banquet in the Citadel. Some five hundred came to enjoy the sumptuous food and drink, whereupon, after much conviviality, they were all mercilessly slaughtered. Some three hundred Mamluks who did not attend the gala fled to safety up the Nile and into the Sudan. There they founded New Dongola on the west bank of the river. Muhammad Ali was furious that a few of his Mamluk enemies had eluded him. But within a generation the Mamluks at Dongola had disappeared, assimilated into Nubian society.

Once he achieved autocratic authority in 1811, Muhammad Ali smashed traditions and brought conservative Egypt tottering into the modern world. He admired the empires of Britain and France, and consequently he sought to create one of his own in Palestine and Arabia, where he occupied the holy cities of Mecca and Medina and became their custodian. In 1821 he launched his invasion of the Sudan in search of gold for his treasury, slaves for his army, and satisfaction of his geographical thirst for the source of the Nile. These were grand imperial ventures, and territorial successes, that have obscured his more lasting revolution of Egyptian agriculture.

At the beginning of the nineteenth century, five thousand years of basin irrigation had adequately supported a population that had changed little since the end of the New Kingdom thirty centuries before. Through times of drought and flood, the maintenance of dikes and canals by authoritarian governments had enabled the basins to produce enough resources to feed the people and secure the state. It could not sustain the plans of Muhammad Ali for the future. Basin irrigation made only partial use of arable land and lost excessive amounts of the Nile waters to the Mediterranean. Muhammad Ali was convinced that both needed to be exploited more fully so that Egypt could produce a cash crop that would finance his personal and imperial ambitions.

The cash crop he had in mind, cotton, is a summer crop, and its cultivation requires water—of which there is very little in Egypt in summer before the annual flood. The first attempts to provide water in the summer as well as in the winter, what is known as perennial irrigation, began in 1820. This effort consisted of excavating the *seifi*, or summer, canals by as much as twenty feet deeper than they were, to allow the limited amount of water in the summertime Nile to flow into the fields. The scheme was a failure, for the accumulation of silt in the canals exceeded the ability of the Egyptians to remove it, and the effort was abandoned in 1825.

If gravity refused to provide a solution for perennial irrigation, then the Egyptians had to find a more efficient way to raise the water by any means possible. The traditional shaduf and saqia were inadequate to the task. Engineers therefore built barrages, or diversion dams, across the canals to raise the water level so they could control the flow. But these regulators were soon immobilized by the rapid rate of siltation, which required an enormous and uneconomical amount of labor to clear. The labor corps mobilized for this job in the nineteenth century, known as the corvée, employed several hundred thousand men every year, fulfilling their obligations to the state by excavating its debris.

The corvée was as old as Egypt. Historically it was an obligation of the peasants to provide their labor to prepare the land during the summer before the inundation and sowing. These were the somnolent months when it was not a burden to spend time at home, repair dikes, check the banks of canals, as part of a community project from which all benefited through mutual aid. The determination to introduce perennial irrigation, and to use it to grow cash crops for the state, changed this reasonable relationship between peasant and landlord, ruled and ruler. It was one thing to prepare a basin for the inundation, but it was quite another to spend the summer months of intense heat in arduous labor extracting the sediment from the canals in order to water the fields of landed estates. In the nineteenth century the historic communal work of the corvée became forced labor, conscripted and driven by the authority of the state for modernization and the personal aggrandizement of its viceroys and khedives. In addition to the structures for perennial irrigation, the labor battalions of the corvée also provided the labor for palaces, the Suez Canal, and the Cairo opera house.

The failure of the seifi canals was followed by twenty years of less than successful canal clearing by the corvée. The frustration of his plans for summer irrigation was exasperating to an aging Muhammad Ali. Help arrived in the form of a French engineer, Linant de Bellefonds, who had long been associated with the viceroy but had recently been off exploring in the Sudan. In 1832 he returned, advising Muhammad Ali to build barrages not in the delta canals but just north of Cairo at the beginning of the delta triangle. These barrages would raise the level of the river and allow it to flow in summer through the canals and onto the fields of the delta. During the flood the sluices would be open to allow the passage of Nile silt, which would avoid the accumulation that had been the downfall of previous schemes for perennial irrigation. Construction began in 1843, and the wall of barrages across the arterial branches and canals that splayed outward from the point of the delta triangle was completed in 1861. Although the system did not work effectively until the 1890s, following the innovations and hydrologic discipline of British engineers, the revolution begun by Muhammad Ali transformed the Nile and Egypt.[12]

Perennial irrigation allowed two, and sometimes three, harvests a year, vastly improving the agricultural productivity of Egypt. And the population grew. According to one modern expert:

It rose in spite of plague epidemics, cholera, conscription, and corvée. More than anything else, this is a tribute to civil order. Improvements in health standards help explain an increased growth rate in later years, but it was civil order, from Mohammed Ali onward, long before modern medicine had any effect, that insured there always was a population increase. One can only conclude that, despite all the difficulties and errors in government, the rulers of nineteenth-century Egypt provided a climate amenable to population growth, something their predecessors notably failed to achieve.[13]

During the nineteenth century, the population beside the Egyptian Nile and in its delta exploded, increasing from 4 million to more than 10 million. After roughly three thousand years of practically unchanged population, in one hundred years it grew two and a half times. Muhammad Ali, with his modernization campaign and agricultural expansion, had set this revolutionary chain of events in motion, one that has led to untold pressures today on the river and its surrounding environment.

8 | *British Engineers on the Nile*

For success in this field the essential factors are competent technical direction
backed by a consistent policy subject neither to political vagaries nor to the
transient vicissitudes of finance. It is something of an anomaly that these
conditions which were present in the days when Egypt was bankrupt
have been lost in times of prosperity.
—*R. M. MacGregor, 10 December 1945*

On 13 September 1882, in the first light of dawn, a British expeditionary force under the command of General Sir Garnet Wolseley destroyed the Egyptian army in thirty-five minutes at Tel el-Kebir, sixty miles east of Cairo. The following day the Turkish pashas surrendered the capital to the British cavalry, and two days later Wolseley triumphantly arrived at noon by train from his headquarters at Ismailia. He had rescued the Suez Canal, the British imperial lifeline to Asia, from the malevolent designs of an Egyptian nationalist, Colonel Arabi Pasha, who threatened to seize the waterway. Wolseley was an instant hero, overwhelmed by adulation and deluged with honors. But his victory imprisoned the British on the Nile, for neither Suez nor Cairo could be defended without control of the river's waters far to the south. To obtain release from their bondage in Egypt, the British sought to decipher the hydrology of the Nile basin in order to restore the prosperity of Egypt, which in turn would ensure their own imperial security at Suez and the preservation of their Oriental empire.

Wolseley may have "saved Cairo," but it was Lord Cromer who saved the Nile. His extraordinary administrative leadership secured the occupation of Egypt and the defense of the Suez Canal for the British empire. Only British officials, he argued, could cleanse Egypt of what he firmly regarded as the Augean stables of Turkish corruption. Their task was to increase agricultural productivity, which would assure political passivity among the peasants, the fellahin. The fellahin have seldom opposed any ruler who provided and regulated the waters of the Nile to the advantage of their cultivations. Cromer understood that British imperial interests, as well as his own personal position as Britain's custodian, depended on the economic prosperity of Egypt. And prosperity required water.[1]

Lord Cromer brought Sir Colin Scott-Moncrieff from India, in 1883, who in turn recruited British engineers from the Indian irrigation service to design and build the schemes for the conservation of the Nile waters. They faced two problems—population and productivity. They had no control over the first: 2 million Egyptians had been added during the first two decades of British occupation, from 1882 to 1900. They could succeed only by improving the second. The introduction of perennial irrigation by Muhammad Ali had transformed the productivity of the fields of Egypt. Egypt was growing a larger surplus than ever of food and cash crops, particularly cotton, which was much in demand by the textile mills of England.[2]

But at the end of the nineteenth century the perennial irrigation structures, which had made possible more Egyptians, were crumbling. The dilapidated system could no longer support the 3 million feddans under perennial cultivation, control flood, or relieve a low Nile. Cromer and his engineers needed to expand and renovate these structures. They then had to devise new schemes to provide water from January to July, long after the Nile flood had passed into the fields and the Mediterranean. The British engineers were vividly reminded of the historic vulnerability of Egypt to the waters of the Nile when the rains did not arrive in 1899 on their former plains in India. Four and a half million Indians perished during the "Great Visitation" of that year, a number equal to half the population of Egypt.[3]

Among the engineers brought from India were Sir William Willcocks and Sir William Garstin. Willcocks was born and educated in India. He visited England infrequently and with distaste. He was another English romantic enthralled by the East. His public behavior was outlandish. His projects for Nile control were some of the most creative engineering schemes in the nineteenth century. Even his intractable opponents grudgingly conceded that he was one of the most brilliant engineers of his time. In 1894 he proposed the construction of a great dam at Aswan, similar to the High Dam that was eventually built, but he had to settle for a smaller structure. Although he officially retired in 1911, he remained in Egypt for the rest of his life, intimidating younger men and being a pernicious nuisance to the British imperial establishment with his arrogance and his conviction that Muslims should become Christians.

Garstin was the antithesis of Willcocks. He was born in India in 1849 and was educated in England at Cheltenham and King's College. He returned to India in 1872 to join the British official elite, the Raj, at the Ministry of Public Works in Delhi. Twenty years later he was recruited by Scott-Moncrieff for the powerful position of inspector general of irrigation for Egypt, and was an instant success at the black-tie dinners in the British residency. He was affable where Willcocks was irascible. He understood water and how it flows; Willcocks understood how to regulate it. Willcocks was a quintessential Egyptian to whom the Nile south of Malakal was an afterthought to Aswan. Garstin disputed this Egyptian parochialism by focusing on the fact that the waters for Egypt came from the whole of the Nile basin. Lord Cromer, in seeking economic regeneration through the conservation of the Nile, depended on Garstin, one of his few close friends, to help him understand the hydrology and thus the strategic importance of the Nile. Garstin "had raised himself to the rank of the greatest hydrologic engineer in this or any other country," according to his entry in the *Dictionary of National Biography*. The Egyptian nationalists regarded Willcocks as a political ally, but they praised Garstin as "the treasure of Egypt."[4]

The third player in the game of Nile control was Murdoch MacDonald. He was born in 1866 in Inverness and grew up in the highlands of Scotland, and he was as different from Willcocks and Garstin as they were from each other. Where Willcocks was brilliant but erratic, and Garstin imperial and steady, MacDonald was practical and productive. He lacked the imagination of Willcocks or the vision of Garstin, but he simply got the job done. Starting as a construction man for the Highland Railway, he worked his way up to engineer. His designs for the Black Isle Railway attracted the attention of Sir Benjamin Baker, the architect of the Firth of Forth Bridge and the City and South London subway, who needed an assistant engineer for the construction of the original Aswan Dam. The dam was the creation of Willcocks, but it was MacDonald who made it work. Willcocks had failed to take into account that heavy discharges would cause massive erosion of the riverbed beneath the dam, which would have undermined and destroyed the structure. MacDonald devised aprons to prevent the scouring, earning the eternal enmity of Willcocks for correcting this flaw in an otherwise stunning scheme. In 1910 he rebuilt the three main regulators of the delta barrage, supervised the construction of the Esna barrage, and to the fury of Willcocks oversaw the heightening of his Aswan Dam in 1929. When Lord Kitchener returned to Egypt in 1912, MacDonald became his undersecretary and later adviser to the Egyptian Ministry of Public Works.

As these strong personalities maneuvered for their projects and their personal advancement in the elegant gardens and dining rooms of the British residency, the population of Egypt expanded exuberantly, requiring more water and more efficient use of it. The principal problem was to increase the amount available to Egypt during the months from January to July after the Nile flood had receded. In 1894 Willcocks proposed a high dam at Aswan that would have inundated the ancient temple on the island of Philae. M. E. Boulé, the French consultant on the Aswan dam, insisted that the temple be saved. Sir Benjamin Baker, Cromer's engineering consultant and close personal friend, scaled down the proposed dam by twenty feet to preserve Philae from permanent inundation. Baker was no conservator of historic monuments, but it would have been political folly to alienate the French by drowning one of the exquisite monuments described by their scholars in the monumental *Description de l'Egypte*. Willcocks was furious.

Cromer organized the administrative and fiscal details for one of the riskiest construction projects of the nineteenth century. The first stone for the Aswan Dam was laid in 1898. Assisted by a fortuitous succession of low Niles, the largest dam in the world was completed within three years, in 1902. It was unlike any other at the time, Willcocks wrote, for "it will allow the early floods laden with the deposits a free and unimpeded passage." After the rich nutrients from Ethiopia fertilized the fields of Egypt, the clear waters were captured. It was an extraordinary achievement. Willcocks was rewarded with a knighthood, which he regarded as inadequate compensation for his original proposal for a high dam at Aswan. Philae was preserved and the perennial irrigation of Egypt expanded. The dam did not have the capacity to store additional water from one year to the next, however; it was a regulator. It had not resolved the fundamental objective of Nile control, over-year storage, which would guarantee a continuous supply of water in high or low Niles for the exploding population of Egypt. This was the goal that later was expanded and came to be known as century storage.[5]

The Anglo-Egyptian conquest of the Sudan in 1898 opened the whole of the Nile basin to hydrologic investigation, which had hitherto been confined to Egypt. In the spring of 1899 Garstin steamed south from Khartoum to determine the most advantageous use of the Nile for the benefit of the Egyptians downstream. Garstin's pioneering surveys between 1899 and 1903 and his two reports published in 1901 and 1904 established the foundation for hydrologic investigations to control and conserve the Nile in the twentieth century. Lakes Albert, Edward, George, Victoria, and Kyoga, on

Construction of the first Aswan Dam, viewed from downstream in 1902 (Reproduced by permission of Durham University Library)

the Lake Plateau, were obvious reservoirs, but it was apparent that their waters would never pass through the swamps of the Nile without enormous loss from evaporation. Garstin's solution was to bypass the Sudd through the massive canal that came to be named for him, the Garstin Cut. Ethiopia and the hydrology of the Atbara, the Sobat, and the Blue Nile were ignored.[6]

The absence of the Ethiopian connection was a serious flaw in an otherwise brilliant exposition of Nile hydrology. Ethiopia provides 84 percent of the water that Egypt receives from the river. Despite their substantial volume and historic contribution, the waters of Lake Tana and the Blue Nile never inspired much interest from British hydrologists in Cairo. Seduced by the waters of the Lake Plateau, British and Egyptians alike were repelled by the geology, geography, and xenophobic isolation of fortress Ethiopia. But following the defeat of the Sudanese in 1898 and the humiliation of his opportunistic French allies at Fashoda, Emperor Menelik II of Ethiopia discarded his exaggerated claims to the east bank of the Nile from Khartoum to Kampala. Hastening to curry favor with the victorious British, he agreed in 1902 not to tamper with the waters of the Blue Nile without proper consultation.

The next year Garstin sent C. E. Dupuis to determine whether Lake Tana could serve as an alternative to a reservoir at Lake Albert. Dupuis concluded in his report of 1903 that a dam at Bahr Dar would not add substantial amounts of water because Lake Tana contributed only 7 percent of the Blue Nile's flow. His conclusion has been confirmed by all those who have come afterward—Grabham and Black in 1921, the engineers from J. G. White ten years later, Pitsugalli in 1939, and the U.S. Bureau of Reclamation in 1964. British and Egyptian engineers remained indifferent, and there were no sustained hydrologic investigations from Cairo during the first half of the twentieth century. Despite its massive hydrologic contribution, Ethiopia remained a cipher in the equation for Nile control.[7]

Also crucial to the British search for Nile control was Henry Lyons, the man in charge of instruments for measuring the river. Lyons did not come from India or King's College. He was a military engineer, trained in instrumentation, and a surveyor. In 1897 Cromer asked him to organize the geological survey of Egypt. By 1901 Lyons had assembled a group of young British hydrologists who were extending the geological survey to include geodesy, meteorology, and the systematic measurement of the Nile. He introduced the use of meters rather than feet in recording the flow of the river at any given time and place. He established the meteorological service of Egypt, and enlarged the Khedivial Observatory and moved it to Helwan. Lyons left Egypt in 1908, a year after Cromer and Garstin, but he left behind a different legacy. His account of "Nile supply . . . periodicity . . . low stage . . . and excessive floods" incorporated what was known of the Nile basin and its hydrology, but it did not provide any schemes or dreams of what to do with it. His instruments and records were more persuasive for MacDonald and Hurst in their pursuit of Nile control than the imperial policies of Cromer or the hydrologic intuition of Garstin.[8]

After the retirement of Cromer, Garstin, Lyons, and Willcocks, the conservation of the Nile languished until 1912, when Kitchener returned, not as commander of the Anglo-Egyptian army but as the imperious, unloved proconsul of the British empire in Egypt. As early as 1898, Kitchener, with the eye of an engineer, had seen the possibility for irrigating the natural slope of the Gezira plain between the Blue and White Niles south of their great confluence. As his adviser for the Nile waters he appointed Murdoch MacDonald, whose drive, charm, engineering skills, and political ambition deeply divided the British community in Egypt and frightened the Egyptian nationalists. In spite of the deep antagonisms Kitchener and MacDonald inspired, Nile control revived.

MacDonald proposed the construction of two dams in the Sudan, one on the Blue Nile at Sennar, and the other on the White Nile at Jabal Auliya, forty miles south of Khartoum. The dam at Sennar would divert the flow of the Blue Nile to irrigate the Gezira plain south of Khartoum for the cultivation of cotton, which would compete on the international market with the principal cash crop of Egypt. MacDonald argued that there was enough water in the Nile basin for both the Sudan and Egypt, and that each would therefore benefit from a dam at Jabal Auliya, which would contain water from equatorial Africa for Egypt after the end of the Blue Nile flood. Determined to demonstrate command, Kitchener insisted that the Egyptian government accept the recommendations of his irrigation adviser, and in the summer of 1914 the British and Egyptian governments approved MacDonald's proposed dams.

In 1914 the Ministry of Public Works recorded the lowest Nile flood since the British occupation of Egypt began in 1882. The director-general of public works in the Sudan, Lieutenant Colonel Macdougall Ralston Kennedy, became convinced that there was insufficient water in the Nile to irrigate the proposed Gezira cotton scheme without reducing the supply of water for Egypt. The issue simmered as the world turned to war but came to a boil in November 1916 when Kennedy confronted MacDonald. He accused him of tampering with the records to win approval of the dams. He was politely rebuffed, but the dam proposal and his accusations soon created a storm of controversy. Alone Kennedy and his accusations might have gone unnoticed, but he found an ally in Willcocks, who had fallen out with MacDonald over the alterations to the Aswan Dam at the turn of the century. Kennedy and Willcocks charged that MacDonald had deliberately falsified the data on Nile flows, and then misinterpreted those records, to promote his dams in the Sudan to the detriment of Egypt. Egyptian nationalists and engineers, having experienced a surfeit of British arrogance and the lowest Nile in a century, took up the charges against MacDonald. To their delight, Willcocks thundered: "The Sudan will take its share of the water high up the course of the river, and Egypt will receive much of its share on paper."[9]

With his inveterate enthusiasm Willcocks enlisted the support of other allies: the prominent British journalist Sir Valentine Chirol, and the Committee of Egyptian Engineers, who represented professional, moderate Egyptian opinion. Together with the Egyptian nationalists they launched an attack on MacDonald in the press and the Egyptian parliament. By 1919 the uproar over the dams at Sennar and Jabal Auliya had percolated into the countryside and, as one British official wrote, "quite ousted all other subjects as a topic of conversation throughout the delta and was a potential lever for nationalist appeals to the fallahin." British demands during the war had stirred discontent among the Egyptian peasantry, and cotton was a combustible commodity that could ignite it. Since the American Civil War the primary source of revenue for the Egyptians was long-staple cotton—which was now to be grown in the Gezira of the Sudan. Any diversion of the waters of the Nile by the British for the benefit of the Sudanese had the potential to turn disgruntled farmers into troops for the Egyptian nationalists.[10]

The Egyptian opposition to MacDonald was not just about dams in the Sudan. It was as much about the relationship between the British and Egyptian officials who measured, analyzed, and made recommendations for Nile control. Egyptian engineers in the irrigation service were frustrated and discontented with their British superiors, who were not about to pander to local politicians or ignorant fellahin, and certainly not to Egyptian subordinates in the Ministry of Public Works. Absorbed in measurements and protected by equations, the British engineers of the irrigation service appeared to be an imperial scientific elite, loyal to Britain and the empire, and therefore not working in the best interests of Egypt. Against this backdrop, in 1920 the Egyptian government—on the advice of the British high commissioner—appointed a commission to investigate the MacDonald affair. The resulting Nile Projects Commission consisted of three hydrologic engineers with impeccable credentials. None had any previous experience in Egypt. Each was ignorant of the hydrology of the Nile. There was no Egyptian representative on the commission, and after its membership was announced no Egyptian would consent to serve. In the minds of the Egyptian establishment, the makeup of the commission confirmed the perfidy of British imperial justice.

Not surprisingly, the media, the politicians, and the populace found MacDonald guilty, but the commission and the supreme consular court of Egypt cleared him of any impropriety. They both concluded: "There had been no falsification or intentional suppression of records nor any fraudulent manipulation of data or gauges by Sir Murdoch MacDonald or by anyone else." Kennedy fled to France and died four years later. Willcocks was found guilty of defamatory libel, but in consideration of his age he was placed on probation, and he no longer played at the table of Nile control. Perhaps as penance for his brilliance and his sins he conducted an evangelical mission in Cairo translating the New Testament into Egyptian colloquial Arabic, seeking to convert misguided Muslims to Christianity, with little success. The architect of Aswan died in Cairo at the age of eighty, in 1932, undoubtedly a relief for himself, the British, and the Egyptians. MacDonald, in spite of his vindication, was hopelessly compromised in his position as the adviser to the ministry. He resigned in 1921, a few months after the Willcocks trial, and immediately decamped for a seat in the House of Commons and a fortune from his consulting firm.[11]

MacDonald's abrupt departure left behind a vacuum of leadership at the ministry, with disastrous results for the hydrologic development of the Nile Valley. He also left his testament, *Nile Control,* a hastily contrived collection of memoranda and computations composed more to deflate the rhetoric of Willcocks and to mollify his critics in Egypt than to inspire its readers with a grand design for the conservation of the Nile waters. It included little tangible construction for Egypt other than a barrage at Nag Hammadi, which was a regulator for irrigation and not a conservator of water. Ethiopia was not completely forgotten. There was to be a dam at a mysterious location, perhaps in the Blue Nile gorge or at Lake Tana. The Garstin Cut was included, as was a remote reservoir at Lake Albert that MacDonald hoped would assuage Egyptian anxieties over the loss to the Sudanese of the waters from the Blue Nile to irrigate the Gezira.

One member of the Nile Projects Commission, Harry Thomas Cory, an American, understood the implications of the Sennar Dam that his British fellow commissioners failed to comprehend. Cory was from Indiana, on the plains of middle America, and had graduated from Purdue University in engineering. He was a cowboy who in 1906 had turned the rampant Colorado into the Salton Sea to save the rich agricultural fields of the Imperial Valley in California. Professional engineers acknowledged his organizational and technical skills. He attained legendary status in the folklore of the American southwest when he was portrayed as the heroic engineer in Harold Bell Wright's popular novel *The Winning of Barbara Worth,* which was made into an even more popular movie in 1926 starring Gary Cooper. He was just the man to champion the oppressed. The Egyptian nationalists immediately singled him out as an American ally when he mingled with his British colleagues at the Gezira Club. But, in his fierce Hoosier independence, his sympathies had been captured by a people even more oppressed than the Egyptians, the Sudanese.

Cory sought the "allocation of water in an equitable manner." He argued that water was a public endowment, one that should be administered "with due regard to the eventual rights of generations yet unborn." He proposed that any additional water conserved from the Nile should be divided equally between Egypt and the Sudan, an approach that became known as the Cory award. The Egyptians, assuming the traditional doctrine of riparian ownership, "first in time, first in right," regarded Cory's idea with implacable hostility. The reaction of the Sudanese was too inchoate to be recorded as public opinion. The British regarded his logic as misguided, derived from democracy on the American frontier without any understanding of the autocratic realities that had ruled the Nile Valley for five millennia. The British were not prepared to sacrifice their national interests by depriving the Egyptians of their historic rights to the Nile waters. The Cory award was ignored in 1921, but it was not forgotten. The ghost of Cory's proposition appeared a generation later at Khartoum and a half century later in Addis Ababa and Kampala.[12]

In Egypt, however, hostility toward imperial rulers from England finally erupted in anti-British riots in 1921. Every class—fellahin, effendia, even the Copts—took to the streets with enthusiasm. In 1922 the British government reluctantly abandoned its protectorate in Egypt, which suddenly became a sovereign state. The unilateral declaration enormously complicated the planning and execution of major engineering works for Nile control throughout the many thousand river miles in the Nile basin. The official representative of Britain in Egypt, by this time called the high commissioner, no longer had the power to decide the political and financial direction of Nile development. The men who held this post following independence found themselves struggling in a swamp of disputatious and frustrating negotiations between Britain and Egypt over their political relationship, the peculiar governance of the Sudan, and the Nile waters.

The position of British adviser at the Ministry of Public Works, whose responsibility had been to supervise the direction and realization of Nile control, was abolished. C. E. Dupuis, a former adviser to the ministry, suggested replacing this powerful official with a "board of control," but the idea was ignored. Without their man at the ministry in Cairo, the British in the Sudanese government decided to organize their own independent irrigation service. Its creation was another manifestation of the determination of British officials in the Sudan to sever all ties with Egypt, in the hope of resolving the financial and construction problems that were preventing the completion of the Sennar Dam. The Egyptians, meanwhile, were convinced that Britain was using the Sudan and its water to sustain its imperial position in Egypt and at Suez.

Their fears appeared confirmed after an Egyptian terrorist assassinated Sir Lee Stack, governor-general of the Sudan and *sirdar* (commander in chief) of the Egyptian army, in November 1924. This was the excuse for drastic action. Outraged, the British high commissioner in Egypt, Lord Allenby, delivered an ultimatum to the Egyptian government without consulting London. He insisted on an apology and a fine, the withdrawal of Egyptian army units from the Sudan, and unlimited irrigation for the Sudan from the Nile. This unnecessary and opportunistic demand for water as payment for the murder aroused the deep, instinctive anxieties of the Egyptians more than apologies or money could. Upon reflection, and strong instructions from the Foreign Office, Allenby sought to control the damage through the appointment of yet another "impartial commission" to study the Nile waters.

This committee produced *The Nile Commission Report* of 1926, by R. M. MacGregor, a British irrigation engineer in the Sudan, and Abdel Hamid Suleiman, the undersecretary at the Egyptian Ministry of Public Works. Their report provided the terms for the Nile Waters Agreement of 1929 between Egypt and the Sudan. These two documents, one after the other, affirmed the principle that Egypt had historic and established rights to the waters of the Nile. Nationalist politicians declared this a substantial victory for Egypt: its claims had been preserved, and it retained the right to review and thereby approve any future conservancy construction. Thereafter the regulation of the Nile waters was a matter of mathematical computation. The Sudan received a modest increase in its allotment rather than all the water Allenby had demanded for unlimited irrigation, but the British had mortgaged the future of the Sudanese by acknowledging the primary right of the Egyptians to their historic needs. The British were absorbed in the development of the Gezira in the Sudan, and they needed a pragmatic agreement for the necessary water without further delay.[13]

The Egyptians were pleased to get on with the construction of their irrigation projects that had been approved long ago. Neither Britain nor Egypt was interested at this time in a comprehensive plan for Nile control, or the administrative machinery to devise it, so long as each obtained expedient and popular results for their own schemes. The limited achievements of the 1929 Nile Waters Agreement can be measured in cement and stone that regulated the flow of water, but did not contribute to Nile control: the Nag Hammadi barrage was finished in 1930; the Jabal Auliya Dam was completed in 1937; the gates of the Asyut barrage opened in 1938. These were parochial projects for irrigation and immediate return in Egypt, irrelevant to the conservation of the lakes and rivers of the Nile basin for those who lived south of Aswan.

The British still had plans for a Lake Tana dam in Ethiopia. After the publication of MacDonald's *Nile Control,* G. W. Grabham and R. P. Black surveyed Lake Tana in 1920–1921. They repeated the recommendation Dupuis had made in 1902 for a regulator dam at the outflow of the lake into the Blue Nile. Their argument came largely from measurements at the Fig Tree Gauge, a block of lava by a giant *warka* fig into which three iron bolts had been driven to monitor the level of the lake. This nilometer was

The Jabal Auliya Dam on the White Nile south of Khartoum (Reproduced by permission of Durham University Library)

more reminiscent of the markers carved by the dynastic Egyptians into their waterside temples than the instruments Lyons had introduced to record Nile flow. In 1925 Grabham and Black published their *Report of the Mission to Lake Tana, 1920–1921*. It was the last gasp in the feeble effort of British hydrologists at the Egyptian Ministry of Public Works to understand the hydrology of the Blue Nile.

But their ignorance of Blue Nile hydrology did not inhibit English or Ethiopian enthusiasm for a dam at Lake Tana. The British began negotiations in 1923 with the powerful Ethiopian regent, Ras Tafari, who was soon to become Emperor Haile Selassie. Historic suspicions divided the two parties, and the negotiations soon failed. But two years later the British sought Italian assistance in securing a dam at Lake Tana, and in return they were prepared to support Italian initiatives in western Ethiopia. This transparent imperialism served only to heighten the fears of Ras Tafari, whereupon he turned to the one power that had no colonial ambitions in Africa, the United States of America, and its private corporations, which did.

Ras Tafari sent a close confidant who was also the Ethiopian ambassador to Great Britain, Dr. Azaj Workneh Charles Martin, to Washington and New York, where he negotiated a contract in 1927 with the J. G. White Engineering Company to complete surveys for the construction of a dam at Lake Tana. The contract, for $20 million, was signed in 1929; it was a lot of money for impoverished Ethiopia, but Ras Tafari hoped it would be recovered through the sale of Nile water. This was another conservancy project that was not integrated into any program for Nile control. Between 1931 and 1934 the engineers from J. G. White conducted extensive hydrologic investigations, and the information was used to produce a friendly agreement between the British in the Sudan and the Egyptians for construction of the dam, although neither needed additional water. In 1935 the Italians invaded Ethiopia, sweeping all these plans down the rapids of the Blue Nile.

During the two decades between the world wars, British engineers and hydrologists employed by the Ministry of Public Works labored in a hostile physical and political environment, with no real leadership. They carried out their duties with no grand design to inspire them, no direction, and only their own rivalries for stimulation. Some established close personal and professional relationships with the growing cadre of Egyptian engineers who were more interested in hydrology than politics. Their only guide was MacDonald's Egyptian epitaph, the two volumes of *Nile Control,* whose evidence was imperfect. They soon turned inward to do their jobs. They collected hydrologic data for no other reason than the intrinsic merit of the information. Hurst, MacGregor, Butcher, R. P. Black, and others continued to amass enormous quantities of facts and mindlessly devise schemes to bring down the water of the equatorial lakes without a coherent plan to control the waters of the Nile basin.

None of these British engineers possessed the authority of former British advisers to the ministry, but it is curious that during twenty-five years of their tenure in Egypt no one proposed a plan for the development of the waters of the Nile basin. They were competent men of narrow vision. They were cautious, suspicious of politicians, often contemptuous of their Egyptian employers. They loathed inefficiency, and this was often their rationale for doing nothing. They were honest, incorruptible, sober, and responsible. They were also dull, rigid, and unimaginative. Reports they could write; dreams they suppressed. Their loyalties were often compromised by being decidedly British in a land where Britain's imperial authority had reigned supreme in the past and lingered after 1922, convincing them that nothing had changed in their scientific investigations of the eternal Nile. They served Egypt well. They should have served the peoples of the Nile Valley better.

Harold Edwin Hurst occupied a special position in the pedestrian band of British and Egyptian engineers. His scientific abilities had propelled him from the magnetic survey of Egypt in 1906 to the Ministry of Public Works, where he became director-general of the physical department in 1915. He was a modest man, content to be the scientific servant to Egyptian politicians, not temperamentally suited for leadership. In 1927 he wrote with pride, "the last twenty years has not been marked by any startling discoveries, but by the collection of accurate numerical information." He never dreamed of following in the footsteps of Garstin or MacDonald, nor would the Egyptians permit him to do so. He was a respected retainer who was kept on in the Egyptian service for a decade after his retirement.[14]

Between the great wars Hurst and his British and Egyptian engineers published six volumes and several supplements under the general title *The Nile Basin*. These publications contained measurements of Nile flows throughout the upper Nile basin, with little commentary and no proposals for Nile control. Ethiopia was ignored. The statistics, however, enabled Hurst to begin responding to the insistent requests from

Egyptian politicians and officials, whom he knew personally and could not ignore, that he design a plan to conserve the waters of the Nile for Egypt. Hurst, with his colleagues from the ministry, set out to create such a comprehensive plan, one that would be the first to integrate the plethora of individual conservancy schemes that had been submitted by British engineers.

The most efficient use of the Nile, Hurst reasoned, required the control and regulation of all waters in its drainage basin. The "most efficient use" was to supply a constant flow that could be regulated to prevent excessive flood without excessive loss from evaporation. MacDonald had conceived of Nile control as over-year storage, or one year's worth of water stored by the dams at Aswan, Sennar, and Jabal Auliya. Hurst figured that true Nile control would require much more: enough storage capacity to protect Egypt against the worst possible sequence of either droughts or floods that might be encountered in any given hundred-year period, a plan he therefore called century storage. He thought this storage capacity could be had from the equatorial lakes, where the rate of evaporation is balanced by rainfall and the geological configuration, which confines their surface area, permits an increase in the volume of water without a substantial corresponding loss from evaporation.

He proposed a great reservoir at Lake Albert, supplemented by regulators at the outflow from Lakes Victoria and Kyoga. "Efficient use" of these reservoirs, however, would require a big canal to carry their water past the voracious Sudd and its massive loss from evaporation. The dams needed were merely a matter of cement. The canal through the Sudd was not, but it became the linchpin for the century storage plan. Throughout the twentieth century proposals for a Sudd diversion canal had been defeated by the lack of understanding of sudd hydraulics, the regimen that determined the behavior of water in the swamp and its floodplain.

British engineers from the Ministry of Public Works had slouched through the Sudd in the 1920s and 1930s seeking answers to the mysteries of sudd hydraulics, and expressing little concern for the Nilotic inhabitants who would have to absorb the dramatic change any canal would create in their environment. A. D. Butcher, who had spent eight years in the Sudd, produced *The Sadd Hydraulics* in 1938. British hydrologists thought it a tour de force. In fact it did not adequately explain the massive loss of water, but it revived the Sudd diversion scheme, the Garstin Cut, also known as the Jonglei Canal. In 1939 John Winder, a British district commissioner in the Upper Nile province of the Sudan, reported that the canal would inflict many hardships on the peoples of his province.

Winder's arguments typified the quiet consternation among British officials in

Khartoum who wanted to help the southern Sudanese and were frustrated by lack of cooperation from Cairo. Butcher was a hydrologic engineer in the employ of the Egyptian Ministry of Public Works. His Jonglei Canal scheme had been reviewed in Cairo and promptly leaked to the press. British officials in Khartoum reacted sullenly to what appeared as yet another condescending insult by their countrymen in Cairo, excluding them from planning for the Sudan that would change the way of life of the Nilotic peoples of the southern Sudan. Butcher had dismissed the environmental impact on the Dinka and the Nuer "as very small," despite his admission that the canal "would open new tracts of territory east of the Bahr al-Jabal hitherto closed to the world." British officials in the Sudan, who deeply distrusted their countrymen at the ministry in Cairo, were determined to launch their own independent study of the proposed canal, and to seek damages for the Nilotes, whom they apparently could no longer protect from canal builders.[15]

World War II interrupted all these plans, keeping most British officials effectively occupied for the duration. But in May 1945, after five years of silence, the Egyptian government informed Khartoum that it was prepared to enter negotiations for the construction of the Jonglei Canal. The request caught the Sudanese government by surprise. The officials in Khartoum sent H. A. W. Morrice, a divisional engineer from the Sudanese irrigation department, to the headquarters of the Egyptian Ministry of Public Works in Malakal to discover from his British counterparts their plans for Jonglei. A. D. Butcher had been replaced as inspector of irrigation for the Egyptian ministry by H. C. Bambridge, who delivered a rude shock to Morrice and his superiors. They had presumed that the project had died during the war, but Bambridge now informed them that the Egyptian ministry was determined to dig the canal, straight as a spear from Jonglei to the Sobat. The new technology of draglines, developed during the war, would make the job possible by reducing the time for construction and consequently the expense. The straight embankment would be ideal for road and rail into equatorial Africa, and the canal would introduce the arrogant and isolated Nilotic people of the upper Nile Valley to the world of the twentieth century. It would bind together the African and Arab Sudan. Most of all, it would resolve a fundamental dilemma for Harold Edwin Hurst: how to bring the water from the equatorial lakes to Egypt without losing it all in the Sudd.

British officials in Khartoum were furious. They had not been forewarned of the revival of the canal, and they were embarrassed that their efforts four years earlier were now to be taken over by British and Egyptian officials from the Ministry of Public Works. Hubert Huddleston, governor-general of the Sudan, responded in November

1945 by appointing a group of senior officials, the Jonglei Committee, to do battle with British engineers and Egyptian politicians in Cairo.

Meanwhile, Hurst was completing his proposal for century storage, including reservoirs at the equatorial lakes and the big canal through the Sudd. The result of his work was *The Future Conservation of the Nile*, by Hurst, Black, and the Egyptian engineer Y. M. Simaika, published by the Ministry of Public Works in 1946 as volume 7 of *The Nile Basin*. In it, Hurst and his associates presented the first comprehensive plan for Nile control, based on their measurements of the river and its tributaries. The Egyptian minister of public works, Abd al-Kawi Pasha, wrote with relief and pride:

> This is the first time that the full development of Egypt has been considered in detail and a new idea, that of "Century Storage" is introduced. The book makes it clear that we can no longer proceed by small stages leaving the ultimate development for future consideration. The new ideas show that on important points a decision must be made now. The main projects are seen to be closely connected parts of one whole, and their connection is a complicated one.[16]

The Egyptian government officially adopted century storage, as proposed by Hurst in *The Future Conservation of the Nile,* as its Master Water Plan in February 1947. The scheme for achieving the storage plan was christened the Equatorial Nile Project by the government, with the Jonglei Canal—the Garstin Cut—as the essential link connecting the chain of dams and reservoirs in the equatorial lakes with Egypt. No one bothered to ask the Sudanese or the Ethiopians for their input. Century storage, as conceived by Hurst, did not include the Blue Nile; a dam at Lake Tana was something the Ethiopians wanted, and it was incorporated as part of the plan, but it was peripheral to the British and Egyptian obsession with the equatorial lakes. The Sudanese were a different matter. They were not prepared to accept the Egyptian plans in the Equatorial Nile Project as the final word on the development of their Nile.

A few short months before he died, in 1945, R. M. MacGregor wrote the epitaph for Nile control in the first half of the twentieth century: "It is difficult to suggest any remedy for this situation or to take a hopeful view of the prospect of advancing these major development projects through any agency now present in the Nile Valley." The remainder of the twentieth century bore witness to MacGregor's pessimism, and by the century's end little, if anything, had changed.[17]

9 Plans and Dams

The best laid schemes o' mice and men
—*Robert Burns,* To a Mouse

The Egyptian government's adoption of century storage caused much consternation among officials in the upstream riparian territories. The principal priority of century storage as designed by Hurst and his Egyptian colleagues was to guarantee a dependable and regular flow of water for Egypt, ensuring its historical rights to the Nile waters. The construction of regulatory structures on the Lake Plateau and the upper Nile would dramatically alter these regions, changing the way of life for the Africans living in the vicinity of its canals and dams. British authorities in the Sudan and Uganda were deeply concerned about the impact on traditional societies, a concern that was shared by the growing number of Sudanese and African elites who regarded Egypt's plans for century storage as irreconcilable with their own national aspirations. Their British guardians, in the twilight of empire, became increasingly sensitive to their responsibilities as "trustees." Their concern for stewardship was made more acute by many close associations they had formed with those they governed, mixed with guilt over the feeling that they were leaving before they had prepared their people for a malevolent wider world. In the end they failed, of course, but in 1947 they rallied from Kampala to Khartoum in defense of Uganda against the dam at Lake Albert and of the southern Sudanese against the Jonglei Canal.

In *The Future Conservation of the Nile,* Hurst, Black, and Simaika had proposed that the waters of the Lake Plateau be concentrated in Lake Albert behind a big dam that would raise the level of the lake dramatically, by forty feet. The geological configuration of the Rift Valley confined Lake Albert so that this reservoir would suffer only minimally from surface evaporation. Although the British governor of Uganda, Sir John Hall, complained about the loss of land around the lake's shores, his real fear was the extension of an Egyptian political presence in East Africa, with the Lake Albert dam as its hydrologic manifestation. Uganda desperately required hydroelectric power for industrialization to provide for an expanding population. Hall mobilized a counterattack led by Brigadier C. G. Hawes, another British irrigation officer from India. Hawes began negotiating in March 1947 with the representative of the Egyptian government, Dr. Muhammad Amin, one of the most able of the new generation of Egyptian hydrologists from the physical department in the Ministry of Public Works. Uganda wanted electric power; Egypt wanted water.

Their negotiations continued back and forth between Entebbe and Cairo for two years. The British in Uganda needed instant hydroelectric power from a modest dam constructed now at the outflow of Lake Victoria, at Owen Falls, not a massive structure sometime in the future to conserve water at Lake Albert. They were suspicious of their countrymen from Cairo, who were not particularly supportive of proposals for hydropower against the demands from Egypt for irrigation water. Uganda was not in a strong position, for it needed Egyptian financial assistance to build the dam at Owen Falls. The parties reached a compromise that resulted in the Owen Falls dam agreement, concluded in 1949. The Egyptians could build a dam at Mutir, downstream from the outflow at Lake Albert, but at a height that would not inundate all its shores. Uganda would be responsible for the construction of a dam at Owen Falls that would not interfere with the natural flow of the river and would raise the level of Lake Victoria about seven feet. Uganda would have its hydroelectric power, but the discharge necessary to produce it from the Owen Falls dam would be regulated by the Egyptian resident engineer in return for Egyptian financial assistance.

Hydrologically, the dam at Lake Albert and the Jonglei Canal were inextricable: there was no need to store water on the Lake Plateau if it could not be delivered to the White Nile without an unacceptable loss in the Sudd. But the Owen Falls dam agreement had an insidious influence on the Equatorial Nile Project. Uganda lost all interest in the Jonglei Canal scheme downstream, which had no benefits for its hydrologic bastion upstream on the Lake Plateau. W. Nimmo Allan, the director of irrigation and later consultant for the Sudan, defined the objectives of Nile control that have since become accepted principles by the ten riparian states: "All projects [in the Nile valley] are so designed and developed to ensure at all stages conditions of life are rea-

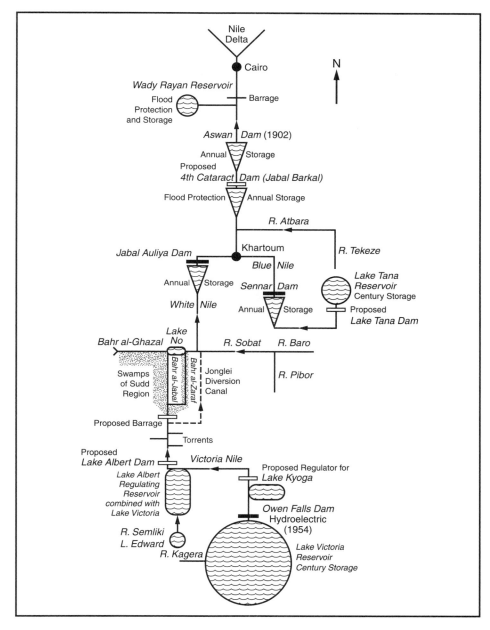

Century Storage: The Equatorial Nile Plan, 1946 (Source: H. E. Hurst, The Nile, *London: Constable, 1952, used by permission of Constable & Robinson Publishing)*

The Owen Falls Dam in Uganda

sonably satisfactory throughout the region affected. [Planning must] ensure that the water resources of the Nile valley are all developed in the most effective manner possible." Neither objective was realized in the Equatorial Nile Project.[1]

Allan, seeking to defend the denizens of the Sudd and their seasonal pastures, became convinced that the Sudan would now have to look after its own interests, for neither Egypt nor British East Africa was going to do so. The time had come to seek remedial measures for the Nilotes, whose lifestyle would be changed by the canal, and "an answer to those critics who suggest that the Sudan Government prefers to convert the Upper Nile province into an anthropological museum rather than make any serious attempt to develop it." The means to this end was to be the Jonglei Committee, and part of its task was to define "compensation expressed in terms of money." Early in 1948 the committee formed the Jonglei Investigation Team, which would be sent to the upper Nile to obtain reliable information that could be used to assess the impact of the canal and propose programs that would ameliorate hardship for the Nilotic peoples of the Sudd.[2]

The Jonglei Investigation Team (JIT) was led by Dr. Paul P. Howell, a former Nuer district commissioner who had gone back to Cambridge to complete his D.Phil. in anthropology on Nuer law. He returned to the upper Nile in 1948 with a sweeping mandate from Khartoum to determine the impact of the Jonglei Canal on the Nilotes of the upper basin. Howell assembled a company of irrigation engineers, agriculturalists, veterinarians, and surveyors to carry out the investigation. They took as their responsibility the study of water, woodlands, grasslands, swamps, animal disease, the regimen of the Sudd, and the effects on the Nilotes of all these factors. Nothing was too good for the Jonglei team. The Sudan had prospered during the Second World War as a supplier rather than a combatant. At the end of the war the fiscal surplus, unknown during the harsh years of the depression, became an embarrassment in Khartoum because of the government's neglect of the south during times of financial dearth. The Sudan now had money to spend on its marginal subjects, and the Jonglei team's mission to understand the environment of the upper Nile in preparation for economic and social change appeared an admirable investment to the Jonglei Committee.

The investigations undertaken by Howell and his team could hardly produce instant results. The JIT's visibility vanished when its members disappeared into the swamps to carry out their research. Moreover, they expended money and energy on mundane matters—housing, refrigerators, wives, children—that had little to do with science and exposed the team to its critics. During the half century of British rule in the upper Nile the empire's representatives were a handful of soldiers, civilian administrators, and Christian missionaries. To their consternation the Jonglei Investigation Team had little interest in military, administrative, or religious obligations. As an autonomous unit with its own budget, the JIT reminded British administrators south of Malakal of nothing so much as the Egyptian Ministry of Public Works.

Furthermore, in the middle of the twentieth century neither the British in the Sudan nor anyone else was prepared to think that environmental effects should determine policy. The British were exhausted by war and beleaguered by a nascent nationalism that neither they nor the Sudanese understood. To Sudanese nationalists, the rise and fall of the water in the upper Nile and the transmigration of its Nilotic peoples were politically irrelevant to their demands for independence. Humphrey Morrice, who later designed the consummate plan for Nile control, bitterly reflected in 1945 on the chasm between the technician and the administrator in the Sudan.

During the last few years I have had the opportunity of seeing them [members of the Sudan Political Service] at work, and have been as much impressed by their intelligence and integrity as dismayed by their attitude towards technical matters.

They regard the scientist or the engineer much as the housewife regards the plumber. For them he is a man whom they call in on occasion to put matters right in some magic way of his own, after which the sooner he makes himself scarce the better. . . . Their capacity for self-deception is unbounded, and I do not delude myself by supposing that I can shake their complacency. They will still sit in their chairs, drinking their whiskey and quietly fiddling away in unison, while something more important than Rome is burning.[3]

Foreseeing the inevitability of independence, officials of the Jonglei Committee in Khartoum began to have serious doubts about spending funds on science and finding a solution to a problem among a savage people in a bloody swamp, all of which would not be their responsibility in the near future. They had also come to accept the reality that the canal was going to be built one way or another—Egypt would see to that—so in February 1949 the committee officially approved its construction as the essential link in the Equatorial Nile Project. It remained the committee's responsibility to determine an appropriate amount for compensation of the damage that would be done to the Nilotes and their way of life. The committee assigned this as the new mission of the Jonglei Investigation Team—to calculate a monetary award that could be used as a starting point in negotiations with the Egyptians—thereby revealing a fundamental difference between the Jonglei Committee and Howell's men. The committee wanted a quick cash fix to throw on the negotiating table. The team regarded itself as an autonomous unit with a serious responsibility to carry out scientific research on the impact of transforming an unknown and complex ecology. "There is more nonsense talked about Jonglei than any other project in the country," Howell wrote, "and some people seem to think we are a bogus scheme like ground nuts than a straightforward commission investigating a specific problem."[4]

In June, A. L. Chick, the financial secretary of the Sudan government and the most powerful member of the Jonglei Committee, proposed that the JIT be disbanded. Everyone was preparing for annual leave, when decisions are usually postponed until after the heat of the Sudan summer. When they returned in December 1949, the cool north wind had stiffened their resolve to dismantle the JIT, which one committee member sarcastically called "four gentlemen writing about fish." Howell stalled for time, setting off a peremptory demand from the committee in July 1950 for remedial measures and costs without further delay. The Sudan is a vast country with few means of communication. Roads, or rather tracks, are impassable half the year. The railway crosses the White Nile only once, at Kosti, two hundred miles south of Khartoum.

Airstrips at Malakal and Juba were hardly more reliable than the river—which has never been dependable. Malakal is three hundred miles of slow water from the railhead at Kosti. Juba is another six hundred miles up the Bahr al-Jabal, where nature unleashes its sudd to obstruct navigation. Safely isolated, Howell and his team discreetly ignored the commandments from Khartoum, until Sir James Robertson, the civil secretary of the Sudan government, became a self-appointed member of the Jonglei Committee in July 1951. He had no interest in Jonglei and was unconvinced of its utility. He joined the committee to see that its resolution to disband the JIT eighteen months earlier would now be consummated by June 1952. Howell was given until 1953 to complete his final report.[5]

These were tumultuous years in the Sudan as it raced toward independence, and in this context Jonglei was irrelevant and the Nile a political rather than a hydrologic symbol. Howell and his team finished writing their final report in the bucolic setting of Christ Church College and its meadows at Oxford during their leave in the summer of 1954. The official report of the Jonglei Investigation Team, titled *The Equatorial Nile Project and its Effects in the Anglo-Egyptian Sudan,* was published in November 1954. Today it would be instantly recognized as an environmental impact study, and its comprehensive coverage would have silenced Howell's critics had not most left the Sudan during the transfer of power to the Sudanese. The report does not have the definitive conclusions expected by the hydrologic engineers, but it demonstrated the complexities of life in the upper Nile, its problems when challenged by transition, and alternative means to resolve them. It is turgid, uneven in style, and without a uniform structure. Fifty years later, however, it remains the only substantial collection of information about the upper Nile. The purpose it was written for—understanding the way of life of the peoples of the upper Nile and their environment, in order to ameliorate their transition to a new world—is now forgotten, and today the report is an unread historical document about the upper Nile province in midcentury.

Even as Howell was finishing the team's report, however, there was deep discontent in Egypt. Fed up with the Egyptian monarchy and the persistence of British influence, a group of army officers led by Gamal Abdel Nasser ousted the king and seized power in a coup d'état, in July 1952. Upon setting up their government, the Revolutionary Command Council, Nasser and his fellow officers needed a spectacular demonstration of the resurgence of revolutionary Egyptian nationalism under their leadership. Within two months they found their symbol in a proposal that had been made many years earlier by an Egyptian-Greek engineer named Adrian Daninos. In collaboration with an Italian engineer, Luigi Gallioli, Daninos conceived of one grand structure at Aswan to guarantee century storage for irrigation, along with enormous quantities of hydro-electric power for industry in Egypt—a high dam, similar to the one Willcocks had proposed at the end of the nineteenth century. The reaction of the hydrologists in the ministry had been cool. Hurst could not accept the huge loss of water that would result from evaporation of a reservoir in the torrid heat of Aswan. The predictions of siltation, seepage, and scouring were also alarming. The Equatorial Nile Project was the adopted plan for Nile control, and no official in the ministry wanted anything to do with Daninos and his dam. As it turned out, the skeptics were irrelevant.

Less than a month after the coup, Daninos met with two engineers he had casually known for years, Samir Hilmy and Mahmud Yunis. They were now members of the Revolutionary Command Council, and as engineers they were delegated to organize the council's technical office. They represented a new generation of Egyptian engineers and hydrologists. Their orientation was with the revolution and Arab socialism, not with the periodicities or century storage of Hurst. They wanted to help the revolution by making certain that the Nile waters were secure. The days of British dominance in matters of Nile hydrology were over.

Soon Hilmy and Yunis were pressing the dam in the Revolutionary Command Council. The council's twelve members were deeply committed to reviving Egypt's prosperity, free of the humiliation of foreign fiscal control in the past. Economically, the dam would provide power and water. Hydrologically, it would discard the century storage of Hurst, which had made Egypt a hostage to upstream riparian states. Financially, the dam was beyond the present resources of Egypt, without new internal sources of income or foreign assistance, which the revolution had pledged to deny. Physically, it presented a challenge for the engineers to build a dam that would have staggered the talents of Willcocks and MacDonald. Politically, it was a daring and expensive scheme, but the dam would be a visible manifestation of the revolution, a monumental symbol that could not be denied.

The argument that demolished any objections, and reduced all previous proposals for the development of the Nile basin to scientific obscurantism or British vanity, was the indisputable location of the dam, at Aswan—within the territorial boundaries of Egypt. After his retirement in 1946, Hurst remained in Egypt as a consultant to the ministry. He accepted the political facts of life and gracefully abandoned his scheme for century storage in the Lake Plateau. He became preoccupied with mathematical calculations for the most efficient regulation of the reservoir that would result from the high dam.

The decision to build a mighty dam at Aswan, the Sadd al-Aali, was taken unilaterally by the revolutionary government of Egypt in September 1952. The interests of the upstream riparian states could mostly be dismissed. Ethiopia and Uganda had been placated with earlier measures. The Sudan, however, was a different matter. The Sudanese astride the middle Nile valley were the intermediary partner with whom Egypt had to come to terms. The Sudan contributes little water to the Nile, but the land of the two Niles lies upstream from Egypt, where the Sudanese can demand a toll for its passage. And there was a more immediate problem. The Sadd al-Aali could not be built at Aswan without an agreement with the Sudan, whose river banks and date palms in Nubia would vanish beneath the reservoir, and whose expanding population required a substantial increase in the meager amount of water for irrigation granted it in 1929.

At first the Egyptians invited their Sudanese brothers to revise the 1929 Nile Waters Agreement, which had been imposed on them by British imperialists. Negotiations that had begun in 1950, two years before the revolution, included Sudanese proposals for the release of more water for the Gezira from the Sennar Dam, a new dam at the fourth cataract, and a greater allocation of Nile water than allowed in the 1929 agreement. These "technical discussions" disguised the essential question—the respective shares of water for Egypt and the Sudan. The talks were unfriendly and unproductive, and they were terminated early in 1951. The representatives promptly retired to their ministries in Cairo and Khartoum to plan projects to meet their own needs for Nile water. Any thought of Nile control that would embrace the whole of the basin—as it had been conceived by Garstin, MacDonald, and Hurst—disappeared when the historical rights of the Egyptians were challenged by the new nationalism of the Sudanese.

After the collapse of the Cairo talks the Sudan arbitrarily adjusted the level of the Sennar reservoir to provide more water for the Gezira. The Egyptians did not object. They did not need the water and were eager to curry favor among Sudanese nationalists by their charity. The Ethiopians, always the odd man out in Nile control, were not consulted. After a half century the Lake Tana dam, whose location presupposed a hydrologic significance it did not deserve, became a symbol of Ethiopian independence, at least to the emperor, from Egyptian and European imperialism. Although there have been periodic invasions from the Sahelian plains below the escarpment, the influence of Egyptians and Sudanese has been ephemeral among the fiercely independent peoples of the historic Ethiopian empire. Little had changed in two millennia.

Egypt was concerned with its revolution, the Sudan with its independence, and both were determined to define Nile control to their own advantage and preferably without consultation, however unrealistic, with xenophobic Ethiopians.

Consequently, the Sudan commissioned Sir Alexander Gibb and Partners to design a dam at Roseires that would capture the waters of the Blue Nile below the Ethiopian escarpment, within the territorial boundaries of the Sudan. As the Egyptians sought to do with their high dam, this would impound water entirely at home, beyond the authority of Ethiopian emperors, Marxists, and democrats who would be inclined to conserve it for themselves. The Sudan and Egypt began new negotiations in September 1953, with Nimmo Allan representing the Sudan government, and Muhammad Amin, who had negotiated the Owen Falls dam agreement, representing the Egyptians. They were amicable antagonists who each respected the other's professional credentials. Allan revived the approach of the memorable Cory award, arguing that the Sudan had a right to an equal share with Egypt of any new water. The Egyptians were prepared to concede a fair share for the Sudan in return for the Sadd al-Aali, but how much was fair?

These friendly but disingenuous chats became more disagreeable the following year with the publication of the report of the Jonglei Investigation Team and the study by Sir Alexander Gibb and Partners for the dam at Roseires. The Egyptians could dismiss the JIT report as academic anthropology about the environment of a swamp that had little to do with the acquisition of its water. They had more difficulty with Roseires, which proved to be the only suitable site on the Blue Nile to store water for the Sudan that would preclude any recognition of Ethiopian rights to the water and, more important, any possibility of tiresome negotiations with them. The Roseires dam would capture 3 billion cubic meters of Nile water, 4 percent of the total Nile flow at Aswan, a diversion that the Egyptians could not ignore with equanimity, although perhaps it would be a fair share in return for Aswan.

The negotiations that reopened in September 1954—during the dying days of the Anglo-Egyptian Condominium and the birth of an independent Sudan—were contentious and competitive. The Egyptians were prepared to trade Roseires for Aswan and a paltry number of cubic meters of Nile waters. The Sudanese did not believe that these terms were equitable or realistic in return for what they were asked to surrender. Roseires was a dam of modest dimensions ready for construction. The high dam was an immense undertaking many years from completion, complicated by the egregious failure of the Egyptian government to officially inform the Sudanese of its construction. Ministers as well as the Sudanese in the market learned from the newspapers that the Sadd al-Aali would drown Sudanese Nubia, requiring the relocation of the Nubians with their five thousand years of history. Aroused, the Sudan demanded its fair share of the Blue Nile, not some sop for the Sudanese cotton farmers in the Gezira. The discussions would have died in September 1954 if not for the fact that both sides desperately needed an agreement that would contain the Nile waters within their own sovereign territory.

For the next four years Egypt and the Sudan continued their unproductive negotiations, characterized by the erosion of trust among the professional engineers thanks to the acrimonious exchanges of political leaders, who conducted a vitriolic campaign to discredit the other side's technicians. The Egyptians wanted the Sudan to assume an equal portion of their loss—the huge amounts of water that would evaporate from the Aswan reservoir—while they eliminated the livelihood of the Nubians at Wadi Halfa. The Sudan could bluster that it would build the Roseires dam without an agreement. The Egyptians insisted that the Sudan must abide by the Nile Waters Agreement of 1929. The Sudanese tartly informed Egypt that it was Great Britain, not the Sudan—which received its independence in 1956—that had signed that treaty. Each side appealed to the principles of international water law, the obscurity of which appeared irrelevant to the hydrologic and political realities of the Nile Valley.

Negotiations resumed in Cairo in December 1957, and were once again abandoned in January, six weeks later. The issues were the same—a fair share of the Nile waters for the Sudan, full compensation for the Sudanese displaced from the Nubian Nile, and the right to build control works that the country needed to utilize its agreed share of the Nile. These futile discussions, however, were very different from those of the past. The Egyptians had a commitment from the Soviet Union to help build the Sadd al-Aali, and they desperately needed an agreement with the Sudanese before construction could begin. Suddenly the virulent Egyptian media campaign against the Sudanese and their ministers and officials evaporated. The press and television in Cairo were controlled by Nasser, and they became effusive in their praise for the understanding and statesmanship of their Sudanese brothers. These fraternal expressions were welcome in Khartoum, but they only convinced Sayyid Mirghani Hamza, the minister for irrigation and the target of much personal abuse from the Egyptian media, to present a new document for Nile control. There was consternation among the Egyptian negotiators, unexpectedly confronted by a plan for the Nile Valley from, of all places, the Sudanese ministry of irrigation and hydroelectric power.

Remembered only by the few connoisseurs of Nile control, the *Report on the Nile Valley Plan,* published in Khartoum in June 1958, was an extraordinary document. It combined the sweeping comprehension of Garstin, a half century of measurements from nilometers, and the hydrologic analysis of Hurst. It also drew on the river experience of Nimmo Allan and the mathematical skills of Humphrey Morrice, its authors. Theirs was the first plan for the Nile—or any other river—devised by electronic computation, what is today called computer analysis. Dr. M. P. Barnett of the Massachusetts Institute of Technology praised it as a "classic study in computer simulation." Morrice and Allan based their work on the principle that "the whole of the Nile Valley should be treated as a hydrological unity." Their plan was elegant, and electronic computation was a powerful tool that soon revolutionized the world. But it was also flawed in several ways: the hydrologic measurements used for its calculations were not necessarily valid predictors of future volumes, and it failed to take into account the hydropolitics of the Nile Valley and the economic demands it made on the poverty-stricken riparian nations. The Egyptians, intent on building their high dam, rejected the plan, which soon vanished and was all but forgotten.[6]

The Ethiopians, meanwhile, understood that the waters of the Nile flowed from their mountain sanctuary, but they also understood, at least since the Anglo-Ethiopian Treaty of 1902, that they would be ignored in any negotiations over Nile control. An impoverished historic kingdom, overwhelmed by Italian imperialism between the world wars, Ethiopia did not have the resources to intervene in the dreary Anglo-Egyptian discussions on dividing the Nile waters. Egypt was well aware that the Ethiopians possessed the water but were incapable of conserving it within their territory. This reality, however, did not inhibit Emperor Haile Selassie's determination to defend the waters of his country from high dams and Nile agreements by downstream riparians. "From 1945, Egypt had sought, without success, to open the question of the Nile waters," wrote one observer. "Ethiopia, in the absence of some valuable *quid pro quo,* had little incentive to enter into an agreement with Egypt to give it a say with regard to Ethiopian waters."[7]

Haile Selassie was determined to build a dam at Lake Tana, but the Ethiopians were profoundly ignorant of their great river, and they had little understanding of the mystical legal rituals that were necessary to defend any obstruction to the flow of the Ethiopian Nile. There was no legal precedent that required an upstream riparian to declare what it intended to do with its water, but Egypt would naturally challenge the Ethiopians to define their needs in the highlands, and this was something they did not know. The Egyptians would produce the reports of Garstin, MacDonald, Hurst, and now the proposals for the Sadd al-Aali, but the Ethiopians had no plans with which to counter them.

In the spring of 1952, Haile Selassie revived his prewar contacts with the United States, where there was a large reservoir of goodwill. Tom A. Clark of the Bureau of Reclamation made a preliminary survey of the River Abbai that confirmed its enormous potential for hydropower and irrigation. He also reported that a comprehensive survey would take ten years. This reconnaissance ultimately led to the massive Bureau of Reclamation study of the Blue Nile basin that began four years later, but disturbing press reports that the West was prepared to provide financial assistance for the high dam at Aswan led the emperor to want more immediate guidance. He turned to British and European consulting firms, whose reports were deeply discouraging to his imperial ambitions for Lake Tana and the Blue Nile. In April 1953, J. Seymour Harris and Partners from Birmingham argued that a regulator at the outlet of Lake Tana would not have any appreciable impact on the contribution of the Blue Nile at Aswan, as the lake accounted for only 7 percent of the Blue Nile's flow. A dam there would never be a significant factor in Nile control. French and Italian firms conducted another survey, beginning a year later, only to report that a Lake Tana dam would produce little power far removed from those who might need it in Addis Ababa.[8]

The emperor and his ministers were perplexed by the discovery that the Lake Tana dam could never be a grand edifice to regulate the Blue Nile as his symbol of the transformation of Ethiopia. Not surprisingly, the emperor demanded another opinion. In 1956 a distinguished Swedish hydrologist confirmed the earlier findings that the future hydrologic development of Ethiopia would be in the great canyon of the Blue Nile and not at Bahr Dar or Tisisat Falls. This conclusion was most unwelcome, coinciding as it did with the construction of the emperor's summer home overlooking Bahr Dar, from whose vista he hoped to gaze upon his dam, his instrument, and negotiate a Nile waters agreement with Egypt as the Sudanese had done. The emperor published his defense of the Ethiopian Nile in the officially sanctioned newspaper, the *Ethiopian Herald,* making clear that his government would not be bound by any Egyptian-Sudanese discussions to divide the Nile between them, and that Ethiopia would reserve the Nile waters within its territory for its own use. Three days after this public declaration the United States, Great Britain, and the World Bank, on 9 February 1956, announced their commitment to finance the first stages of the high dam at Aswan. The Ethiopians immediately responded with a flood of diplomatic notes to Cairo and Khartoum reserving their rights to utilize the water resources of the Blue Nile for the benefit of the Ethiopian peoples, irrespective of any measures for Nile control by the downstream riparian states.[9]

Challenged by Egyptians and Sudanese, and suspicious of Europeans of any nationality, Haile Selassie turned once again to the United States. If they could finance a dam at Aswan, they could build one at Lake Tana. In the spring of 1956 he called on his nephew Zewde Gabre-Sellassie, great-grandson of the emperor Johannes IV, educated at Balliol College, Oxford, to perform an important task. He sent the young man to Washington, accompanied by Robert D. Scott, an international lawyer with whom he had negotiated Italian war reparations for Ethiopia in 1952. Ostensibly he was to conclude loan agreements for highways and Ethiopian airlines. He could not resist the opportunity, and Scott's Washington connections, to press the United States government to recognize the rights of the upstream riparian states to their equitable shares of the Nile waters.

The two engaged in vigorous discussions in May at the Department of State with Herbert Hoover Jr., the undersecretary of state, George Allen, the assistant secretary for Near Eastern, South Asian, and African affairs, and Leo Cyr, the director of African affairs. Between the two great wars Haile Selassie had sought American assistance to preserve his country and was abandoned to Italian fascism. Twenty years later the United States was not prepared to desert the Ethiopians to the Pan-Arabism of Nasser by refusing them the rights to their waters in the highlands. Zewde and Scott could not have found a more sympathetic audience. At a press conference in May 1956, President Dwight D. Eisenhower warned the Egyptians that American support for the Aswan dam had to be conditioned on a recognition of the rights of the upstream riparian states.[10]

When he returned from Washington later that month, Zewde needed few arguments to persuade the emperor to establish a Department of Water Resources that would help press for Ethiopia's rights to the Nile waters. Haile Selassie met with Vice President Richard Nixon in March 1957, and he expressed his disappointment that the United States had not consulted him about financing the high dam, when Ethiopia supplied 84 percent of the water to be stored at Aswan. The vice president was seeking African allies, and he reaffirmed his president's statement of the previous year that the development of the Nile waters should be a cooperative effort of all its riparian states, including Ethiopia and those under British colonial rule. In August, Zewde Gabre-Sellassie signed an agreement with the United States for a comprehensive study of the Blue Nile basin, to be conducted by the Bureau of Reclamation, an agency of the U.S. Department of the Interior.

The resulting Blue Nile Basin Study Plan required five years of intensive investigation. With characteristic conviction, the Bureau of Reclamation included not just the river but the whole of the Blue Nile basin. The study comprised a multitude of stream-flow measurements along the length of the river and its many tributaries, as well as reconnaissance by the air force, topographical maps from the army, and hydrologic soundings from the U.S. Coast and Geodetic Survey. The Americans absorbed much of the cost, but the contribution of $10 million from the Ethiopian treasury was a substantial symbol of its importance to the emperor and Ethiopia. Although it was a brief encounter compared with the half century of investigation by the Egyptian Ministry of Public Works in the basin of the White Nile, the bureau eventually completed a report of seventeen volumes, *Land and Water Resources of the Blue Nile Basin: Ethiopia,* which outweighed Egypt's eleven tomes of *The Nile Basin.*

The report by the Bureau of Reclamation identified thirty-three irrigation and hydroelectric power projects, which would require an estimated 6 billion cubic meters of water from the Blue Nile and its tributaries. It proposed a conservancy scheme that would eliminate the annual flood of the Blue Nile by impounding its water behind four dams on the river (at Kardobi, Mabil, Mendaia, and Border). This would give the river a constant flow, and a hydroelectric capacity three times that of Aswan. The amount of water available to downstream riparians would actually increase. At the same time Ethiopia could "maximize hydropower without considering the interest of Egypt and the Sudan [for] the amount of water available to the downstream riparians would not be substantially affected." Ethiopia would capture the Blue Nile flood of 50 billion cubic meters, but it could actually release more water to reach Roseires on the plains of the Sudan than any time in the past because of the minimal loss from evaporation in the Blue Nile gorge, 3 percent, or 1.5 billion cubic meters, rather than the 6 billion cubic meters, or 12 percent, of the Blue Nile water that would evaporate in the Aswan reservoir. Since the Blue Nile dams would be managed in conjunction with the Roseires reservoir, water could be released in May, as "timely water," without sustaining the enormous loss from evaporation at Aswan.[11]

Egypt, however, would no longer be the beneficiary of additional water in years of high flood, which would be stored behind the Blue Nile dams rather than at Aswan. The lower level of the reservoir at Aswan would limit loss from evaporation, but it would also reduce the hydroelectric capacity of the high dam. In return Egypt would receive additional water for irrigation, sustaining its historic economy as an agricultural nation with only marginal industry, a prospect the Egyptians could not be expected to view with equanimity. If relations between downstream and upstream riparians became hostile, Ethiopia could presumably withhold water it did not need, threatening the Sudan on its Sahelian plain and Egypt in its desert—just as the pharaohs, sultans, and warlords of the Nile Valley have feared for five millennia. Such

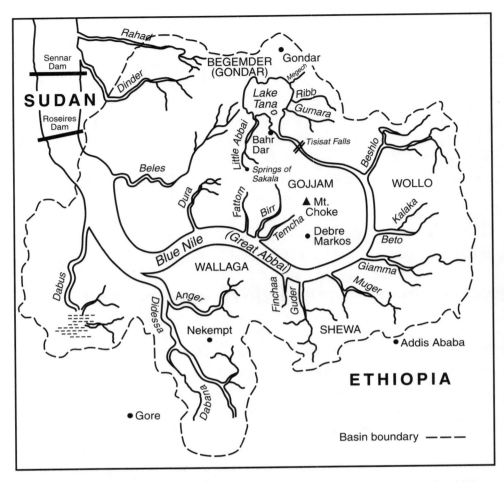

The Blue Nile Flood: Runoff Distribution (Source: U.S. Bureau of Reclamation, Land and Water Resources of the Blue Nile Basin, *1964)*

a prospect could not but rekindle ancient Egyptian fears of Ethiopian control of the life-giving waters.

But back in 1957, before the survey was begun and the report published, the Egyptians chose to ignore the Ethiopian initiative to enlist the Americans. They were busy negotiating for outside financial and technical assistance to build the high dam, as well as attempting to bully the Sudanese into accepting the dam and the inundation of Sudanese Nubia. Egypt, as part of its propaganda effort, declared that the unity of the Nile would bind its unfamiliar and hostile brothers to it, and sought to bargain approval for Aswan in return for a little more water behind the Sudanese dams at Roseires and Sennar. In the euphoria of independence, no Sudanese minister was willing to accept such an exchange. But in November 1958, General Ibrahim Abboud over-threw the elected government of the Sudan, seizing power in a military coup, and events took a turn in Egypt's favor. President Nasser immediately recognized the new government of fellow soldiers, and he soon received word that the Sudan no longer opposed the Aswan high dam in principle.

By March 1959 Abboud had no choice but to ask Nasser to reopen negotiations over the Nile waters. The Sudan had a more immediate problem than Egypt had. The first stage of the Managil extension of the Gezira irrigation scheme was complete. The second stage was under construction, and the third stage was ready to begin canaliza-tion. The Sudan's need for Nile water stored behind the Roseires dam was immediate, and the country lacked the resources to build it. Nasser's willingness to restart the ne-gotiations was assisted by a feeble effort from Great Britain in the twilight of empire to call for an international Nile waters authority, in which Britain would be a nonri-parian member. The idea of a Nile valley authority has never died, but neither the Egyptians nor the Sudanese wished to have the British return as a protagonist to muddy the waters of Nile negotiations.

The Egyptian government, too, was under subtle but intense pressure to reach an agreement with the Sudanese. Nasser himself had whipped up popular enthusiasm for the high dam, making it a matter of national pride, and the public's urgency was growing and becoming more intolerant of delay. Relations between the two govern-ments were more cordial, now that military men were in control of both, than they had been under the politicians. Salah Salim, the ebullient Egyptian minister for Su-danese affairs, was quoted as saying that "one session between officials of the two sides would be sufficient to produce a satisfactory settlement."[12]

These developments were well known in Ethiopia, where the Americans were con-ducting their comprehensive survey of the Blue Nile basin. The survey was still several years from being finished, however, so it was of no use in defending Ethiopian rights to the Nile waters against the imminent prospect of a high dam and a potential agree-ment between Egypt and the Sudan to divide the water between them. Haile Selassie responded as he had many times in the past, by turning to yet more outside consult-ants. Whenever his Lake Tana dam or the Blue Nile waters had appeared threatened by the British or the Egyptians, he immediately recruited foreign experts who quickly produced reports responding to the specific terms of their profitable commissions. These reports were never part of any comprehensive plan for the development of the Blue Nile basin, because one did not exist.

This time it was the British engineering firm of Bolton, Hennessey and Partners, which confirmed the findings of its predecessors. The Tana dam could never be a regulator for Nile control, but the engineers did recommend that during any future negotiations Ethiopia should demand 20 percent of the Blue Nile waters for its own use, "with a view to future bargaining." There was little hydrologic justification for this arbitrary assessment, but it inspired articles in the *Ethiopian Herald* about "Ethiopia's legitimate and major interests and rights as the greatest supplier of the waters of the Nile." The Egyptians and the Sudanese did not respond to such talk, and they remained equally aloof when informed by the British government on behalf of its East African territories that Kenya, Uganda, and Tanganyika would reserve 1.75 billion cubic meters, 2 percent of the total Nile flow, for their future irrigation needs.[13]

The representatives of the military governments of Egypt and the Sudan reopened their negotiations in Cairo in October 1959 amid much fanfare and expressions of friendship. The Egyptians had generated considerable goodwill in Khartoum during the summer by withdrawing their troops from a contentious border on the Red Sea and ignoring the unilateral abstraction of water from the Sennar reservoir for the Managil extension of the Gezira. Optimism became buoyant when the two governments reached an agreement that resolved tawdry but emotional disputes on customs, currency, and trade, which appeared to augur well for a successful conclusion to the difficult Nile water negotiations.

The result was finally achieved, after years of desultory talks, on 8 November, when the two parties signed the Nile Waters Agreement of 1959. Zakariya Mohieddin, the Egyptian minister of the interior, and General Talaat Farid, the Sudanese representative, led their respective delegations amid much hand-shaking, hugs, and kisses. This was a historic achievement, for the first time dividing the Nile waters between two of the riparians. The Anglo-Egyptian treaty of 1929 was concerned more with regulation of the Nile waters than with their parting. The 1959 agreement ignored any rights, equitable or historic, of Ethiopia or the other seven colonies and territories on the river. In 1959 their claims were in the future, and the needs of Egypt and the Sudan for plans and dams were in the present.

The agreement made possible the immediate construction of dams at Aswan, Roseires, and Khashm al-Girba, without which Nile control for Egypt and the Sudan could not be achieved. The future division of the water was more contentious. In return for Sudanese recognition of their established and historic rights, the Egyptians agreed to share equally with the Sudan any additional water obtained by future conservancy schemes—the old Cory award, which the Nile Waters Commission of 1921 had refused to adopt after strenuous Egyptian objections. Both Egypt and the Sudan unashamedly staked out substantial increases in their now mutual established and historic rights. The Egyptians received an additional 7.5 billion cubic meters, for an annual guarantee of 55.5 billion cubic meters. For Egypt, this has remained the nonnegotiable figure from which all discussions with upstream riparians must begin. But at the time, when the Egyptian negotiators proposed that the Sudan should receive as its share 18.5 billion cubic meters, the Sudanese seemed overwhelmed by their benevolence. This was a dramatic increase of 14.5 billion cubic meters from the 1929 agreement, and far more than the Egyptians had offered in any previous negotiations.

The Egyptians could afford to be generous. The expansion of the Gezira scheme could never absorb this amount of water, which permitted the Egyptians to give the Sudanese a huge amount on paper knowing that they were unlikely to use it. According to the laws of gravity, the surplus would flow downstream into the reservoir at the Aswan High Dam, where it would be used to reclaim the Egyptian desert with Sudanese water. Proud and independent, the Sudanese accepted the responsibility for the development of their vast Sahelian plain, now that they had a guarantee for the

The Roseires Dam on the Blue Nile, 1966 (Photograph by J. F. E. Bloss, reproduced by permission of Mrs. C. M. L. Bloss and Durham University Library)

water to do it. Although both sides have subsequently grumbled that their share of water was inadequate, it is difficult to believe that in 1959 they could have expected more. The advantages to both outweighed the disadvantages. Nasser got his high dam. The Sudan got Roseires. The inundation of Sudanese Nubia and the resettlement of its inhabitants were an embarrassment, but these problems lay in the future. The hostile atmosphere that had characterized Egyptian-Sudanese relations since 1952 had been replaced by a sensible if misguided optimism.

Less spectacular was the agreement's establishment of the Permanent Joint Technical Commission (PJTC), composed of four representatives each from Egypt and the Sudan, to plan and carry out the necessary hydrologic studies for future conservation projects throughout the Nile basin. The commission was installed in a handsome building near the Hilton Hotel in Khartoum. Its members were new men, internationally known hydrologists—Yahia Abdel Magid, Abdullahi Mohammed Ibrahim, Mohammed A. Mohammedein, and Bakheit Makki Hamad. But they were just as infatuated with the waters of the Lake Plateau as any British hydrologist before them. They were convinced that the future of Nile control was in devising a means to bring water to Aswan from the equatorial lakes—the Jonglei Canal, the Equatorial Nile Project, century storage. They could not admit that the future was in the basin of the Blue Nile, and Ethiopia was not included in their plans. There was no need for any future conservation projects in the Blue Nile basin when the Equatorial Nile Project would bring the waters of the great lakes down for storage behind the ultimate facility for Nile control at Aswan, the Sadd al-Aali.

10 *The Nile Ends at Aswan*

These gigantic enterprises may in turn prove but the preliminaries
of even mightier schemes, until at last nearly every drop of water which
drains into the whole valley of the Nile . . . shall be equally
and amicably divided among the river people, and the Nile itself,
flowing for three thousand miles through smiling countries,
shall perish gloriously and never reach the sea.
—Winston Churchill, The River War, *1899*

The decision in September 1952 by Gamal Abdel Nasser and the Revolutionary Command Council to construct a high dam at Aswan was an attempt to solidify their political power by building, in effect, a Great Pyramid. With a rapidly increasing and discontented population, they hoped that a regular supply of water would ameliorate future economic, political, and social crises. If the water could be contained behind a lofty dam in a vast reservoir within the borders of Egypt, the Egyptians could never again be held hostage by upstream nations. The newly independent governments would undoubtedly wish to assert their own rights to the Nile waters, and their political instability would limit their interest in Nile control. These concerns, however, were for the future. In 1952 there were two immediate unresolved questions about a high dam at Aswan—feasibility and finance. Could this enormous monument be built with current engineering technology, and who would pay for it?

Egyptian engineers in the army and the universities were understandably confident that it could be done. The civil servants and hydrologists at the Ministry of Public Works were less encouraging. They had devoted their careers to the idea of century storage and, still under the influence of Hurst, were deeply concerned about the huge loss of water from evaporation and seepage. As loyal Egyptians with a new and popular government, however, they reluctantly agreed to the project, but only as another edifice to complement the structures upstream for century storage—which the High Dam most certainly was not. Dr. Hassan Zaki was one of the High Dam's few enthusiastic supporters in the ministry. He had earned a doctorate in irrigation many years earlier, from Birmingham University, and served as undersecretary of state for hydroelectric development, a program the government of King Faruq had displayed little interest in. Now, at sixty, he was a professional bureaucrat invigorated by his appointment in September as director of the High Dam Authority.[1]

Two months after the decision in September 1952 to build a great dam at Aswan, Zaki traveled to Bonn to commission two German engineering firms, Hochtief and Dortmund Union, to prepare feasibility studies for the dam. The German government provided funds for the studies as a way of giving something to the Arabs to balance the compensation it was then paying to Israel for the Jewish Holocaust. Hochtief and Dortmund formed a large consortium of British, French, and German firms, which two years later presented a proposal based largely on the principles of soil mechanics developed by Karl von Terzaghi. A Hungarian professor of engineering at Harvard, Terzaghi had demonstrated in the 1930s that different soils, if properly utilized, could provide as much stability for large structures as concrete.

Terzaghi's concepts were fundamental to the German design. Given the dramatic seasonal fluctuations of the Nile at Aswan, it was impractical, if not impossible, to exclude the river's water from the site of construction. The solution was to create, through coffer dams and diversion tunnels upstream and downstream, dead water in which the dam could be constructed, starting with a central core of hardened clay and built up with rock fill and vibrated, compacted sand. At Aswan there is no dearth of sand, granite, and clay. The proposed dam, four miles upstream from the old Aswan Dam built in 1902, would be three miles long, rising to a height of 350 feet above the Nile bed and stretching in a crescent shape half a mile across the river.[2] Zaki argued for further hydrologic review, hoping that this would persuade the international community to provide financial assistance to build the dam; the Germans had made it clear that they could not afford the enormous project, preoccupied as they were with their own recovery from World War II.

A panel consisting of seven internationally known hydrologic engineers was recruited, including members from Germany, France, and the United States, whose representative, not surprisingly, was Karl von Terzaghi. In December 1954 the panel endorsed the Hochtief-Dortmund plan, calling it "as safe as the safest among the existing earth and rock fill dams resting on sediments." The cautious Zaki, still seeking to win over the engineers in the Ministry of Public Works who had been influenced by Hurst and the British hydrologists, sought one more review of the design, this time from a British firm. When it was again approved, the next step was to find the $1.3 billion to pay for it.[3]

At the time Egypt had substantial holdings in British sterling, but the dam would still require $400 million in foreign exchange. The government first sought financing from the International Bank for Reconstruction and Development, commonly known as the World Bank, in November 1954. The bank's president, Eugene Black, considered the project technically sound and economically beneficial, but he was also cautious about Egypt's ability to repay such a large loan with local currency. The issue was complicated by difficult Anglo-Egyptian negotiations over the withdrawal of British troops from the Suez Canal zone, and the humiliating defeat of the Egyptians in the Gaza Strip by the Israelis in February 1955. The defeat in Gaza caused Nasser and the Revolutionary Command Council to decide in September 1955 to rearm the Egyptian army at great expense, $80 million, with weapons purchased from Czechoslovakia with Soviet assistance, a decision taken partly because of the Western embargo on arm sales in the Middle East since the Arab-Israeli war of 1948.

The United States and Great Britain promised financial support for the dam, however, making an offer in February 1956 of a package that included a $270 million loan from the World Bank, and grants-in-aid of $56 million from the United States and $14 million from the United Kingdom. But British prime minister Anthony Eden and U.S. secretary of state John Foster Dulles were increasingly concerned about Egypt's growing ties with Czechoslovakia and the Soviet Union, particularly any expansion of Soviet influence in the region, and they placed stringent conditions on the financial package they offered. The Egyptians considered the terms patronizing and unacceptable. Eugene Black sought to allay Nasser's reservations regarding World Bank monitoring of the Egyptian economy, but Egypt's relations with the bank, Britain, and the United States continued to deteriorate during the winter of 1955–1956, exacerbated by personal animosity on the part of Eden and Dulles toward Nasser. Nasser's denunciation of the Baghdad Pact (later known as the Central Treaty Organization), and the conclusion of a second and more expensive $200 million arms agreement with the Soviet Union, confirmed their suspicions. Although Nasser had agreed to the World Bank's conditions as a challenge to Dulles, the secretary of state withdrew the American financial commitment on 20 July 1956, on the pretext that the Egyptian economy could not afford the strain of building the dam. Eden soon followed suit, and without the resources of the United States and Britain any proposal from the World Bank became irrelevant.

A week later, on 26 July, Nasser retaliated by announcing the seizure of the Suez Canal from its British and French owners and its nationalization under Egyptian control. His plan was to pay for the construction of the Aswan High Dam with the toll revenues collected from ships passing through the canal. The resulting international crisis over the Suez Canal led to the November military expedition by Britain, France, and Israel to reclaim the canal zone, and eventually the intervention of the United States and the Soviet Union to put a stop to the hostilities. The ensuing two years of crisis in Egypt prevented any progress on plans for the dam at Aswan. The nation was forced to use its revenues to replace weaponry lost during the Suez Crisis and to provide compensation for Egyptian accounts abroad that were frozen by the Western powers. Western companies had no incentive to become involved in plans for construction at Aswan.

In June 1955, however, Soviet foreign minister Dimitri Shepilov had casually mentioned to Nasser that the Soviet Union would be interested in providing financial support for the High Dam. This was diplomatic small talk that revealed a change in Soviet policies toward nonsocialist Third World countries following the death of Stalin in 1953. During the next three years Egypt's foreign trade shifted toward the Soviet Union. The decision by Dulles in July 1956 to withdraw financing for the dam presented an opportunity for the Soviet Union to exploit relations with Cairo for Moscow's benefit. On 23 October 1958, Soviet premier Nikita S. Khrushchev, with his characteristic dramatic flair, offered a loan of 400 million rubles ($220 million) at 2.5 percent interest for the first stage of construction, plus other credits for industrial development. Nasser eagerly took the Russian money, and soon reached a second agreement, on 27 August 1960, for another $120 million for the second stage of construction. The High Dam, the Sadd al-Aali, had become a financial reality.

Not surprisingly, the Soviet agreement excluded the participation of any other countries in the operation, or even the purchase of equipment from them, so the Aswan High Dam became a construction project of the Soviet Union. Responsibility for building it went to the Hydrological Research Institute, known as Hydroproject, an agency of the Soviet Ministry of Electric Power Station Construction. Hydroproject and its chief engineer, Nikolai Malyshev, had just completed the Kuibyshev Dam on the Dnepr River, and they were given the job of design and construction at Aswan. Shortly after the agreement a delegation of Soviet engineers visited Egypt to discuss the plan for the High Dam with their Egyptian counterparts. Meanwhile, in Moscow, the staff at Hydroproject assembled models of the dam, the bed of the Nile, and the ancillary structures required to build it. In January 1959 the Hydroproject engineers produced a plan for the dam that differed little from the Hochtief-Dortmund design. When Hassan Zaki reconstituted his international consultants to review the Russian design, they could hardly object to the same German proposal they had approved in 1954.[4]

During the culmination of the Nile Waters Agreement in the autumn of 1959, Musa Arafa, the minister of public works, along with Hassan Zaki and other Egyptian engineers, were invited to the dramatic closing of the Dnepr River by the Kuibyshev Dam at Kremenchug. The purpose of the visit was not only to witness a spectacular engineering achievement but to impress upon the Egyptians that the High Dam could be erected using the same construction methods that had built the great hydroelectric dams in the Soviet Union. The Aswan project used many of the same people, as well. In addition to chief engineer Malyshev of Hydroproject, Ivan Vassilievich Komzin, production manager at the Kuibyshev Dam since 1950, became the construction boss at Aswan. The success of these men at Kuibyshev had doubtless been due in part to their administrative skills, but in addition they commanded all the resources they needed from a totalitarian state, including the army, factory managers, and an inexhaustible supply of labor from the Gulag and prisons. This turned out to be an important difference in their experiences in Egypt.[5]

On 9 January 1960 President Nasser pushed a button that ignited ten tons of dynamite, demolishing twenty thousand tons of granite into fragments on the east bank of the Nile. On the following day the president pushed another and more important switch to start the first turbine installed in the old Aswan Dam. The electrification of the old dam provided the energy without which the construction for infrastructure at the High Dam—communications, roads, rail, housing—would have been impossible using unreliable and expensive sources of petroleum. Old Aswan was soon generating power, although it took another year, until April 1961, before all its turbines were operating and churning out 1.8 million kilowatts.

The first dam-building equipment arrived at Aswan in February 1960, but then it had to lay idle for lack of fuel, parts, and mechanics. A coffer dam upstream was needed to divert the Nile into a channel at Khor Kundi to form the dead water at the dam site, where the clay and rock and sand would be deposited for the dam. Downstream, another coffer dam would prevent the waters from surging back upstream and undermining the dam's foundations. In all, 11 million cubic meters of hard granite and loose sand had to be removed for the diversion channel and deposited where the dam would go. The Hydroproject engineers predicted that the upstream coffer dam would be completed by the middle of 1964. By the end of the first year of construction, there were 80 Soviet and 120 Egyptian engineers at Aswan, and about 2,000 Nubians chipping away at the granite. A railway from the old river port of Shellal had been cut through the granite for hauling the millions of tons of desert sand to the site, and builders had put up workshops and a water tower, but not much more had been done. Although enthusiasm was high at an elaborate ceremony held on 9 January 1961 for the first anniversary of construction on the High Dam, there was actually little to celebrate.

By the time of the second anniversary at Aswan on 9 January 1962, only 1 million of the total of 11 million cubic meters of rock and sand had been excavated, and it was clear that things were not going well. Supply was not keeping up with demand at the work site, there were shortages of both skilled and unskilled labor, and the leaders were clashing over political ideology. There were a number of reasons for the problems. Neither Nasser nor his engineers could command the kind of human and material resources that the pharoahs had mobilized for their big projects, or even that the Soviets had for the great hydroelectric dams in Russia. The Egyptian Ministry of Public Works and its bureaucrats had never undertaken a project of this size. The Egyptian engineers, accustomed to Western machinery, were contemptuous of the inferior Russian equipment they were forced to use. And having lived by the Nile from birth, they were arguing to the Russians that the strategic upstream coffer dam had to be completed soon, during the early 1960s, before a great annual surge that could not be contained came along to destroy the coffer dam and inundate the diversion tunnels. The Egyptian and Soviet bureaucrats in charge of managing supply and demand were hampered by the lack of a common language and experience.

Meanwhile the Russians, although determined to make the High Dam a symbol of state enterprise in the Third World, were the prisoners of Soviet production culture and all its inefficiencies. The Soviets failed to take advantage of the knowledge and experience of White Russian engineers in Egypt who were fluent in Arabic and English. Gregory Tscheborarieff, a student of Karl von Terzaghi and director of the Laboratory of Soil Mechanics at Giza, and Serge Lelyarshy, among another half dozen Russian hydrologists with long experience in Egypt, could have assisted greatly. The Soviets and the Egyptians both underestimated the amount of time required to complete the channel and tunnels and excavate all those tons of rock and sand, in spite of the more prudent predictions of ten years that had been made by Hochtief-Dortmund.

Nasser, in characteristic fashion, decided to take charge of construction of the High Dam, along with his remaining Free Officers and the network of British-oriented Egyptian engineers. He and the High Dam Supreme Committee tacitly agreed to ignore previous commitments to buy Russian equipment. The Russians were furious, but their lamentable performance at Aswan no longer gave them credibility or control of the rubles transferred to the Egyptian government. Nasser turned over the Soviet-provided funds to the Egyptian engineers to purchase reliable construction equipment from the West, including Swedish drills for the hard granite and British hydraulic pumps, excavators, and trucks. For the construction job, they turned to Egyptian contractors—capitalists who were paid in Soviet foreign currency. These included a company called Arab Contractors, which in March 1962 was awarded the contract for the excavation of millions of cubic meters of rock and sand. The company was directed by Osman Ahmed Osman, who had completed major projects at the Suez Canal, the Cairo airport, and in Kuwait, Saudi Arabia, and Libya, and by the end of the year it had ten thousand workers excavating and filling the dam at Aswan. Another company, the Misr Group, won a subsidiary contract to secure the tunnels, the hydroelectric station, and the rock faces with cement.

Construction of the High Dam was transformed when it became a project of the Egyptians backed by Russian rubles. New personalities injected new life. Ivan Komzin retired to Russia and was replaced by Aleksandro Aleksandrov. Musa Arafa was given a desk job in Cairo, and the dynamic young engineer Sidki Suleiman took his place at Aswan. Gamal al-Batrawy replaced Amin al-Sherif as the director of operations for Arab Contractors. After the fumbling of the early years, excavation now proceeded with ruthless determination, supported by the power of the Egyptian state. Arab Contractors and the Misr Group offered cash incentives to meet the construction schedule. By July 1963 there were 34,000 laborers from Arab Contractors completing the tunnels for the hydroelectric station and the coffer dam.

The project reached a turning point on 15 May 1964, when the Nile began to rise against the upstream coffer dam. Fed by extraordinary levels of precipitation in the equatorial lakes, the river reached its highest flood in a century. The coffer dam held. The Nile disappeared at Khor Kundi down through the channel gorge cut from the granite of the Aswan dike. The great dam could now be built.

Gamal Abdel Nasser did not live to see his pyramid finished, although the dam was operational when he died in September 1970. Five months later, in January 1971, his successor, Anwar el-Sadat, and the Soviet president Nikolai Podgorny presided at the official opening ceremonies. The dam was a tremendous engineering achievement. The foundation of the dam was a deep grout curtain dug 665 feet below the riverbed to rest on the immovable Aswan granite. Above the grout curtain the clay core of the dam rose 364 feet, buttressed upstream by more than a half mile of impacted sand and rock to sustain that core against the weight of the world's greatest reservoir. The crest of the dam, 130 feet across, sweeps majestically in a great curve for two miles. The massive hydroelectric powerhouse, with its twelve turbines, annually generates 10 billion kilowatt-hours from the water pouring through six diversion tunnels. The dam and power station together cost $820 million.

Beginning as early as 1948, critics both internal and external had denounced this folly on the Nile, and the completion of the Sadd al-Aali in 1971 caused them to coalesce in their opposition. In Egypt those who opposed the dam confronted a dilemma. It was a patriotic symbol of Egyptian nationalism and independence from an imperial past, but the engineering and environmental problems for them vindicated their political opposition to Nasser and his revolution. A popular Egyptian novelist, Sunallah Ibrahim, expressed this quandary with greater insight than the engineers:

> In the beginning [of the revolution] the goal is simple and clear and everything is either black or white, with or against. There is enthusiasm and faith in the future and the ability to change the course of history. Not a time for reflection and analysis. Then the revolution is accomplished and another stage with a slower rhythm begins: tasks are more complex, objectives are less clear, and shadows of gray begin to smear the whiteness and the blackness. This becomes the time for thinking. What about? The mistakes of the first stage and the possibilities of the future.[6]

The shadows began to fall across the reservoir as it filled after the completion of the coffer dam in 1964. Six years later the High Dam could contain a great lake of 162 billion cubic meters, twice the average annual flow of the Nile. Eight miles across and extending south for more than 300 miles into Sudanese Nubia, the surface covers more than 2,550 square miles. Known as Lake Nasser in Egypt and Lake Nubia in the Sudan, this vast reservoir will have a long but diminishing life. Throughout the ages Egypt has been annually restored not only by water but by the nutrients that wash down from the soils of Ethiopia. The water entrapped behind the dam can be passed through turbines and sluice gates, but the sediment carried in suspension by the river silently drops to the bottom in the quiet water of the reservoir. The heaviest silt sinks

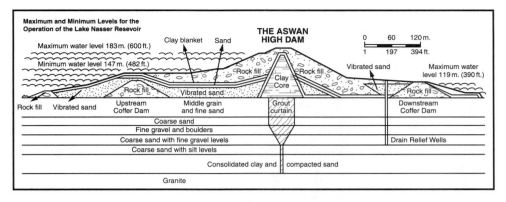

Profile of the Aswan High Dam (Reprinted from Rushdi Said, The River Nile, © *1993, p. 233, with permission from Elsevier Science)*

at the beginning of the reservoir, and the finer grains gradually fall to the bottom farther along. Known to hydrologists as "dead storage," this accumulation of silt over time reduces the capacity of live storage, the water, in the artificial lake. Every obstruction on a river, whether from a lava flow or a cement barricade, has a finite life when its reservoir is filled with dead storage. The Sadd al-Aali is no exception. The hydrologic life of the High Dam has been variously estimated at four hundred to five hundred years, a factor of more geologic interest than Nile control in the twenty-first century.[7]

The rising waters soon inundated lower Nubia, the dwelling place of one hundred thousand Nubians and five thousand years of history. There was greater interest in history than in people. A massive international campaign led by UNESCO was launched in 1955 to preserve temples, tombs, fortresses, and the Nubian past soon to be swallowed by the reservoir. The Nubian salvage scheme was the inspiration of Christiane Désroches-Noblecourt, curator of Egyptian antiquities at the Louvre in Paris, but the driving forces were Saroit Okacha, minister of culture in Egypt, and Thabit Hasan Thabit, director of antiquities in the Sudan, who persuaded their governments and in turn Dr. Vittorino Veronse, director of UNESCO, to finance the preservation of Nubian monuments. In October 1959 Veronse organized an international conference of archaeologists with experience in Nubia to determine how to proceed in saving the ruins. In March 1960, supported by enthusiastic commitments from Egypt and the Sudan, Veronse formally launched an international appeal for the Nubian salvage scheme. The Egyptians established a documentation center at Cairo, and in October a working

The Aswan High Dam, aerial view

group, the International Committee of Experts, began meeting at Wadi Halfa under the indefatigable William Y. Adams of the United States, H. A. Nordstrom from Norway, and Thabit from the Sudan to define the sites and their priorities.

The monuments of Nubia had been seen by everyone who passed south of Aswan over the previous thousand years, but their methodical archaeological inspection began only during the first decades of the twentieth century under George Andrew Reisner, who led expeditions from Harvard. Half a century later the Nubian salvage scheme under the Egyptians, the Sudanese, and UNESCO captured popular and political interest, symbolized by the towering stone statues of Ramses II at Abu Simbel. The campaign would require $87 million and "an effort of cooperation [that] has never been undertaken on such a scale in the domain of archaeology," wrote Tom Little, author of *High Dam at Aswan*.[8]

Many rushed to preserve the past. Twenty-three rescue missions from as many countries conducted extensive surveys and excavations, carefully allocated by the committee to avoid national rivalry over the assigned digs. There were many sites, but some were more desirable than others. The Poles were at Faras, the Argentinians at Aksha, the Spanish at Irgin, the Ghanaians at Debeira, the West Germans at Kalabsha, the French at Amada, and the Americans at prehistoric sites in upper Egypt and lower Nubia. In an extraordinary effort President John F. Kennedy extracted $10 million from Congress for the preservation of Nubian monuments. Temples were moved to higher ground. Some were donated to countries in return for their generous financial and scholarly assistance. The Roman temple from Dandur is now in the Metropolitan Museum of Art in New York.

The evocative symbol of the Nubian salvage scheme was the great temple of Ramses II at Abu Simbel. The four colossal statues of Ramses II, his temple, and statues of Queen Nefertari and their children were the legacy built by the longest reigning and most powerful pharaoh of dynastic Egypt. Ramses ruled for sixty-six years in the thirteenth century B.C.E., during the New Kingdom. His statues were first uncovered in 1817 by Giovanni Battista Belzoni. Born in Padua, Belzoni was six feet eight inches tall and had worked his way through British and European theatricals as a muscular strong man, arriving in Alexandria promoting heavy hydraulic machinery, in which the Egyptians expressed no interest. The British consul general Henry Salt, still in competition with the French well after the Napoleonic wars had ended, sent Belzoni up the Nile to gather artifacts, which he did with the enthusiasm of the tomb robbers that have been in business since Cheops was laid to rest in his pyramid at Giza in 2567 B.C.E. At Abu Simbel in 1817 he penetrated the protective wall of sand deposited throughout the millennia to enter the huge inner temple. It was another seventy-five years before the sand had been removed, in 1892, to permit entry by the few who ventured south of Aswan. Another three-quarters of a century later the colossi and temples could now be rescued. Not everyone wanted to save Abu Simbel, for there were those who argued that the great cost could be better used for humanitarian concerns, but its imposing presence from the past proved irresistible.

By November 1963, $19 million had been pledged from forty-five countries, and the Egyptians, reviewing numerous salvage schemes, selected a design by the Swedish consulting company Vattenbyggnadsbyran, which proposed cutting the sandstone rock colossi and temples into sections with fine high-tempered wire knives, lifting them out, and reassembling them on the heights above the reservoir. Contracts were signed with a consortium organized by Hochtief of Germany, designers of the High Dam, and including Impreglio of Italy, Grands Travaux de Marseille International of France, Santab and Skamba of Sweden, and Atlas from Egypt. The United States contributed one-third of the cost to raise the temples. Protected by their own coffer dam, the brooding statues ascended to greater heights, a journey every pharaoh had obsessively planned for his afterlife.

On 13 May 1964 President Nasser and Chairman Khrushchev arrived on the yacht *Ramses* at Khor Kundi and the pavilion erected above the coffer dam. On the following morning they mutually pulled the switch to close the coffer dam. During the jubilant ceremonies no one appears to have noticed the absence of President Ibrahim Abboud of the Sudan, whose Nubians three hundred miles to the south were being shabbily displaced. The international community had rallied to preserve the sandstone monuments of Nubia; the relocation of the Nubians was not its responsibility. The Sudanese government had agreed to the loss of their date palms, homes, and land, ac-

Abu Simbel, the Temple of Ramses II, uplifted from the waters of Lake Nasser

cording to the terms of the Nile Waters Agreement of 1959 with Egypt, and received compensation for it. This expedient compact made possible the financing for the Nile dams at Aswan in Egypt and at Roseires in the Sudan. It did little for the Nubians.

During the negotiations the difference of a few million pounds in compensation for the Nubians had been more contentious than the larger issue of dividing the precious Nile waters. The Sudanese demanded 36 million Egyptian pounds. The Egyptians offered £E9 million. The Sudanese countered by asking for £E20 million; the Egyptians stood firm at £E10 million. The deadlock was broken by the personal intervention of President Nasser, who suggested splitting the difference at £E15 million. This seemingly dramatic gesture by the revolutionary leader of the Arab world melted the Sudanese resistance, and in their admiration and naïveté Abboud and his generals thought his proposition a sensible compromise. It proved to be a disastrous mistake.

This fixed sum provided only 40 percent of the estimated funds needed to relocate fifty thousand Nubians. It had no provision for endemic inflation or inevitable uncertainties. The Nubians were not the Arab immigrants who came to the Sudan in the sixteenth century. They were the descendants of Taharqo and the kingdom of Kush who had lived south of Aswan for many millennia. Their reaction was violent. Riots were firmly suppressed by the Sudanese army, tarnishing the image of the Abboud military regime, which never recovered. Nubian farmers from Wadi Halfa were removed to an alien environment at Khashm al-Girba on the Atbara River, among the pastoral Shukriyya people. The generosity of the Sudanese in signing the Nile Waters Agreement in 1959 required them to pay for the resettlement from a meager treasury. Forty years later the Egyptian contribution, a pittance, is bitterly remembered by disaffected Nubians who have not prospered from the dislocation to Khashm al-Girba. The reservoir behind the dam is now half filled with Ethiopian soil in dead storage, and consequently it holds less water, exacerbating the historic tensions between Nubian immigrant cultivators from the Nile, the Halfawis, and the traditional owners of pastures, the Shukriyya of the Butana.[9] Khashm al-Girba became a microcosm of the environmental problems produced by the great dam at Aswan.

The Khashm al-Girba Dam on the Atbara River (Photograph by J. F. E. Bloss, reproduced by permission of Mrs. C. M. L. Bloss and Durham University Library)

The High Dam guaranteed water and power for Egypt, but at a great cost that was not merely financial. The Russians provided most of the foreign currency to build the dam, and Egypt carried the labor burden, but the environmental impact of the Sadd al-Aali remains irreparable. Opponents and even supporters of the dam had serious concerns before it was built, and their fears have proved well founded. Since the beginning of history human intervention has disrupted the rhythms of the environment, and Aswan is no different. The problem is not so much the edifice of the High Dam itself but the huge reservoir it created. South of Aswan the crust of the earth is laced with fractures in the Nubian sandstone, and the dam had impounded a tremendous weight of water on fragile fault lines. On 14 November 1981 a major shock, 5.3 on the Richter scale, occurred at Kalabsha, forty miles southwest of Aswan. The massive dam of clay, sand, and rock remained stable, but the great weight of its reservoir has created further instability throughout the many faults underneath, precipitating a dramatic increase in seismic activity, tremors, and earthquakes.

There is magic and power in free-flowing water; when it is confined, there is death and decay. Oxygen in moving water sustains phytoplankton, which in turn keeps fish, and ultimately humans, alive. But the High Dam has disrupted the even distribution of oxygen in the water now collected in the giant reservoir. Worse, the rich sediment from the Ethiopian highlands carried by the Nile and now deposited in the lake brings nutrients, especially nitrogen. Nitrogen acts as a fertilizer, producing the dreaded blue-green algae, Cyanophyta. The algae consumes the oxygen that is vital to plankton and other aquatic life in a process that eventually leads to eutrophication, the aging and dying of a lake. The change in water quality has been enormous. Many species of fish have died, some eaten by the carnivorous Nile perch, whose fillets are on every menu from Kampala to Cairo.

In addition, the nutrient-filled sediment from Ethiopia carried by the Nile, estimated in billions of tons or cubic meters, no longer passes through Egypt to the Mediterranean as it once did. Many people expected that the deposition of the silt would fall evenly across the bed of the reservoir, but anyone who has been on free-flowing rivers knows that is not how they behave. Upon reaching the quiet waters of Lake Nubia, between 1978 and 1990 the Nile dropped a billion and a half cubic meters from Ethiopia into the first hundred miles of the lake between the Dal and the second cataract at Wadi Halfa, with its forest of flooded date palms. The remaining tonnage trickled northward, leaving a veneer of nutrients on the bed of Lake Nasser that would never reach the fields of Egypt, which are now in need of chemical fertilizers. The most immediate harm from the loss of Ethiopian sediment was sustained not by

Lake Nasser and Lake Nubia, the great reservoir behind the Aswan High Dam

farmers but by the historic Egyptian brick industry, which once produced a billion bricks a year from the river's dregs. Deprived of their primary ingredient, the brick makers began to buy, at premium prices, thousands of tons of precious and irreplaceable topsoil from the fellahin.

The damage to farming from the loss of the natural sedimentary fertilizers has ultimately been just as great. The agricultural ingenuity of Egyptians and imperialists has constantly expanded the productivity of the Nile Valley, but even after the High Dam the Egyptians still had to confront the implacable forces of nature, sand, drainage, the quality of its water, and the changes required in the historic and complex system of crop rotation. Throughout the millennia, the Nile and Egypt have always been surrounded by sand, and Lake Nasser is no different. The awesome sandstorms of the Sahara are known by many names—including *khamsin, habub,* and *harratan*—to nomads, trans-Saharan caravans, and cultivators by the Nile. The sands of the western Egyptian desert have been blown into the Nile since the Pleistocene era. The High Dam has not changed the unpredictable regimen of nature, but it has changed the results. In the past the sands of the Sahara carried into the Nile Valley by the wind were flushed down the river by the force of moving water in flood. When the Nile no longer flowed vigorously after the flood, the wind-driven sand accumulated in great dunes on the western bank, encroaching on the narrow floodplain and burying the monuments of dynastic Egypt. The dam builders could excavate sand at Aswan and teams from the Nubian salvage scheme could remove the sand covering Abu Simbel, but neither had any control over the khamsin that carried many tons of Saharan sand into Lake Nasser. It sank to the bottom of the reservoir to mix with the Ethiopian sediments, further raising the level of dead storage. And at the end of the river, on the shores of the Mediterranean Sea, there are even greater environmental concerns.

For thousands of years the coasts of the eastern Mediterranean had been replenished by Nile silt that flowed through the delta, to be distributed by eastward currents and winds along the seashore to Palestine and the Levant. By the 1970s the Mediterranean coast of Egypt was in full retreat, accumulating large sand dunes from unstable beaches and offshore winds. The Coastal Research Institute of the Ministry of Public Works has been investigating the complicated relationship between river and sea, but at the turn of the millennium the answers remain unclear. Many attribute the degradation of the delta coastline to the dearth of sediment, and the decline of profitable sardine fishing to the disappearance of its nutritious rich silt. Others argue that the retreat from the coast is a result of global warming and the rise of the seas. At the least, the Sadd al-Aali has undoubtedly contributed to the Egyptian coast moving inland, but it has existed only briefly so far and probably cannot bear the full responsibility for the encroachment of dunes, the creeping inundation of sea water into peripheral lakes and lagoons, or reductions in the drainage of the delta.

Decreases in drainage of the Nile Delta, waterlogging of the soil, and increased soil salinity first appeared in the nineteenth century with the introduction of perennial irrigation. In the past the waters from the seasonal flooding of the basins beside the river and in the delta would drain to the river and the sea. During the twentieth century continuous perennial irrigation enabled crops to be grown in winter and summer as well as the *nili* crops from the flood of the old basin irrigation. The steady supply of water grew wheat in winter, maize in summer, in addition to clover, rice, and the vegetables, beans, lentils, and onions that are the stuff of the Egyptian diet. This steady supply of contained water was a great burden on the soil and its fertility. The subsoil water level rose, strangling crop roots. Soil salinity increased when the sedimentary salts were no longer flushed to the sea but instead sank into the soil to permeate and pollute it and reduce its productivity. The salinity of perennial irrigation was compounded by the retreat of the coastline, which permitted the intrusion of brackish water. No longer flushed by drainage from the Nile flood, the coastline is now dependent for its protection on man-made structures and its deep underground aquifer.

Furthermore, without sediment, a clear river generates greater energy, scouring its bed more effectively in direct proportion to the increase in flow. Engineers determined that the amount of water released at the dam could be controlled to contain the damage to the riverbed, but the barrages and regulatory works downstream from Aswan are particularly vulnerable to increased scouring. To keep the barrages from being undermined by erosion, in the 1980s the water level of each reach between the barrages at Esna, Nag Hammadi, and Asyut was lowered by a few inches to produce stability. According to Rushdi Said, "the stark reality . . . of this delicate balance is that the present Nile channel does not allow for greater releases" from Aswan unless the three downstream barrages are rebuilt.[10]

The Sadd al-Aali was not responsible for perennial irrigation—that was the perspicacious idea of Muhammad Ali in the first half of the nineteenth century. The Aswan High Dam, however, made it permanent and productive at an environmental cost not figured into the calculations of those who built it. No longer able to carry Ethiopian nutrients to the delta and unable to launder the increasing municipal, industrial, and agricultural waste dumped into it, the Nile died at Aswan. Below the dam its flow, manipulated by engineers, is no longer a river but a grand canal.

In the hydrologic development for the most effective use of the known waters from the Nile basin, the Sadd al-Aali is the wrong dam in the wrong place. Perhaps the Egyptians can ameliorate the environmental damage by reform of river management and the necessary resources in their endless efforts to manipulate nature. The environment is not, however, the price Egypt has to pay for the High Dam. The evaporation of more than 10 billion cubic meters from its great reservoir in the extreme heat of the Egyptian desert is the dam's annual unrecoverable cost. Ten billion cubic meters lost to the atmosphere represents nearly 9 percent of the average annual flow of the Nile waters that reach Aswan. It is a quantity of water sufficient to quench the thirst of 20 million Egyptians and help to feed them. This evaporation can never be managed or recovered. The enormous loss was the principal reason why Hurst and the engineers of the Ministry of Public Works opposed the High Dam until they were overwhelmed by political reality. The Egyptians, from the fellahin in the fields to the president in his palace, were and are prepared to pay the price of 10 billion cubic meters of Nile water for symbolism and security.

To the Egyptians the symbolism of the High Dam as a monument to modern Egypt and its revolution remains untarnished by environmental concerns. It is a great achievement accomplished by Egyptian engineers with Russian rubles that gives them security. It was built in Egypt by Egyptians to provide power and water for increased industry and agriculture without being hostage to African peoples or their politicians upstream. Thirty years have passed since the completion of the Sadd al-Aali. A new generation has been born in Egypt, people who are now secured by the waters in Egypt behind their dam. The pharaohs would have understood and approved.

11 *Jonglei*

No sooner had the construction of the Sadd al-Aali become a reality than the unknown mechanics of global climate contrived to produce dramatic and unpredictable
rainfall on the Lake Plateau between 1961 and 1964. It was an extraordinary and mysterious event. Since the imperial occupation of East Africa by the British and Germans at the end of the nineteenth century, recorded rainfall had followed a consistent
pattern of an oscillating ten-year cycle. Suddenly in 1961 the skies over eastern Africa
opened in a torrential downpour that lasted four years, dumping huge amounts of
water on the equatorial lakes. Lake Victoria rose eight feet, adding 170 billion cubic

meters to its waters. Lakes Kyoga, Albert, Edward, and George together accumulated an additional 84 billion cubic meters. Within four years the Lake Plateau had amassed three times the historic annual average flow of the Nile at Aswan. At the time there was no rational explanation other than nature run amok, "a freak," in the words of one hydrologist.[1]

Forty years later our understanding of the influence of the oceans on global climate and rainfall explains the deluge in eastern Africa as less a freak than a manifestation of El Niño. In the 1920s Sir Gilbert Walker, professor of meteorology at the University of London, proposed the theory that the oceans determine the world's climate. In the 1960s a Norwegian meteorologist at UCLA, Jacob Bjerknes, confirmed Walker's hypothesis from data accumulated by the scientific investigations during the International Geophysical Year, 1957–1958. In 1969, Bjerknes presented a more complete definition of the relationship between oceans and atmosphere, in which El Niño, an abnormal accumulation of warm water in the central Pacific, "triggered severe droughts, floods, and other climatic anomalies throughout the tropics"—the most plausible explanation for the four-year deluge over the Lake Plateau.[2]

The great rains began to diminish after 1964 to more normal levels, but not before causing extensive flooding of villages around the lakes. The Bantu and Luo people scattered around the lake shores were not numerous and were able to move to higher ground. But the Dinka and the Nuer living below the lakes on the horizontal pastures of the Nilotic plain—a million Africans—had nowhere to go. The water poured from the lakes in white waves down the Bahr al-Jabal and into the Sudd, where it broke out of its aquatic prison to inundate the seasonal pastures, the *toic,* of the Nilotes. The Nuer elders remembered the flood of 1918, *pi lual,* red water, that brought great suffering, but only for the year. The waters that came down from the lakes after 1961 remained at high levels in the Sudd for two decades. In the Kongor district whole forests became skeletons, the *awaithar,* brooding over a plain of water. Zaraf Island in the heart of the Sudd disappeared. Old Fanjak town, an island and hostelry in the swamps for a hundred years, was deserted. The village of Jonglei vanished beneath the waters. From 1961 to 1980, the average annual discharge from the Lake Plateau down the Bahr al-Jabal into the Sudd nearly doubled, from 27 billion to 50 billion cubic meters. The water spilled relentlessly through the aquatic walls surrounding lagoons, expanding the irretrievable permanent swamp to six times its normal size, and twice that of the remaining seasonal floodplain.[3]

Deprived of grass in the inundated toic, 120,000 cattle perished. Without them, thousands of Nilotes died from famine—mature women, children, the old, the infirm.

The strong young men and women fled for survival to the northern Sudan, where their presence visibly demonstrated the deep differences between southern and northern Sudanese. Although southern Sudanese had been enslaved and brought to the northern Sudan to serve as soldiers and domestics since the opening of the Sudd in the mid nineteenth century, the number of free Nilotes in the twentieth century was not large. They much preferred their Garden of Eden, protected by the Sudd and the British policies of segregation between northern and southern Sudan during the first half of the twentieth century. The great floods of the 1960s dramatically changed their traditional way of living. No longer restrained by British efforts to contain them in their pastures and cattle camps, the Nilotes were driven by the rising waters to the alien and urban environments of Khartoum and Omdurman.

The flight from the flood by young Nilotes coincided with a building boom in Khartoum, fueled by new petrodollars from the Organization of Petroleum Exporting Countries (OPEC) seeking investment for surplus capital. The builders desperately needed cheap migrant labor. The oil-producing states had always been dependent on food imports, and they saw the Sudan, with its enormous acreage and modest population, as their opportunity to turn a friendly Arab country into "the breadbasket of the Middle East." In the offices and housing developments of Khartoum, the dam sites at Roseires and Khashm al-Girba, and the irrigation canals of the Gezira the displaced Nilotes found work—but it was at the bottom of the economic and social scale. Here the proud Nilotic refugees from the upper Nile basin experienced many forms of discrimination, subtle and not so subtle, and the reality of the *abid* (slave) mentality that northerners had learned from their folklore. The southerners were refugees, migrant workers with no choice but to try to make life tolerable, earn some money, buy radios, and learn the ways of cultures different from their own—and not only because those ways were Arab and Muslim. Once the flood finally subsided, they returned to the upper Nile, equipped with new ideas and the experience of modernization in all its manifestations. They did not disappear into the Sudd, for their warrior traditions had been transformed into a political militancy far more intense and sophisticated than the gentle savage described by romantic Englishmen.

In 1961, Tanganyika, a British mandate, became independent. (Two years later the country merged with the island of Zanzibar and became known as Tanzania.) Independence soon came to the British colonies of Uganda and Kenya as well, in 1962 and 1963, respectively. In the face of the great flooding, these newly independent East African states were naturally more concerned with ameliorating the damage to their own citizens than with the deprivation of the southern Sudanese. Their solution was simple: pass the excess water from Lake Victoria through the sluices of the Owen Falls Dam. Throughout the millennia, the pharaohs had been just as fearful of too much water as too little. The completion of the first dam at Aswan in 1902 gave power to the new pharaohs to eliminate the threat of flood for the Egyptians downstream. The completion of the dam at Owen Falls in 1954 gave power to the new East African nations upstream to regulate the waters of the equatorial lakes. Those in between, as usual, were the losers.

The decision by the East African states to increase the outflow at the Owen Falls Dam was hardly an ebullient demonstration of independence until Julius K. Nyerere, the first president of independent Tanganyika, invoked what became known as the Nyerere Doctrine. "Former colonial countries had no role in the formulation and conclusion of treaties done during the colonial era, and therefore they must not be assumed to automatically succeed to those treaties," was the general thrust of it. Uganda and Kenya soon achieved their independence as well, and both invoked the Nyerere Doctrine, claiming they were not bound by treaties Great Britain had signed for them. Specifically, on 4 July 1962, Nyerere's government informed Great Britain, Egypt, and the Sudan that "the provisions of the 1929 [Nile Waters] Agreement purporting to apply to the countries under British administration are not binding on Tanganyika." (Egypt dismissed this argument eighteen months later, insisting that the agreement remained in full force.) Belgium, the other colonial power in the region, had never been a party to the Anglo-Egyptian agreement of 1929, so its newly independent former colonies—Congo, Burundi, and Rwanda—had no obligations as to the dispensation of the Nile waters. All bets were off for the waters of the Lake Plateau.[4]

For the Sudan and Egypt, the solution was the same as it had been at the beginning of the twentieth century—the Garstin Cut. The El Niño rains had demonstrated nature's ability to produce an amount of water Hurst had calculated would take many decades, or even a century, to accumulate. Had it not been for the Owen Falls Dam and the geological formations at the outlets from the equatorial lakes, the volume of water flowing across the Nilotic plain would have destroyed even more animals and people than it did. The waters that inflicted so much hardship on the Nilotes would support an expanding population in Egypt and the Sudan if only they could pass the Sudd, that voracious consumer of water, by the canal known as Jonglei.

The idea for the Garstin Cut, the Jonglei Canal, underwent numerous permutations during the first three-quarters of the twentieth century, resulting in more investigations "than any other major development project in the Third World." During that time nine specific proposals for allowing the equatorial waters to bypass the Sudd were designed before the Egyptian and Sudanese governments accepted a final plan in 1974. Records, reports, and surveys—together a massive amount of documentation— have created much confusion and distortion. Information collected under different conditions and for a different purpose usually produces conclusions no longer applicable for the present. After seventy years of successive surveys the Egyptian and Sudanese engineers finally discovered a new technology that could make the canal a reality. But first, a way had to be found of dealing with the southern Sudanese, the restive Nilotes living in the region of the Sudd, with their incompatible perceptions of the canal to be dug through their homeland.[5]

In 1969 another colonel, Jaafar al-Numayri, came to power in Khartoum, with the avowed purpose of ending the debilitating war in the southern Sudan. Before seeking a solution to the civil war in the south, however, he had to confront the northern Sudanese conservatives and Communists. The Ansar, the disciples of al-Mahdi in the nineteenth century and the followers of his successors in the twentieth, refused to accept the legitimacy of another presumptuous junior military officer and admirer of Nasser. Numayri contained them by destroying their sanctuary at Aba Island in the White Nile, 150 miles south of Khartoum. A year later, in July 1971, he suppressed an attempted Communist coup d'état after a three-day battle. By 1972 he could no longer ignore the Southern Problem. He had successfully confronted his enemies on an island in the Nile and in the suburbs of Khartoum, but the southern insurgents, the Anya-Nya, led by Joseph Lagu, were gaining strength with arms supplied by Israel out of the abundance captured from the Egyptians in 1967 during the Six Day War.

Numayri granted his plenipotentiaries full powers to end a seventeen-year war that he could never win. Timely mediation by Emperor Haile Selassie brokered a peace treaty at Addis Ababa in February 1972. Numayri transformed the agreement into law, the Southern Provinces Regional Self-Government Act, which established a single, autonomous region in the southern Sudan governed by a popularly elected People's Regional Assembly and a High Executive Council that would enforce the laws of the legislature for the whole of the southern Sudan. The Sudanese government retained control over defense, foreign affairs, customs, and the waters from the Lake Plateau and the upper Nile basin. Effective control of these waters depended on excavation of the Jonglei Canal.

President Numayri basked in the approval of the international community for his prudence, political realism, and statesmanship in taking the initiative to end a debilitating civil conflict. Responsibility for implementing the agreement in a devastated and isolated land fell to the interim Southern Regional Government, led by Abel

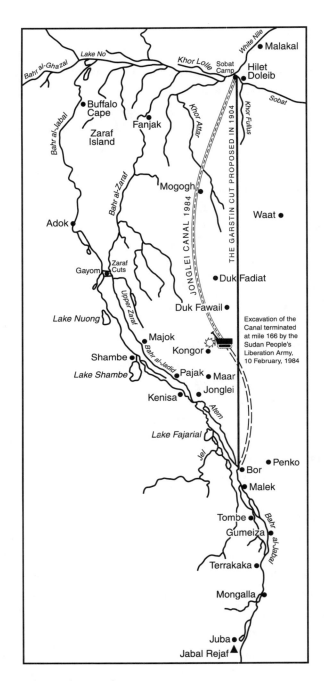

The Jonglei Canal

Alier, who had played a critical role at Addis Ababa as Numayri's minister for southern affairs. Under his direction, more than a million refugees were repatriated to their homes; the Anya-Nya were integrated into the national army; and a free election returned their representatives to the People's Regional Assembly of the southern Sudan, which first convened on 6 February 1974. Six days later, Numayri signed an agreement for political and economic integration of the Sudan with Egypt. In March the Permanent Joint Technical Commission presented its respective governments a revision of the canal Hurst had planned for the Equatorial Nile Project, and in June the Egyptian and Sudanese ministers for irrigation signed the agreement to build the Jonglei Canal. Egypt and the Sudan would share the cost, as well as the water.

The decision to build the Jonglei Canal was not the culmination of a half-century obsession with the abundant waters of the Lake Plateau; it was only the beginning of a grand design by the Egyptian Ministry of Public Works to conserve and transmit the waters from the Lake Plateau and the entire upper Nile basin to the great reservoir of Lake Nasser behind Aswan. Once there, it could be used for massive new reclamation projects in Egypt's western desert, Sinai, and the Fayum. In addition, the canal would complete the imperial dream of Cecil Rhodes for a Cape-to-Cairo route. It would also shorten the tortuous river journey south to Juba by two hundred miles. The canal would be wide enough to be navigable by Sudanese government steamers, with an all-weather road built parallel to it for vehicular traffic.

The canal was to be dug in a straight line for 175 miles, from the mouth of the Sobat River due south to the huts of Jonglei on the Bahr al-Jabal. The ditch was designed to deliver 4.7 billion cubic meters every year into the White Nile at its confluence with the Sobat, near the town of Malakal. From Malakal it is 1,700 miles under a Sudan sun, through savanna, Sahel, and desert, downstream to Lake Nasser. There, 20 percent of the additional water would be lost to implacable evaporation, reducing the total to 3.8 billion cubic meters. Half of this, 1.9 billion cubic meters, was guaranteed to the Sudan by the 1959 Nile Waters Agreement.

It was the same plan as the old Garstin Cut, proposed seventy years earlier, made possible by new technology. Those responsible for Nile control, from Garstin to the Permanent Joint Technical Commission, had always assumed a Jonglei Canal, but no one had ever devised the means to dig it. During most of the twentieth century dredgers and draglines excavated canals. Draglines were more efficient than dredgers, but it would take them twenty years, and enormous expense, to excavate the longest navigable canal in the world, 175 miles through the Sudd. Completing the canal would also require a dam at Lake Albert to store and regulate the outflow into the Bahr al-Jabal.

The invention of the Roue-pelle, the Bucketwheel, eliminated the need for draglines, dredgers, and fifty years of discussion, memoranda, and reports on the most efficient means of digging the canal. Adapted from iron strip-mining machinery in Germany for the French conglomerate Compagnie de Constructions Internationales, it proved extraordinarily efficient during the construction of the Chasma Jhelum Link Canal, from the Indus to the Jhelum River in Pakistan, in 1964. Modified for use in the Sudd by Pierre Blanc and Guy Charlère, the Bucketwheel could excavate more than a mile of the new canal every six days at only 14 percent of the cost of dredgers and draglines. The mighty wheel suddenly made the Jonglei Canal economically feasible, by reducing the time needed to dig it by two-thirds, and by replacing the Lake Albert dam as the regulator for the waters flowing down the Bahr al-Jabal from the equatorial lakes.[6]

But in 1974, when the decision was made to go ahead with the canal, the Nilotes were angry. The floods of the 1960s and the civil war of the 1970s had driven many thousands to the north, where they had experienced the harsh realities of survival in a world far different from their isolated sanctuary in the land beyond the rivers. Many acquired some formal education, and from them emerged an intellectual elite with advanced degrees from universities abroad. A few had even read the report of the Jonglei Investigation Team; some knew of its conclusions. Those who had stayed behind listened to those who had left the swamps. There were those who refused to accept the Addis Ababa Agreement and sought refuge in the Baro Salient in Ethiopia to retaliate against northern Sudanese domination. There were those who had been ignored in the scramble for patronage by ministers of the Southern Regional Government, and they were prepared to exploit an explosive issue like Jonglei. Abel Alier and his ministers, of course, knew of the Egyptian-Sudanese agreement to dig the canal, but the first elected southern Sudanese, who had only recently convened at Juba, did not. Overwhelmed by returning refugees and reconstruction, the regional government in Juba had no time and no vehicles to consult with the chiefs or their people before the signing of the agreement in June 1974. The euphoria of autonomy could not hide a history of distrust and seventeen years of civil war, all of which aroused deep suspicions in the southerners.

Joshua Dau Diu from Fanjak in the Sudd was the first to curse the canal in the assembly at Juba. In the upper Nile there was discussion among the chiefs, but little organized opposition. Their pastures had been destroyed by the flood waters. Jonglei might divert or regulate their dangerous flow, but in Juba the representatives from the upper Nile in the assembly argued with Nilotic enthusiasm that the agreement to construct the canal had been signed before any studies to identify its impact on the inhabitants. This was more rhetoric than reality. A few southern Sudanese leaders knew the findings of the Jonglei Investigation Team, but most of the newly elected members of the People's Regional Assembly were ignorant of its report and no one had read its four volumes. Moreover, no southern Sudanese had any knowledge of the plans for Nile control safely locked in files of the Egyptian Ministry of Public Works in Cairo and, after 1959, at the offices of the PJTC in Khartoum. It did not matter. Their inherent distrust of anyone north of Malakal was confirmed by rumors that six thousand Egyptian fellahin would be settled in the canal zone to plow the toic that for centuries had produced the grass for Nilotic cattle. The government in Khartoum made no effort to dispel the rumors. One erroneous prediction fed another to conjure a cataclysm whereby the fish would disappear, the rainfall would cease, and hostile deserts would encroach on their Garden of Eden. Three months after the signing of the agreement to excavate the Jonglei Canal, the Southern Regional Assembly denounced the decision.

In the assembly, members opposed to Alier's Southern Regional Government, which they contemptuously called the Dinkarachy, were led by Joseph Oduho, a respected teacher from the Latuka in Equatoria and an outspoken intellectual in favor of an independent southern Sudan. In October 1974 the opposition used Jonglei to mobilize demonstrations against the administration in the ironstone gravel streets of Juba. When rumors circulated that Egyptian troops were in Khartoum preparing to escort the Egyptian fellahin to the upper Nile, the students of the commercial secondary school marched through Juba to the offices of the High Executive Council. Many local citizens joined them. Neither the students nor their supporters from the town had any interest in Jonglei except to bring down the Dinka in control of the regional government, which the local Equatorians considered an enemy as malevolent as those from Khartoum or the peasants from Egypt. Police intervened. The demonstration turned into a riot, and three people were killed by the security forces.

The regional government tried to control the damage by appointing three committees, composed of members of the High Executive Council and the regional assembly, to investigate and respond to the violence. The committees were sent to the upper Nile to dismiss the rumors of the fellahin invasion and to emphasize the benefits the canal would bring to the southern Sudanese. Promises were made. The Nuer and Dinka of the canal zone would have schools, medical care, veterinary services, clean drinking water, agricultural extension services, bridges and ferries to cross the canal to the verdant toic pastures. The National Council for the Development of the Jonglei Canal Area, appointed by presidential decree, would organize the modernization of the upper Nile. Abel Alier, president of the regional government, a Bor Dinka, and later a member of the World Court, issued a statement to the regional assembly denouncing the rumors. The regional government was not prepared to accept underdevelopment and poverty, he said.

> The Regional government does not wish and will not associate itself with politics that tend to maintain and perpetuate the present economic status quo in the Region. . . . We are [not] to remain as a sort of human zoo for anthropologists, tourists, environmentalists and adventurers from developed countries of Europe to study us, our origins, our plights, the size of our skulls and shape and length of customary scars on our forehead. I wish to say that although this [Jonglei] is a Central Government project, the regional Government supports it and stands for it. If we have to drive our people to paradise with sticks, we will do so for their own good and the good of those who come after us.[7]

With that, the Jonglei Canal, the great engineering scheme to prevent the loss of irreplaceable water from the equatorial African lakes for Egypt and the northern Sudan, was transformed into an ambitious program of social and economic development in one of the most isolated regions in the world. President Numayri had learned that he could not suppress the southern Sudanese as he had the Ansar and the Communists. Characteristically he sought to defuse the dissent by creating yet another organization. He established the National Council for the Development of the Jonglei Area, to "formulate socio-economic development plans for the Jonglei area and the promotion of studies of the effects of the construction of the canal on the lives and livelihood of the local inhabitants." The council was responsible for procuring funds, establishing programs in agriculture, industry, and public works, and implementing all these projects. Rhetoric was cheaper than bullets; patronage was a small price to pay for support from a broad spectrum of politicians and civil servants appointed to the national council in return for their acceptance of the military regime. Numayri had become a convert to progress by embracing economic and social development rather than arms and political repression. The members of the national council met irregularly, and continued to receive their direct and indirect perquisites. The task of translating the president's promises into reality was delegated to the Jonglei Executive Organ (JEO) and its small but dedicated staff. Everyone's best intentions were soon subsumed in the politics of diverse interests and compromised by the dearth of resources.[8]

Although the outcry against the canal was never silenced, the arrest of the opposition leaders after the Juba riots, combined with the presidential promises, at least diverted it. The appointment of the council was symbolic. The appointment of its executive, the JEO, created an impecunious rival to the Permanent Joint Technical Commission. The plans generated by the JEO for the socioeconomic development of the canal zone were seldom compatible with the engineering projects of the PJTC. Although given sweeping authority by Numayri's hastily conceived decrees, the JEO was only a coordinating body with no power to coerce. The engineers and hydrologists of the PJTC were principally concerned with digging a canal. They represented decades of experience and resources and possessed the power of coercion. They found their schemes to control the waters of the river challenged by the JEO and its plans for social, economic, and environmental development to control the land. Tensions between the two were inevitable. They would have been more acute if not for the common sense and willingness to compromise of individual members of these two antagonistic agencies.

Engineers from the PJTC, led by the distinguished Sudanese hydrologist Yahia Abdel Magid, were not to be intimidated by social scientists from the JEO. In late July 1976 the contract to dig Jonglei was awarded to the Compagnie de Constructions Internationales (CCI), a subsidiary of the large French construction conglomerate Grands Travaux de Marseille International, whose chairman and chief executive officer, François Lemperiere, became the driving force behind the Jonglei Canal. The PJTC was to act as the principal consultant and employer. Thanks to the Bucketwheel, the cost of excavation was a relative pittance—$43 million for a navigable canal 175 miles long, in a remote region, that would provide an additional 3.8 billion cubic meters of water from the Lake Plateau.[9] The Bucketwheel was taken apart in Pakistan and shipped to the mouth of the Sobat, where in June 1978 it sputtered to life, and the excavation of the Jonglei Canal began.

It was an awesome machine. It stood five stories tall and weighed twenty-three hundred tons. Its great wheel was forty-one feet in diameter, and from it hung twelve buckets that held three cubic meters apiece, all revolving once every minute and rotating from side to side 180 degrees every five. It was guided by laser beams and operated precisely on grade in a plain where the slope is four inches per mile. A conveyor belt deposited the clay soil on the eastern bank for the all-weather road to be constructed alongside the canal. The machine dug a trench 130 feet wide, and it consumed eleven thousand gallons of fuel each day.

Before it could get started, however, a new barrage of criticism erupted in 1977,

The Bucketwheel excavating the Jonglei Canal

this time from the international environmental community, against a canal that it claimed would destroy the ecosystem of the Sudd and its Nilotic inhabitants. The critics had apparently never heard of Humphrey Morrice, who had been sent to Malakal in 1945 to report on the impact of the Garstin Cut on the Nilotes, or of Hurst's report, *The Future Conservation of the Nile,* published in 1946. They had apparently never read the four volumes of P. P. Howell's Jonglei Investigation Team, one of the first environmental impact studies, printed in 1954.

The hue and cry was first heard from members of the United Nations Environmental Programme in Nairobi, and it was soon picked up by the European press, particularly in France and Germany, and their environmentalist constituencies. Sometimes thoughtful, often strident, frequently ignorant, these critics produced a steady stream of copy from a coalition of environmental groups in Europe and the United States known as the Environmental Liaison Centre, with headquarters in Nairobi, demanding an immediate moratorium on excavation in the canal zone. The academics held seminars; the United Nations held conferences. In Nairobi, the United Nations Conference on Desertification in 1977 provided a global forum for those determined to denounce the canal. Jonglei would drain the Sudd of water, they argued, turning it into an arid wasteland that would invite the implacable march of Saharan and Sahelian sand, in turn altering the climate of northeast Africa. "Here is a canal being built in an area that could easily be Africa's next desert," one critic said. When the groundwater was exhausted, the savanna would become uninhabitable for African cultivators and herdsmen. The Nile perch would perish. The great herds of gazelle would die when they could not cross the canal. The rhetoric culminated in a vocal, standing-room-only meeting of the Royal Geographical Society on 5 October 1982 titled "The Impact of the Jonglei Canal in the Sudan," which was full of sound and fury but not much connected to reality.[10]

There was little substance to these criticisms. The Jonglei Investigation Team had demonstrated twenty-five years earlier that the canal would have no effect on precipitation in the Sudd. All later research has confirmed this conclusion. Others feared that groundwater in the Sahel to the north would diminish when diverted by the canal, but the Sudd is separated from the sandstone below by a layer of impervious clay, and the wells of the Sahel and the Sahara are recharged by the floods of occasional rains, not from the swamps of the Nile. The critics argued that the canal would eliminate most of the toic pastures beloved by Nilotic cattle, but at no time had they listened to the complaints from the Nilotes that they were the victims of too much rather than too little water.[11]

The engineers of the PJTC and CCI quietly ignored the environmental critics of Jonglei, whom they regarded as ecofreaks. The JEO listened more politely, citing evidence to refute their wildest charges while commissioning studies to investigate others, but had little success in convincing the Nilotes that its schemes for their modernization would improve the quality of their lives. With funds from the United Nations Development Programme, the U.N. Food and Agricultural Organization, the U.N. Capital Development Fund, the European Economic Community, and bilateral aid from the Netherlands, numerous research studies and pilot schemes were launched. The International Landuse Company of Arnheim, a subsidiary of Euroconsult, began a mechanized farming project on the Penykou plains east of Bor in 1976, financed by the government of the Netherlands. The U.N. Development Programme, under the direction of the dynamic anthropologist Charles la Munière, channeled 25 percent of its total funds to develop Sudd fisheries, and a more ambitious project of integrated rural development at Kongor and its satellite village of Panyagoor. The project was to be the visible proof of the government's concern to assist the people of the upper Nile through the traumatic adaptation to the Jonglei Canal. What was learned by the transformation of Kongor would then be applied to other communities scattered along its path.

During the birth of these pilot projects, the JEO convinced the EEC's European Development Fund to finance a research program on the ecology in the canal zone. The traditional engineering firm of Babtie, Shaw, and Morton of Glasgow combined with the more fashionable environmental consulting company of Mefit-Babtie of Rome in 1979 to undertake a comprehensive survey of the environment and ecosystems of the canal zone. Teams of scientists descended upon the upper Nile to investigate range and swamp ecology, livestock, water supply, and their impact on the Nilotic inhabitants. Their inquiries embraced every aspect of the Sudd—cattle, vegetation, wildlife, water, limnology and plants, invertebrates and fish, and the impact of the canal on the environment. Their report filled fourteen volumes containing an enormous amount of information artistically presented and poorly organized.[12] It confirmed that Jonglei was indeed the most researched and published project in the Third World. Like the studies that preceded it, particularly that of the Jonglei Investigation Team decades before, the conclusions were neither definitive nor helpful for those seeking practical solutions to intractable problems in a land isolated by rivers and the Sudd. Those who supported the project, those who paid for it, and those who carried out the many studies were fortunate that neither their research nor their findings were ever scrutinized by peers, justified by costs, or validated by results. The renewal of the civil war in May 1983 rendered their recommendations stillborn three months before publication.

The arrival of the scientists coincided with the explosive excavations of the Bucketwheel. Its success in the sandy alluvial soils of the Indus River valley could not be repeated in the cotton soil of the upper Nile—hard, consolidated clay, viscous mud in the rains, cement in the dry season. Two years after its reconstruction from Pakistan at the mouth of the Sobat, the Bucketwheel had managed to move its ditch only eighteen miles. At that rate it would arrive at Jonglei, after much tiresome and unprofitable effort, eighteen years later. Draglines would have equaled that performance. So the Bucketwheel was reconfigured. With a newly automated guidance system, increased power, and new tempered steel buckets for cutting through the clay, by the spring of 1981 it was advancing through the toic of the Sudd at a thousand feet a day—over a mile a week—toward Jonglei.

The village of Jonglei, where the Sudd begins, had long been the place designated for the canal to split off from the Bahr al-Jabal on its journey northward, but the great rains in the 1960s had changed all that. Hydrologic studies made after 1976 revealed that this voluminous discharge down the Bahr al-Jabal had destabilized its channel between Bor and Jonglei, reducing the village to a few beleaguered *tukls,* huts, and leaving only its name above the flood. The few remaining shelters could no longer serve as a terminus for the canal, and even the environmentalists, engineers, and politicians were surprisingly in agreement that it would have to be extended to Bor, where in fact Garstin in 1904 had planned to start his Cut. Here the riverbed of the Bahr al-Jabal was stable, and its banks were well-defined and firm enough to support the construction of the regulators needed to maintain a constant discharge between river and canal. The realignment to Bor added another 50 miles to the canal, making a total length of 225 miles. It would also bypass the concentration of Dinka on the Duk ridge, a mound of cotton soil clay that rises a few feet above the Sudd plain between canal and river.

There was no alternative. With the blessing of the Egyptian and Sudanese hydrologists from the Permanent Joint Technical Commission, CCI and the Sudanese Ministry of Irrigation signed an agreement on 13 March 1980 to lengthen and realign the canal. The extension escalated the price by $125 million—three times the original estimate—which was made worse by OPEC's decision to raise the price of oil for everyone, including a Bucketwheel consuming eleven thousand gallons a day. The French government and French commercial banks had to scramble to keep the project alive with additional financing.[13]

The Bucketwheel continued relentlessly digging its ditch through the canal zone. The money came from Europe, but the labor came from the upper Nile, where it was abundant and available. A thousand Nilotes were recruited to tend to the insatiable needs of the Bucketwheel, but only two dozen men, French engineers, Pakistani technicians, and Nilotic operators, were needed to keep the automated Bucketwheel on grade in the Sudd plain. There was little margin for error in making certain that the waters from the equatorial lakes would flow downstream rather than up. Lasers placed a mile in advance of the Bucketwheel raised and lowered its gigantic wheel to maintain the grade. Bulldozers cleared the path. Draglines finished the banks.

The teams from Mefit-Babtie were not far behind. In April 1983 ten volumes of their report were delivered to the office of the Jonglei Executive Organ in Khartoum, but before its few officials could read or comment civil war returned to the Sudan on 16 May. All the scientific studies and social schemes suddenly became irrelevant when

Digging the Jonglei Canal

the garrison of the 105th Battalion of the Sudan army at Bor refused to surrender after being confronted by troops sent from Juba by the Southern Command. After a fierce firefight and many casualties the survivors of the 105th retired eastward across the Pibor River, to the Baro Salient, and sanctuary in Ethiopia. Their defiance of the central government was a repetition of a more rustic mutiny by the Second Battalion of the Equatorial Corps in August 1955, this time made more violent by automatic weapons. The southern Sudanese officers and men at Bor were veterans of the Anya-Nya insurgency who had been integrated into the regular Sudan army by the terms of the Addis Ababa Agreement. They were disenchanted, disaffected, and unpaid.

By 1983 President Numayri had dissipated the goodwill generated by the Addis Ababa Agreement both at home and abroad. He had little real interest in economic development in the southern Sudan, and he sought to appropriate recent oil discoveries and Jonglei water for the north. He did not consult the elected officials of the autonomous Southern Regional Government. Exasperated by their petty and personal controversies, Numayri considered the south an impotent giant that he could emasculate by integrating the Anya-Nya into the regular army and transferring them to garrisons in the northern Sudan. In March he sent Lieutenant Colonel John Garang de Mabior to resolve the festering discontent at Bor over pay and the prospect of reassignment to the arid posts in the north. Garang appeared to be the ideal choice.

He was a Bor Dinka from Wangkulei who had made his way by perseverance and patronage to the Magambia secondary school in Tanzania, Grinnell College, and Iowa State University, where he completed his doctoral dissertation on the Jonglei Canal. Upon his return to the Sudan in 1971 he joined the Anya-Nya and the following year was integrated with his fellow Sudanese into the regular army after the Addis Ababa Agreement. He had served in the 105th and in 1983 was director of research at army headquarters in Khartoum, where he had gained intimate knowledge of corruption in the regime and observed Numayri's maneuvers to unravel the autonomy for the south agreed at Addis Ababa in 1972.

He had argued in his dissertation at Iowa State that Jonglei would disrupt the traditional regimen of Nilotic life and "end up merely containing and managing poverty and misery in the area." The solution for the upper Nile was not the canal but drainage, irrigation, and mechanized farming, which could be accomplished only by the reorganization of the countryside into compact village centers. Rain-fed agriculture at Kongor was more reliable than irrigation projects in the northern Sudan. Whereas the JEO had based its development strategies on traditional livelihoods that defined the use of the land, Garang was advocating a more sweeping economic and social revolution whose centralization was inimical to the fierce individualism of the Nilotic peoples. Garang did not take part in the battle of Bor, but the following morning he followed the men of the 105th into Ethiopia, where he organized the former Anya-Nya, whose aging cadres were now swollen by angry young men. Units of the southern Sudanese police, prison guards, and army with their weapons joined him in the Ethiopian sanctuary of the Baro Salient. During the summer of 1983 he consolidated his insurgency by founding the Sudan People's Liberation Movement and its military forces, the Sudan People's Liberation Army (SPLA).[14]

President Numayri publicly dismissed the Bor mutiny as a nuisance, but he retaliated by seeking to undermine the southern autonomy he had opportunistically conceded at Addis Ababa ten years earlier. He divided the traditional provinces of the southern Sudan into administrative units that encouraged local animosities—ancient disputes that immobilized any concerted opposition. In addition, his personal and political conversion to a more strict adherence to Islam led him to impose the Shari'a, or Islamic law, of the Quran. By Presidential Decree Number 1 of June 1983, one month after the rebellion at Bor, he promulgated his September Laws, implementing Shari'a throughout the Sudan. To John Garang and the mutineers from Bor, this arbitrary declaration confirmed the justice of their insurgency. The SPLA was now fighting for religious as well as political freedom. Southerners of every ethnic and political persuasion denounced the "rising tide of Muslim fundamentalism" that "threatened to unsettle the spirit of tolerance characteristic of the Addis Ababa decade."[15]

In October 1983 Mefit-Babtie submitted its final report. A month later the Jonglei Executive Organ convened a development conference for the Jonglei Canal at Bor. It was the first time the southern Sudanese had a forum in the canal zone to express their views. Many leading southerners were now able to attend. The Nilotes had watched the Bucketwheel eating a mile a week through their pastures. The southern Sudanese elite and their members from the national council for Jonglei searched in vain for the fulfillment of promises made by the government after the Juba riots of 1974. The Penykou Development Project was immobilized by cotton soil, and the bureaucracy of the United Nations had proved incapable of resolving logistical problems in the demanding and isolated environment of the upper Nile. Southern disillusionment with Jonglei erupted at Bor. Angry Dinka and Nuer forcefully expressed their frustration, which was often more emotional than rational. Members from Mefit-Babtie, who had just completed their report, provided more reasonable criticism. Both the people and the scientists confirmed Garang's convictions that the Jonglei Canal was not the instrument for the modernization of the southern Sudan.

Garang was determined to destroy the canal, and with it the regime of President Numayri. Three months after the Bor Conference, the SPLA attacked and demolished the Sobat camp of CCI, on 10 February 1984, halting the canal's excavation at mile 166. To this day, the Bucketwheel continues to rust at the bottom of its trench, surrounded by a debilitating war with no defeats and no victories. The southern Sudanese have since experienced the worst of all possible worlds—living in a land ravaged by war, decimated by famine, and pillaged by Arab militias from the north, the murahiliin. Their grievances against Jonglei were substantial, but these were neither cause nor catalyst for the resumption of war against the Sudanese government by John Garang and the SPLA, whose agenda was more political and religious than hydrologic. The human and material devastation from the conflict has been far worse for the Nilotic peoples than any accommodation to an environment that would have been disrupted by a canal. Independence, drought, floods, and civil war have demonstrated that the southern Sudanese can no longer enjoy the splendid isolation of the past, but their painful, destructive inclusion into the wider world has complicated the intractable problem of Nile control.

Egypt's determination to acquire additional water from the equatorial lakes through Jonglei will not be fulfilled in the near future. Peace in the Sudan will not end the hostility of the southern Sudanese toward the canal, which means that it will be very difficult to reach any peace agreement that includes completion of the canal as a condition. The Egyptians have always regarded Jonglei as a prototype for larger parallel canals to carry the waters of the Nile basin out of Africa. Any projects in their master water plans to construct the canals and regulators to control and transport the waters of the Lake Plateau and the Congo and Ethiopian watersheds can no longer be contemplated without the consent of the southern Sudanese—whether they are independent, autonomous, or a region of the Sudan. Meanwhile, frustrated French canal builders patiently wait in Paris to return to finish Jonglei. The canal has not moved forward since the renewal of the civil war in 1983, and the war continues despite the efforts of itinerant international mediators in search of a peaceful conclusion.

12 *Who Owns the Nile?*

> *If Sadat wants to protect the Nile basin because water is life to his*
> *people, he must know that the Nile has one of its sources in the Ethiopia*
> *he wants to destroy. It is from here that comes the dark blue alluvial soil*
> *so dear to the Egyptian fellahin. Furthermore, Ethiopia has a head of*
> *state who cares for the lives of his people.*
> *—President Mengistu Haile Mariam, 16 February 1978*

> *We depend upon the Nile 100 percent in our life, so if anyone, at any*
> *moment thinks to deprive us of our life we shall never hesitate to go to*
> *war because it is a matter of life or death.*
> *—President Anwar el-Sadat, May 1978*

When the Aswan High Dam was completed in 1971, there was certainly determination, but no great urgency, to find new water. Although Nile flows at Aswan during the early years of the 1970s were below average in volume, this was offset by water that had been allocated to the Sudanese by the Nile Waters Agreement of 1959 that they did not use. The Sudan's depressed economy and the consequent deterioration of its agricultural infrastructure rendered it incapable of utilizing its share of the Nile waters. From the shaded windows overlooking the Blue Nile at the headquarters of the Permanent Joint Technical Commission and the Sudan Ministry of Irrigation in

Khartoum, Sudanese officials watched in dismay as their gift to Egypt of 4 billion cubic meters passed silently below. The Sudan has been understandably reluctant to publicize its inability to consume its share of the Nile. The Egyptians characteristically have remained as inscrutable as the Sphinx, delighted to receive the annual Sudanese contribution to Lake Nasser in the expectation that conditions in the Sudan would make permanent what the terms of the Nile Waters Agreement could not. Egyptian optimism only increased when two great Nile floods, in 1974 and 1975, added to the unused Sudanese water. Between 1974 and 1978 the Nile delivered abundant water to Egypt that by 1979 had filled Lake Nasser almost to capacity.

In this world, however, there is no free water, and during the decade of plenty Ethiopia also sought to assert its historic claims to the Nile in return for its generous contribution to Egypt. The Egyptians could dismiss with impunity the feeble claims of the Bantu and Nilotic peoples to the waters of the upper Nile basin, but they could not ignore the Ethiopians, who contribute 84 percent of the Nile waters along with rich nutrients from their highlands. The great reservoir behind the High Dam, with its size and permanence, produced a false sense of security, but it could not entirely erase the Ethiopian connection and the age-old fear that the Ethiopians might obstruct the flow of the Nile. Relations between Egypt and Ethiopia, the two most powerful states in the Nile basin, have swung periodically between acceptance and bellicosity. Emotional disputes over religion and territory have erupted from time to time, but the eternal quarrel was the Nile. Late in the twentieth century the pattern has remained much the same, perpetuated by the bravado of new colonels who came to power in the 1970s, Anwar el-Sadat in Egypt and Mengistu Haile Mariam in Ethiopia, who overthrew Emperor Haile Selassie in 1974 and seized power with his ruling council, the Derg. In addition to the ancient tensions between the two countries, Sadat and Mengistu personally and politically despised each other.

Mengistu and his tamed press sought to revive deep-seated Ethiopian fears of a Muslim jihad arising from Egyptian territorial aspirations in the Red Sea and the Horn of Africa, arms for the Somalis in the Ogaden, and support for Eritrean irredentism. Never one to be upstaged, Sadat opened fire with salvos in the Egyptian press about Mengistu that referred to him as a corrupt Communist puppet of the Soviet Union and threatened him "with military intervention if he dared touch the waters of the Nile." The verbal warfare and hostile rhetoric in the press was soon reduced to the fundamental issue, the Nile waters. Mengistu lost no time in playing upon the ancient Egyptian fears that the ruler of Ethiopia could contain the Nile. The *Ethiopian Herald* conducted a campaign of denunciation against Egypt through the winter and spring of 1978, but in May it shifted its attention to demanding that the Ethiopians use the waters for themselves. "No one in his right senses can question Ethiopia's inalienable right to her natural resources for the benefit of her struggling masses," it wrote. "Revolutionary Ethiopia would like to make it emphatically clear that she is at full liberty and within her rights to utilize her natural resources for the advancement of her people."[1]

In 1979, Wondimneh Tilahun of Addis Ababa University published *Egypt's Imperial Aspirations over Lake Tana and the Blue Nile*. This was an academic, and therefore presumably legitimate, compilation of Mengistu's views on the Nile waters. It regurgitated the millennia of Egyptian-Ethiopian hostility, particularly the Egyptian invasion by Khedive Ismail in 1875–1876, but its principal theme was a new twist on "utilizing her natural resources." The threat to Ethiopia was no longer Egypt sequestering the Nile waters behind the High Dam at Aswan. "It is clear that Anwar Sadat's sabre-rattling intimidates neither the Ethiopian masses nor the allies that would assist us in the exploitation of our resources. With the realization of this aspiration, Lake Tana and the Blue Nile would cease to be the fifth-columns of nature planted in the heart of Ethiopia beckoning and tempting Egyptian aggressors to disturb her peace and security. . . . The great danger of unutilized rivers to Ethiopia is that it creates an insane desire on the part of her neighbours to see to it that she will never attain the capacity to utilize these rivers." Tilahun's book was widely distributed by the government and the university press to eager readers and government officials who were particularly fond of quoting his more stylistic phrases to local audiences. It had the greatest influence, ironically, among the Egyptians, who avidly read the Arabic translation published in Cairo.[2]

The verbal invective, however, came to a halt in 1981. On 6 October of that year, President Anwar el-Sadat was assassinated. His successor, Hosni Mubarak, was a pragmatist, trained in the Egyptian air force, who sought stability for Egypt after the tumultuous years of Nasser and Sadat. One of Mubarak's most important advisers was Boutros Boutros-Ghali, scion of one of the great Christian Coptic families of Egypt. His grandfather, Boutros Ghali, had been a founder of the *majlis milli,* a community council seeking acceptance for Copts in modern Muslim Egyptian society, and he served as foreign minister and prime minister of Egypt from 1908 until he was assassinated in 1910. His grandson Boutros Boutros-Ghali, educated in Egypt and France with a doctorate in international law, was the leading Coptic intellectual of the twentieth century. As a professor and the director of the Center for Political and Strategic Studies at Cairo University, he was a prolific writer and lecturer, adviser to Nasser on

Nile waters, and minister of state for foreign affairs under Presidents Sadat and Mubarak. He became famous for his negotiations that led to the Camp David Accords and peace between Israel and Egypt in 1978, and then as secretary-general of the United Nations from 1992 to 1997, but he was also the principal architect of Egypt's African Nile policy.

As early as 1963, Boutros-Ghali published an influential article titled "The Foreign Policy of Egypt," in which he identified "the challenge of the Nile" as Egypt's primary concern. "From Cheops to Muhammad Ali," he wrote, "from Muhammad Ali to Gamal Abdel Nasser, Egyptian foreign policy has been dominated by two challenges: the first has been the physical task of mastering the waters of the Nile; the second has been the moral task of deciding how the Egyptian rulers should use the wealth resulting from the cultivation of the Nile Valley. To master the Nile waters was a challenge which demanded centuries of back-bending toil . . . to carry the river water to the greedy desert. . . . The second challenge also remains unchanged. How shall the rulers of Egypt make the best use of Egyptian wealth?"[3]

In the same year, 1963, the Organization of African Unity (OAU) was established, with its headquarters, significantly, in Addis Ababa. Nasser immediately perceived that vigorous Egyptian participation in the organization would improve his and Egypt's image on the continent and particularly in the Nile basin. Boutros-Ghali and other Coptic intellectuals produced a flood of publications seeking to turn Egypt from isolation to the legitimate concerns of its upstream neighbors, especially Ethiopia and the equatorial nations. In 1965, Boutros-Ghali founded *Al-Siyasa al-Duwaliyya* (International Politics), a quarterly published by *Al-Ahram* (the regime's unofficial newspaper) that became the most influential journal of Egyptian foreign policy. He argued that Egypt should promote cooperation and stability in Ethiopia and the equatorial states rather than confrontation. He became Sadat's principal adviser on matters African and Nilotic, and minister of state for foreign affairs in 1977.

Anwar Sadat, who became president in 1970 following Nasser's death, sought to replace Nasser's revolutionary rhetoric of Pan-Arabism and reliance on the Soviet Union with old-style Egyptian nationalism, including an unholy but pragmatic combination of Western liberalism and Islamic radicalism. When Boutros-Ghali became responsible for Egypt's foreign policy, he argued that Egypt should seek stability in the region through cooperation with upstream riparians. Economically impoverished and politically unstable, these states were no immediate threat to Egypt, but they lay astride the waters of the Nile and could not be ignored. Intemperate rhetoric and rattling of sabers would only precipitate an equally vehement response. It would be better for

Egypt to embrace its African brothers in a spirit of unity, through dialogue, sweetened by funds for local projects. The Egyptians were masters of diplomatic discourse, and none of the riparians could match the technical knowledge of their hydrologists and engineers. Conferences and conversations would inspire mutual sharing of a scarce resource, leaving Egypt free to continue its plans for the conservation of waters from the equatorial lakes and the reclamation of its deserts from the reservoir at Aswan. Boutros-Ghali wrote later:

> I tried repeatedly to convince Sadat of my views and maintained that Egypt's national interest required us to establish relations with Ethiopia, where 85 percent of the Nile waters originate. To guarantee the flow of the Nile, there is no alternative to cooperation with Ethiopia, particularly in view of the Ethiopian irrigation project at Lake Tana, which could reduce the Nile waters reaching Egypt. As long as relations between Cairo and Addis Ababa were strained or hostile, we risked serious problems. Preserving Nile waters for Egypt was not only an economic and hydrological issue but a question of national survival. As Herodotus declared, "Egypt is the gift of the Nile," and our security depended on the south more than on the east, in spite of Israel's military power.[4]

Not all Egyptians agreed with Sadat's Christian minister of state for foreign affairs. Egyptian Islamists had a very different opinion about their country's relations with non-Muslim Africans upstream, particularly Ethiopians led by the unbeliever Mengistu Haile Mariam. There was a great outpouring of anti-Ethiopian literature in Arabic, reinterpreting the message of the prophet Muhammad "to leave the Ethiopians alone" and reviving memories of the devastating Muslim invasion of Ethiopia by Ahmad Grañ in the sixteenth century. Al-Azhar University, the great repository of Islamic learning in Cairo, was the center of radical Islam, and it issued publications denouncing Christian oppression of Ethiopian Muslims. When Boutros-Ghali reminded the Egyptian minister of defense, General Abd al-Ghani al Gamasi, that Ethiopia was the Nile and should not be regarded as an enemy, he "seemed to believe that I was favoring Ethiopia because it is a Christian state."[5]

To those like the Islamists who believed in Egyptian unilateralism, the construction of the Aswan High Dam seemed the ultimate solution to the tyranny of dependency. It was not. The High Dam produced as many problems as it resolved. Egypt has always been totally dependent on the Nile, and it remains so. There are few thunderstorms in that dry land. The underground sandstone aquifers of the western desert can supply abundant water for the oases of Kharga, Dakhla, Farafra, Bahariya, and

Siwa, but their water, which cannot be replenished, can never meet the needs of the Egyptians by the Nile. Groundwater in the eastern desert and Sinai is sparse, and attempts to dam spate wadis have failed. The Nile provides the only meaningful amount of water in Egypt, as always.

Furthermore, for five thousand years the Egyptians had the Nile waters to themselves. Except for a few Nubians, the Egyptians were the only cultivators who annually absorbed the waters of the Nile and its Ethiopian nutrients on their fields. Based on their historical claim, reinforced by the regular rhythm of the Nile, the Egyptians developed a firm belief in their continuing right to the waters. Dependency, backed by the knowledge that without the Nile flood government and society tended to collapse, only deepened the power of this belief. This conviction of Egypt's right to the Nile waters came to resemble religious dogma, transfixing pharaohs and priests, sultans and ulama, landlords and fellahin.

Monopolies are historically inefficient, squandering their resources when unlimited control provides no apparent incentive to conserve them. The Egyptians were no different. Until the dramatic increase in the Egyptian population in the twentieth century there was ample water, and until the completion of the first Aswan Dam in 1902 frequently too much. Rushdi Said has described the prevailing attitude toward water:

> Among the pervasive beliefs in Egyptian culture is that water, like air, is God-given and free. Any pricing system and controls on its use are totally unacceptable and almost blasphemous. The perception that water is abundant is sometimes manifested in frivolous but revealing ways. A former President of Egypt offered to channel part of the water of the Nile to Jerusalem as a gesture of good will; a prominent member of Parliament once submitted a proposal to construct a pipe line from Lake Nasser to Saudi Arabia to supply it with fresh water; and some investors presented projects to divert the "excess" waters of the Nile to the desert.[6]

But when historic fantasies were measured by contemporary nilometers, there was no excess water to be found in the Egyptian Nile and barely a sufficient flow to satisfy current demand. Between 1977 and 1981 the Egyptian Ministry of Public Works and Water Resources compiled the hitherto unknown data to determine how water was consumed or wasted in Egypt. The findings, known as the Egyptian Master Water Plan of 1981, were published in seventeen volumes, equal in quantity and weight to those of the U.S. Bureau of Reclamation for the Ethiopians, but the results were deeply disturbing. The ratio of available water to population was no longer abundant.

Indeed, water was becoming a scarce resource that required conservation and management as careful as that of an endangered species.

The Nile is the tie that binds upper and lower Egypt, and the feluccas navigating the river and its canals are a crucial part of that connection. To keep them afloat during the winter months, the survey found, half a billion cubic meters are discharged from Aswan to make the Nile navigable. To preserve the turbines generating electricity at the High Dam another 2 billion cubic meters are released during the same months, disappearing into the depths of the Mediterranean Sea. Domestic needs for water in the heat of the Egyptian deserts are greater and more wasteful than in states with temperate climates: Egyptian homes together consume 3 billion cubic meters annually, two-thirds of which disappears or is no longer recyclable. Industrial usage demonstrates the same pattern of exuberance by swallowing more than 3 billion cubic meters, but the return is infiltrated with toxic pollutants whose effects, unmeasured and uncontrolled, can be seen by every fellahin on the river and in every irrigation canal. All this is in addition to the 10 billion cubic meters that evaporates from the surface of Lake Nasser every year.

Factories, feluccas, households, and turbines were wasting water but their extravagance could not compare to the loss of water in agriculture. The fields of Egypt require approximately 50 billion cubic meters annually, or 84 percent of the total amount of the Egyptian Nile. The implacable increase in population has contributed to this level of consumption, further complicated by the enterprising agricultural sagacity of fellahin and landlords exploiting the predictable release of water from the Aswan High Dam. Like their ancestors, they adjusted, changing the pattern of crop rotation, planting nontraditional summer crops like corn and sorghum, and growing more wheat and vegetables, less cotton and rice, over the 14 million acres devoted to Egyptian agriculture, all of which meant more crops of different varieties and greater profit. The price for this significant change was water. Since the completion of the Aswan High Dam in 1971, Egypt has annually required approximately 61 billion cubic meters drawn from Lake Nasser, of which 50 billion are absorbed by cropland and evaporation in transit. Domestic, industrial, navigation, and hydropower needs consume another 9 billion cubic meters. This leaves only 2 or 3 billion cubic meters for the reclamation of new land.

The instinctive response to these findings, and the need to feed an expanding population, was to find new sources of water rather than to manage the available supply. Egypt has a constant if variable supply of water behind the High Dam. Efficient management can increase the amount of water that hitherto flowed to the sea during the canal closure and cleaning in winter by retention in the lakes and lagoons of the northern delta. Additional water has been pumped from groundwater aquifers, and drainage water has been recycled. These efforts contribute only a modest amount to that available from the Egyptian Nile, and even the most rigorous measures for control cannot provide the quantity needed for a rapidly expanding population. Conservation of existing water supplies, in California or Cairo, has historically been a palliative to satisfy immediate needs produced by the demands of population or the tyranny of drought. It has never been the solution to an increasing demand for freshwater. New lands to feed new people can be cultivated only with new water.

There were four ambitious projects to find new water from losses on the plains of the upper Nile basin, the Sudd, and in Lake Nasser. Some had been proposed earlier in the twentieth century, but they were not given official sanction until incorporated into the Egyptian Master Water Plan of 1981. All of these projects were far in the future and shrouded in economic and political uncertainties, but they were taken seriously by Egyptian and Sudanese engineers of the Permanent Joint Technical Commission from their headquarters in Khartoum. They were bold designs by a new generation of Egyptian hydrologists unfettered by the ghost of Hurst, and together they could yield 14 to 20 billion cubic meters of new water, which would increase the annual Nile flow by an astounding 24 percent.

One of these projects depended on additional storage in the equatorial lakes. Every student of Nile basin water development since Garstin had advocated using the lakes as reservoirs. Although the completion of the Aswan High Dam in 1971 resolved the question of over-year storage, the great rains of the 1960s on the Lake Plateau made the prospect of containing additional water in the lakes all the more attractive. To guarantee a constant supply of water the Egyptians would have to raise the Owen Falls Dam, build a regulating barrage at Lake Kyoga, and resurrect the much discussed dam at Lake Albert to create a vast reservoir system totaling 170 billion cubic meters in the equatorial lakes. These proposals were vintage Hurst, century storage repackaged, but, as before, the reservoirs would be of no value if there was no conduit to convey the water through the swamps. This plan called for a canal very different from the original Jonglei. The new and larger canal would be constructed beside the original one, doubling the amount of water that would pass into the White Nile and providing an increase of nearly 9 percent in the total mean annual Nile flow reaching Aswan.

North and east of the Sudd in the lowlands beneath the Ethiopian escarpment lie 2,536 square miles of swampland, the Machar Marshes. This huge swamp is quite separate from the Bahr al-Jabal and the White Nile, and even more isolated and mysterious than the Sudd. No major rivers flow through its labyrinth of lagoons and channels, and the aquatic vegetation provides little sanctuary for man or beast or even birds. The marshes catch the torrents cascading from the Ethiopian highlands and contain its thirty-two inches of annual rainfall. Under the Master Water Plan, the water trapped here would be diverted into another canal, this one excavated for 250 miles through the heart of the Machar Marshes to the White Nile at Melut. Despite its length, cost, and questionable hydrologic benefits, it would add another 4 billion cubic meters to the White Nile.

Impounding the equatorial lakes, traversing the Sudd, and taming the Machar Marshes left only the waters of the ironstone plateau and the Nilotic plain to incorporate into the Egyptian Master Water Plan. There are many rivers that rise on the Congo-Nile watershed to flow through the Bahr al-Ghazal in the Sudan and disappear into the great swamps of the Sudd. Officials from the Egyptian Irrigation Department had measured the flow of these tributaries for decades, but the region was considered the least promising source of new water from the upper Nile basin. At the beginning of the century Garstin dismissed the Bahr al-Ghazal as a worthless contribution to the water needs of Egypt. This judgment was premature.

The rivers of the Bahr al-Ghazal region generate an estimated discharge between 13 and 20 billion cubic meters a year before a sluggish trickle makes its way to Lake No and ultimately the White Nile. The solution proposed by the Permanent Joint Technical Commission and incorporated into the Master Water Plan was to construct a series of small dams and barrages below the Congo-Nile watershed on the tributaries at the edge of the ironstone plateau. The impounded water would then be released through yet another extraordinary canal 250 miles long to Lake No that would circumvent the absorbent swamps. This canal would divert another 7 billion cubic meters, but as Garstin and Willcocks had long ago observed, Lake No acts as a reservoir and the blocking effect from the flow of the Bahr al-Jabal would push the water back into the Sudd to be lost. Ever resourceful, the Egyptian engineers planned to correct this anomaly by a second canal, another 140 miles long, from Lake No to join the Machar Marshes diversion canal at Melut on the White Nile. This chain of canals would be reinforced by a second diversion canal that would tap the waters of the rivers from the Congo-Nile watershed into the Bahr al-Jabal near Bor.

There is imagination and grandeur in all these plans and projects but an equal unreality. The states of the Lake Plateau have experienced years of political instability. The upper Nile basin has been devastated by civil war. In all the calculations by Egyptian, European, and Sudanese engineers and hydrologists there has been little consultation with the southern Sudanese who would be most affected by the construction of regulators for Nile control or the environmental impact in their aftermath. Economically, the proposals can be completed only at great cost supported by dubious financial and hydrologic return. These massive projects, on a scale to dwarf those of the pharaohs, have to be excavated in one of the most isolated regions of the world, across an incalculable number of natural obstacles, where the primitive infrastructure has not been improved by two destructive decades of war. The hydrologic demand for new water, however, is insatiable and in the end may prove more powerful than ethnicity, politics, or religion to revive in the twenty-first century Jonglei and its supportive dams and canals.

The Egyptian Master Water Plan ironically owed much to an African initiative. The years of independence in East Africa had coincided with the unpredictable and unprecedented rainfall of 1961 to 1964 on the equatorial lakes. This aberrant abundance may have been a symbol of African nationalism, but the volume of precipitation was inexplicable and its waters destroyed communities on the lakeshores. In 1961 the independent East African governments requested that the World Meteorological Organization and the United Nations Food and Agricultural Organization make a survey of the Lake Victoria basin. Two years later the consultants from these organizations recommended an expanded hydrometeorological study for the whole of the Lake Plateau and its equatorial lakes.

In the euphoria of African brotherhood at independence, Egypt and the Sudan were invited to participate. They agreed with alacrity. The agencies and personnel of the United Nations were equally enthusiastic to make them members. They regarded the hydromet survey as a giant step in regional cooperation and integrated river basin development. Cooperation may have been the spirit of the times, but translating the rhetoric of unity into political agreements to achieve it was an illusion. The principal supplier of Nile water, Ethiopia, waited ten years before deciding to join the coordinating committee in 1971, and then only as an observer. Observation costs nothing. The Ethiopians listened but refused to discuss a Lake Tana dam agreement, or for that matter any project proposed by Egypt and the Sudan during the years of rhetorical hostility.

Motivated by a growing sense of their national interests, Burundi, Rwanda, Tanzania, and Uganda sought in 1969 to establish an organization for development of the Kagera River basin. None of them had the human or material resources to carry out such a project, but with advice and cash from the United Nations Development Programme the Kagera River basin survey was brought under the administrative umbrella of the hydromet survey in 1971. By 1977, when the Egyptians realized they should

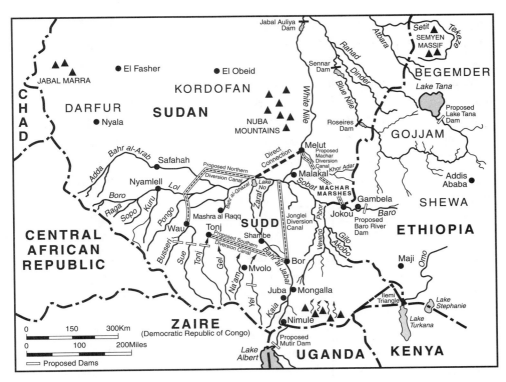

The Egyptian Master Water Plan, 1981: Proposed Dams and Diversion Canals (Reprinted from Rushdi Said, The River Nile, © *1993, p. 229, with permission from Elsevier Science)*

emulate their riparian neighbors by creating their own Master Water Plan, the Norwegian and Swiss consultants had already produced thirteen volumes, including a proposal for a Kagera River Basin Organization that would oversee development and management. This organization came into being on 5 February 1978. Its officials proposed a dam at Rusumu Falls on the Kagera River for hydroelectric power, but its other recommendations were soon overwhelmed by political instability, civil strife, and the inability of the regional governments to match their financial commitments to their hydrologic interests.

Meanwhile the Egyptians and the Sudanese pursued their own priorities. They continued to press at first for a Nile basin commission, which appeared all the more urgent because of drought and nationalism. By 1979 the dearth of water that was to last for a decade had begun, and the immediate impact convinced each riparian state to look after its own needs. Kenya created the Lake Basin Development Authority to initiate irrigation projects utilizing the waters of Lake Victoria and the seven rivers from Kenya that flow into it. Tanzania revived an old scheme proposed by the Germans before World War I to drain water from Lake Victoria to the Vembere Plateau. Since Egypt and the Sudan had no control over supply, it became increasingly imperative to sequester what was available to them in times of dearth. In March 1981, President Numayri of the Sudan argued, unsuccessfully, for an agreement to develop the Nile basin as a whole. In June he persuaded presidents Mobutu Sese Seko of Zaire and Milton Obote of Uganda to issue the Badolite Declaration, which advocated an agency to coordinate and develop the Nile basin. During these months an Egyptian-Sudanese team from the Permanent Joint Technical Commission assiduously toured the capitals of the upper riparian states attempting to arrange a meeting in Khartoum or Cairo in September 1981 to consider basinwide planning by a proposed Nile valley authority to combat the deepening drought.

Their appeals were politely rebuffed, but the leaders of the upper basin states could not ignore the adoption by the Organization of African Unity at Lagos in 1980 of a "Plan of Action for the Economic Development of Africa," which emphasized the need for regional development agencies. Armed with this manifesto, the Egyptians and the Sudanese pursued their diplomatic offensive. Samir Ahmad, the Egyptian ambassador to Ethiopia, delivered a series of lectures in 1983 titled "Egypt and Africa: On the Road to Cooperation" that offered Egyptian technological assistance but studiously ignored any sharing of the waters. Boutros-Ghali aggressively pursued his African Nile diplomacy, which resulted in the Nile basin states accepting an Egyptian invitation to a conference at Khartoum in 1983. Amicable discussions at the confluence of the Blue and White Niles produced no agreements, but Egypt, the Sudan, Uganda, Zaire, and the Central African Republic did create an informal organization known as UNDUGU (from *ndugu*, the Swahili word for brotherhood). This convivial club continued discussions and drafting plans for the development of the waters of the upper Nile basin with funds from the United Nations Development Programme. Burundi, Rwanda, and Tanzania later joined. The Ethiopians were polite but unresponsive, and the others ignored them.

During the next ten years UNDUGU held sixty-six meetings at the technical and ministerial level, producing more rhetoric than results. The United Nations Development Programme drafted expansive and expensive plans to increase agricultural lands under irrigation and an electricity grid that spanned the Nile basin states from Enga in Zaire to Aswan in Egypt. These unreal dreams for development were the work of altruistic planners at the United Nations and unproductive discussions at UNDUGU meetings, which were symptomatic of the economic and political instability of the upper Nile riparian states. Their internal and communal disarray precluded any coherent policy for using the waters of the Lake Plateau, leaving Egypt free to pursue its own hydrologic development independent of those upstream. The Egyptians were generous with friendly gestures and financial aid in an effort to help transform UNDUGU into a group that could produce substantive proposals rather than just dialogue. Egyptian policy was one of "confidence building," so long as the projects that resulted did not threaten the flow of the Nile. Meanwhile, Egypt continued to develop its infrastructure for irrigation and land reclamation without interference from impotent but potentially troublesome riparian neighbors. The chummy get-togethers with UNDUGU were a parody of British imperial designs for Nile control that soon dissolved in drought.

Three months after the Sudan People's Liberation Army destroyed the French base camp at Sobat and terminated the excavation of the Jonglei Canal in February 1984, the annual rain clouds from the south Atlantic did not arrive in the Ethiopian highlands. There was no water, only drought, and despite massive international aid death from famine and disease for more than a million Ethiopians and an unknown number of Sudanese. The Egyptians would have suffered commensurately, as they had throughout the ages, if not for the water stored behind the Aswan High Dam. But even the Sadd al-Aali could not protect Egypt from the lowest Nile in the twentieth century. Even the theoretical models constructed by Hurst for his periodicities never contemplated Nile flows as low as those recorded from 1984 to 1988. In 1984–1985 only 35 billion cubic meters arrived at Aswan, nearly 60 percent less than the annual average. The Egyptians would have to do more with less, but worse was yet to happen.

Given the measurements from nilometers, the statistical analyses, and the application of probability theory to models of best and worst scenarios, no one could have predicted the precipitous plunge in Nile flows over the years from 1979 to 1988. The Egyptians needed at least 61 billion cubic meters every year to quench their thirst and that of their fields, but during the decade of drought the Nile had shrunk to 49 billion cubic meters, 42 percent less than the historical average. President Mubarak, in an unprecedented gesture, invited President Mengistu to a symposium at Cairo University in March 1987, the conclusions of which vigorously proposed what Boutros-Ghali had been arguing for a decade: that cooperation with the upstream riparians was essential for Nile control. The same theme was published the following year by the Center for Arab Studies in Cairo as *The Crisis of the Nile Waters: Where To?* In it, a galaxy of intellectuals, including the Egyptian Rushdi Said and the Ethiopian Wondimneh Tilahun, argued for coordination of Nile planning. But the drought continued, and in July 1988 Lake Nasser fell to a record low, 494 feet above sea level, and contained only 38 billion cubic meters out of a potential capacity of 170 billion. This was a level

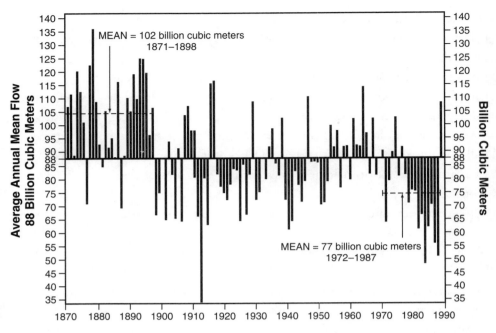

Annual Flows of the Nile at Aswan, 1870–1988 (Source: P. P. Howell and J. A. Allan, eds., The Nile: Sharing a Scarce Resource, *1994, reprinted with the permission of Cambridge University Press)*

only 12 feet, or 7 billion cubic meters, above the minimum amount needed to feed the hydroelectric turbines without danger of implosion. The dam had been generating half of Egypt's electricity in the 1970s, but in 1988 it produced less than 18 percent, and the country was becoming increasingly dependent on fossil fuels. Egypt had to decide whether it would sacrifice water for crops or for hydroelectric power.[7]

This was a new and perplexing situation for the Egyptians. The Sadd al-Aali was meant to release Egypt from the tyranny of drought and famine, but even Hurst had not contemplated the changes in global atmospheric patterns that were taking place. Whether these patterns are random or predictable remains unclear, but they appear to be governed at least in part by El Niño, formally known as the El Niño Southern Oscillation. First described scientifically in 1895, El Niño is the product of an interaction of atmosphere and ocean that affects global climate, and consequently the flow of the Nile. Normally the seawater along the Pacific coast of equatorial South America is cooled by the upward surge of the Humboldt current from Antarctica combined with frigid surface water from the Northern Hemisphere. Periodically and unpredictably, massive amounts of warm water from the vast expanse of the tropical Pacific move

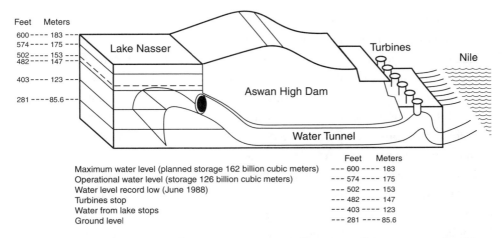

	Feet	Meters
Maximum water level (planned storage 162 billion cubic meters)	--- 600 ----	183
Operational water level (storage 126 billion cubic meters)	--- 574 ----	175
Water level record low (June 1988)	--- 502 ----	153
Turbines stop	--- 482 ----	147
Water from lake stops	--- 403 ----	123
Ground level	--- 281 ----	85.6

The Egyptian Nile Water Crisis of 1988 (Source: Arnon Soffer, Rivers of Fire, *1999, reprinted by permission of Rowman and Littlefield Publishers)*

eastward to invade these normally stable cold waters. The power of these meteorological forces affects both the Southern and the Northern Hemispheres, producing, paradoxically, floods, storms, and tidal surges in some places and a dearth of rain leading to severe drought in others. In Africa, El Niño retards the flow of the tropical eastern jet stream that governs the movement of the intertropical convergence zone from the south Atlantic northeastward across the continent, impeding the rain clouds that carry the waters that become the Nile.

During the years of El Niño the eastern jet stream did not move the ITCZ to the upper Nile and Ethiopia with vigor or the normal quantity of water, resulting in 5 to 15 percent less rain over the Nile basin, particularly during the first years of the 1970s and most decidedly in the 1980s. Conversely, years in between these El Niño events have produced an inverse effect, known as La Niña, in which rainfall was 5 to 10 percent higher than the average throughout the Nile basin. But El Niño defies predictability. The correlation between El Niño and the Nile has been calculated retrospectively for the past 120 years of accurate meteorological and Nile measurements. Unfortunately, the figures cannot reconcile the discomforting evidence from three El Niño years, 1891, 1917, and 1932, during which Nile flows nevertheless were normal, nor do they account for the exceptionally low Nile of 1914 that came two years after the El Niño of 1912.[8]

The most dramatic demonstration of La Niña was the high Nile flood of 1988 that finally broke the decade of deficient Nile flows. Just as Egypt was on the brink from the effects of the great drought, the clouds from the south Atlantic suddenly deposited more rain than in any previous year of the twentieth century, and far more than any recorded in the nineteenth century. On 4 August the ITCZ moving north collided with a violent line of squalls from the southeast just north of Khartoum, dropping nine inches of rain in twenty-four hours on a city with an average annual rainfall of seven inches. At the same time less dramatic but greater quantities of water fell on Ethiopia and the Atbara watershed. Ninety-three billion cubic meters, 9 percent above the century's average, surged down the Nile to break the terrible drought, flush through the turbines, and water the fields.

In spite of the great Nile drought of the 1980s, no Egyptians perished from lack of water. The Ethiopian experience was quite different and more devastating. While the Egyptians survived because of the water stored behind their High Dam, a million Ethiopians perished from famine and thirst when the rains did not arrive. They had no dam. They did not even have a master water plan as Egypt did, although they did produce one in 1990, but even that was more speculation than reality. The country had little infrastructure by which to reach its rivers and few competent personnel in the agencies for planning and development of Ethiopian waters. Despite efforts to expand the number of gauges and organize the collection of their readings, without a coherent and defined proposal it was impossible to draft a plan or legislation for the conservation of the abundance of the country's water. In addition, President Mengistu and the Derg were forced from power in 1991, and they were replaced by a democratic government led by Meles Zenawi. The country had limited financial resources, and the new government was forced to concentrate on establishing its stability, containing an insurgency by the Oromo people, continuing its historic conflict with Somalia, and waging war on the border with Eritrea—all of which consumed the energies and resources available to the Ethiopian government and its leaders. Millions of dollars for arms and the mobilization of its peoples precluded the evolution of a coherent Ethiopian water plan.

The return of the Nile restored the faith of Egyptian fellahin in their High Dam, but the country's rulers were deeply shaken. The able and experienced Egyptian engineers and hydrologists could no longer guarantee delivery of sufficient water to sustain and provide for a million new Egyptians every year. The Nile waters come from upstream states. Since 1963, Boutros-Ghali had been arguing in the staterooms of Cairo that Egypt, despite its High Dam, could not continue to ignore those who sat by the springs, lakes, and rivers of the Nile thousands of miles to the south. The time had finally come for the Egyptians to begin a meaningful dialogue with their African neighbors to protect their vital interests.

13 *The Waters of the World and the Nile*

> *Water is the true wealth in a dry land; without it, land is worthless*
> *or nearly so. And if you control water, you control that land*
> *that depends upon it.*
> —*Wallace Stegner,* Beyond the Hundredth Meridian

At the beginning of the new millennium the expanding population of the world is voraciously consuming its available supply of freshwater, from the Nile as well as elsewhere. The oceans, whose water is undrinkable and unusable except to ships and fish, monopolize 96 percent of the world's water. Glaciers in the Arctic, Antarctica, Greenland, and the mountainous cordillera contain only 2 percent of global water, but they immobilize an estimated 69 percent of the world's freshwater in their frozen wastelands. There are twenty-eight lakes, most of which are in the Northern Hemisphere, that have accumulated 85 percent of the available freshwater as the result of tectonic fractures in the earth's crust and glacial erosion. Equally important are the artificial lakes created by dams, some of great antiquity like the Marib Dam constructed by the Sabaeans across the Wadi al-Dhana in Yemen during the seventh century B.C.E. The great obsession with dam building, however, is a phenomenon of the twentieth century, and the technology to do it has increased the world's volume of impounded freshwater tenfold, to more than 156,000 square miles. Of these, the Nile reservoirs, Lake Nasser and Lake Victoria behind the Owen Falls Dam, are the largest.[1]

Lakes, rivers, and reservoirs are dependent on the global movement of water from ocean to land and back again by gravity to the sea. Although the relationship between ocean and atmosphere, including El Niño and La Niña, and the hydrologic cycle that creates freshwater remain a matter of controversy, there is no dispute that a huge quantity of water evaporates into the sky from the surface of the ocean to become rainwater, 90 percent of which falls on the sea whence it came. Only 10 percent manages to reach the shore in drizzle or torrential downpour. An equal or even greater amount of rainfall on the land is generated by lakes, glaciers, and reservoirs scattered across the globe; of this freshwater, a third flows back into the oceans. Every individual in every society learns from childhood that the crucial course of the hydrologic cycle brings renewal. The rainy season or the monsoon returns to give life to the land, and is celebrated with elaborate ceremonies and rituals to thank the gods or nature. In some years the gods give too much, and there is destruction. In other years nature gives too little, and there is death. Whether in plenty or in dearth, the flow of new water contains the awesome power of renewal.

From time immemorial humans have sought to predict climate. The weather remains a primary topic of conversation at the beginning of each day in every society and culture, particularly those addicted to the Weather Channel. Every country has its meteorological agency, as well as an army of scientists, social scientists, amateurs, and astrologers, plotting and forecasting the weather. Innumerable institutes in governments and universities, the most ambitious of which is the International Research Institute for Climate Prediction at Columbia University, seek to add to the level of sophistication in these matters. The technological revolution at the end of the twentieth century has enabled the meteorologists to absorb and analyze a huge quantity of data, but predictability still eludes them all.

Everyone can agree that the distribution of the world's rainfall and its runoff is extremely uneven. Eighty percent of global water falls in northern and equatorial lands with relatively modest populations. In the temperate continents, where most people live, the flow of water is limited and unequal. The amount of rainfall throughout the millennia has fluctuated from year to year and decade to decade, but the average quantity of accessible freshwater has remained historically constant, while the population of the world has not. In the middle of the nineteenth century a few more than a billion people inhabited this earth. By 1990 the world's population had increased to 5 billion, and in the year 2000 to 6 billion. In 1850 there was abundant freshwater for everyone, an estimated 30 million cubic meters for each. In 1990 there were only 8 million cubic meters for each person, and today there is even less.[2]

This huge population explosion has deeply disturbed the renewal and purification of streams, rivers, lakes, and reservoirs. With their profligate reproduction, their constantly increasing economic activities, and their implacable determination to exploit resources, humans have transformed every major river of the world, including the Nile. Water has been withdrawn and consumed for expanding urban and rural populations, industry that pollutes, and agricultural irrigation, whose returnable water carries salts and insecticides. Irrigation is the greatest consumer, using 86 percent of the world's freshwater, and its thirst in Egypt is even more voracious. Four percent of global freshwater is needed to serve industry, particularly the cooling of power plants, and 3 percent is used by cities, towns, and villages for their drinking and sanitary needs. Evaporation from reservoirs results in major losses of freshwater—7 percent of the available renewable supply—and this water, unlike that used in agriculture, industry, and city sewers, is not recovered or recyclable. Every year 10 billion cubic meters of the Nile waters disappear into the atmosphere from Lake Nasser.[3]

As the world's population continues to grow, so too will the need for freshwater. The most dramatic growth in demand for water began in the 1950s and 1960s, and it steadily increased throughout the remaining decades of the twentieth century.[4] During decades of dearth the consumption of water for irrigation, industry, and municipalities has often absorbed the entire flow of rivers and their reservoirs. In the late 1980s, Egypt consumed all the water it received from the Nile. Increasing economic development will always require more water, but the global supply, on average, does not change. In 1950 per capita use and the average amount of renewable water were in balance. By 1980 the available water in North Africa, northeast Africa, and Central Asia had significantly diminished, although in northern Europe, Canada, Alaska, South America, and Oceania there was abundance. At the beginning of the new millennium the rains have returned to the Nile, demonstrating that there is no uniformity in the distribution of the waters of the world, least of all in the Nile basin.

The United Nations predicts an increase of Malthusian proportions in global population, which is expected to exceed 8 billion by 2025, and 10 billion by 2050. All of these people will consume a fixed amount of freshwater.[5] During the last half of the twentieth century, the number of inhabitants in the basin states of the Nile increased by 40 percent, and their explosive annual population growth of 3 percent will undoubtedly continue, contributing proportionately more to the global total than most countries. Egypt and Ethiopia are expected to double their populations by 2025, but they are not alone; it is estimated that all the other upstream riparian states will follow this same pattern. Ostensibly, this should not be a critical problem for the states of the Lake Plateau and Ethiopia, where the amount of rainfall may be annually unpredictable but is historically dependable. There is a general rule among some water planners that a country is deficient when its annual renewable freshwater is less than one thousand cubic meters per person per year. If this rather arbitrary but reasonable definition is applied to the states of the Nile basin, Burundi, Kenya, and Rwanda became water scarce at the turn of the twenty-first century. Egypt and Ethiopia are projected to have less than a thousand cubic meters per person by 2025.[6]

Scientific debates about global warming or global climatic cycles have yet to be unraveled, but in fact they are academic to those who fearfully stand by the banks of the Nile praying that the waters will flow. Water can be stored. It can be moved from those who have to those who have not—at great cost and with difficult political arrangements. But there is no substitute for water. The Nile basin is the immediate worry, for its finite waters, which serve 250 million people today, must provide for 600 million in 2025. The Nile waters that flow north from Burundi and the great lakes of equatorial Africa mostly evaporate and disappear into the air in the Sudd. Without the annual flood cascading from the Ethiopian plateau down thousands of streams and rivers, carrying 84 percent of the Nile, Egypt would have only sand and rock and wind. For thousands of years, as today, the abiding fear in Egypt and the Sudan has been that the Nile would cease to flow, or that the Ethiopians would somehow interfere and put a stop to it.

The power of this paranoia is understood by every president and peasant in Egypt. When the British occupied the country in 1882, they mobilized all their diplomatic, economic, and military might to defend Cairo and the Suez Canal by securing control of the Nile waters from Lake Victoria to the Mediterranean Sea. Under their imperial shield the British sought to plan for Nile control, the development of the Nile basin for the most efficient conservation of its waters. They failed, a failure symbolized by the defeat of the Anglo-French military expedition to reoccupy the Suez Canal after the Egyptian nationalization in 1956. Triumphant, Gamal Abdel Nasser sought a monument for the hydrologic security of Egypt by the construction of the High Dam at Aswan. Completed in 1971, this massive edifice may be the wrong dam in the wrong place, but despite its critics it sustained the people of Egypt during the decade of drought in the 1980s and protected them from the enormous floods of the 1990s. The dam creates an effective illusion that Egypt, for the first time in five thousand years, is free from the danger of being a hostage to upstream riparians.

The years of African independence and population increases have created strident and avaricious demands for Nile water. The development of the water resources in the Nile basin remains shackled by historical rivalries, ethnic conflicts, and religious antagonisms, hostilities that have consumed millions for war, leaving a pittance for the peaceful development of a precious resource, water. History is awash with the ironies of Nile civilizations and their myths. There is no greater irony at the beginning of the twenty-first century than the truth of the Arab proverb: those who have drunk from the Nile must return to drink again from the waters of the coy fountains of Herodotus bubbling at the foot of tall mountains. In a new century of self-determination and democracy, even those who are most dependent on the Nile recognize the need for equitable use by all those who drink its water. To define and agree on what constitutes equitable utilization, however, will be a perilous passage down a long river, from the shimmering surface of its great lakes through the Stygian Sudd, along narrow defiles of deep canyons, to the terror of turbulent cataracts and the sea.

Notes

Introduction

1. Loren Eiseley, *The Immense Journey,* New York: Random House, 1946, p. 15.

Chapter 1: The Tyranny of Dependency

1. The flow of water is measured by the international community in cubic meters, and great rivers run to billions of cubic meters. The measurement of the annual discharge of any river is normally taken near its mouth in order to include all the possible contributions, but since the last tributary of the Nile is the Atbara, 1,700 miles from the Mediterranean Sea, the official confirmation of the Nile flood is that which is released at Aswan. The measurement of the inflow of Nile waters is now made at Dongola in the Sudan at the head of the Lake Nasser reservoir. Here over the past century the average annual mean flow of the Nile has been 88 billion cubic meters; the comparison figures are, the Amazon, 5,518 billion cubic meters; the Mekong, 470 billion; the Mississippi, 562 billion; and the Rhine, 70 billion. Rushdi Said, *The River Nile: Geology, Hydrology, and Utilization,* Oxford: Pergamon, 1993, p. 9.

2. Sedimentary rock deposits that best display the Sahara in this wet phase are found in the Gilf Kabir. The Gilf is a large plateau that rises some 3,000 feet in southwest Egypt 190 miles west of Abu Simbel on the Nile. The Gilf was the location of the Academy Award–winning film *The English Patient.*

3. T. Evans, "History of Nile Flows," in *The Nile: Sharing a Scarce Resource,* ed. P. P. Howell and J. A. Allan, Cambridge: Cambridge University Press, 1994, pp. 27–63; M. A. J. Williams and D. A. Adamson, "Late Pleistocene Desiccation Along the White Nile," *Nature,* vol. 248, April 1974: 584–586; F. Alayne Street and A. T. Grove, "Global Maps of Lake Level Fluctuations Since 30,000 yr. BP," *Quaternary Research,* vol. 12, 1979: 83–118; M. A. J. Williams and D. A. Adamson, *A Land Between Two Niles,* Rotterdam: Belkama, 1980; and M. A. J. Williams and H. Faure, *The Sahara and the Nile,* Rotterdam: Belkama, 1982.

4. Although the duration of the flood has been measured since the reign of Pharaoh Djur of the First Dynasty (circa 3050 B.C.E.), the most reliable measurements are from the twentieth century. According to Rushdi Said: "Of the 46 floods of the years 1890–1935, it was less than 75 days in four years and more than 125 days in twelve years. The maximum duration of the flood was in 1894 when it lasted for 162 days between May 17 and October 26. Out of 207 years in which both the minimum and max-

imum levels were recorded, the rise of the Nile began in the month of June approximately 75 percent of the time. . . . The maximum rise of the river occurred in the latter part of September and the early part of October in approximately 87 percent of the time. In 5 percent of the time the maximum rise occurred in November. There was no record of a maximum rise before August 7 or after November 27." Said, *The River Nile,* p. 97.

5. The literature on Roda is large and impressive. The most exhaustive study is William Popper, *The Cairo Nilometer,* Berkeley: University of California Press, 1951. See also Ali Mubarak, *Al Khitat al Taufiqiya al Jadida* [The New Tawfik Survey of Egypt and Its Towns and Villages], 20 vols., Cairo: Bulaq, 1886–1899, reprinted 1958–1967; Capt. Henry G. Lyons, *The Physiography of the River Nile and Its Basin,* Cairo: Survey Department, 1906; Amin Sami, *Taqwim el-Nil,* 6 vols., Cairo: National Printing Department, 1915; O. Toussoun, Prince, *Mémoire sur l'histoire du Nil,* Cairo: Mémoire Institut d'Egypte, 1925; Kamel Ghaleb Pasha, "Le Mikyas au nilomètre de l'Ile de Rodah," in *Mémoires de l'Institut d'Egypte,* Cairo, 1951: 78–92.

6. The correlation between Nile flows and the dark ages in dynastic Egypt has been demonstrated in Barbara Bell, "The Oldest Records of the Nile Floods," *Geographical Journal,* vol. 136, 1970: 569–573; Barbara Bell, "The Dark Ages in Ancient History, I: The First Dark Age in Egypt," *American Journal of Archaeology,* vol. 75, no. 1, 1971: 1–26; Said, *The River Nile,* pp. 138–140.

7. Barbara Bell, "Climate and the History of Egypt, the Middle Kingdom," *American Journal of Archaeology,* vol. 79, no. 3, 1975: 223–269; Said, *The River Nile,* pp. 149–150.

8. Said, *The River Nile,* p. 152. The importance of Kush in the Nile Valley and the "Corridor to Africa" still remains, paradoxically, unappreciated if not unknown by those concerned with Africa and dynastic Egyptian studies, let alone the knowledgeable audience interested in the Nile despite the enormous amount of scholarly studies about Kush (Nubia). For an excellent introduction to Kush and its extensive bibliography see Derek A. Welsby, *The Kingdom of Kush: The Napatan and Meroitic Empires,* Princeton: Markus Wiener, 1998.

9. Said, *The River Nile,* pp. 164–165. The flood of 967 has been calculated at 54 billion cubic meters, compared with those of 1984, at 42 billion, 1987 at 45 billion, and 1913 at 45.5 billion.

10. Al-Maqirzi Abu al-Abbas, *Al-ilmaam bi akhbar man bi-ard al-Habasha min hulul al-Islam,* Cairo, 1895, quoted in Said, *The River Nile,* p. 166.

11. G. Belzoni, *Narrative of the Operations and Recent Discoveries . . . in Egypt and Nubia etc.,* 3d ed., vol. 2, London: John Murray, 1822, pp. 28–29.

12. Sa'id 'Abd al-Fattah 'Ashur, "Ba'd adwa' jadida 'ala al-'alaqat bayna misr walhabasha fi al-'usur al-wusta" [Some New Lights on the Relations Between Egypt and Ethiopia in the Middle Ages], *Egyptian Historical Journal,* vol. 14, 1968: 1–43. See Haggai Erlich, *The Cross and the River: Ethiopia, Egypt, and the Nile,* Boulder, Colo.: Lynne Rienner, 2002, p. 46.

13. Said, *The River Nile,* p. 165; Ludovico Ariosto, *Orlando Furioso,* Canto 33, st. 106, trans. B. Reynolds, London, 1981, p. 305.

14. Evans, "History of Nile Flows," pp. 40–51; Said, *The River Nile,* p. 161; C. S. Jarvis, "Flood Stage Records of the River Nile," *Transactions of the American Society of Civil Engineers,* vol. 101, 1935: 1013–1071; H. E. Hurst, "Long-Term Storage Capacity of Reservoirs," *Transactions of the American Society of Civil Engineers,* vol. 116, 1951: 770–799; H. E. Hurst, R. P. Black, and Y. M. Simaika, *Long Term Storage in Reservoirs: An Experimental Study,* London: Constable, 1965.

For the dispute over the integrity of the records of Nile flows see Robert O. Collins, *The Waters of the Nile: Hydropolitics and the Jonglei Canal, 1900–1988,* Oxford: Oxford University Press, and Princeton: Markus Wiener, 1990 and 1996, respectively, pp. 114–144; Hurst's analysis is in Sir Murdoch MacDonald, *Nile Control,* Cairo: National Printing Office, 1921.

The search for periodicity has been a vigorous scientific industry. See H. J. Riehl and J. Meitin, "Discharge of the Nile River: A Barometer of Short-Period Climate Variations," *Science,* vol. 206, 1979: 1178–1179; F. A. Hassan, "Historical Nile Floods and Their Implications for Climatic Change," *Science,* vol. 212, 1981: 1142–1144; S. Hameed, "Fourier Analysis of Nile Flood Levels," *Geophysical Research Letters,* vol. 1, 1984: 843–845; E. Aguado, "A True Series Analysis of the Nile River Low Flows," *Annals of the Association of American Geographers,* vol. 72, 1987: 109–119; F. A. Hassan and B. R. Stucki, "Nile Floods and Climatic Change," in *Climate: History, Periodicity, and Predictability,* ed. M. R. Rampino, J. E. Sanders, W. S. Newman, and L. K. Königsson, New York: Van Nostrand and Reinhold, 1987, pp. 37–46.

15. H. E. Hurst, R. P. Black, and Y. M. Simaika, *The Future Conservation of the Nile,* vol. 7 of *The Nile Basin,* Cairo: Physical Department, Ministry of Public Works, 1946; Hurst, Black, and Simaika, *Long Term Storage;* H. E. Hurst, R. P. Black, and Y. M. Simaika, *The Major Nile Projects,* vol. 10 of *The Nile Basin,* Cairo: Physical Department, Ministry of Water, 1966.

Chapter 2: The Lake Plateau

1. Fréderick Stracke, "Caput Nili, l'Urundi, les Barundi," *Grand Lacs,* Revue Générale des Missions d'Afrique, 1 February 1949: 16.

2. E. J. Devroey, "Les sources du Nile an Congo belge et au Ruanda-Urundi," *Bulletin des séances,* vol. 21, 1950: 268–269.

3. Sir William Garstin, ed., *Report upon the Basin of the Upper Nile,* London: His Majesty's Stationery Office, 1904, p. 55.

4. Thomas Heazle Parke, *My Personal Experiences in Equatorial Africa,* London: Sampson Low, Marston, 1891, pp. 217, 220; A. J. Mounteney-Jephson, *The Diary of A. J. Mounteney-Jephson: Emin Pasha Relief Expedition, 1887–1889,* ed. Dorothy Middleton, Cambridge: Cambridge University Press, 1969, pp. 255, 341.

5. Unlike the Nile in Egypt the hydrologic environment of Lake Victoria and the Lake Plateau has been measured only in the past century, and the record is inconsistent, unreliable, and skewed by the extraordinary rainfall between 1961 and 1964. Like Egypt throughout the millennia, however, the cumulative record provides a remarkable hydrologic portrait of the Lake Plateau that is more understandable on the whole than in its individual parts. See Said, *The River Nile,* pp. 111–113; K. V. Krishnamurthy and A. M. Ibrahim, *Hydrometeorological Studies of Lakes Victoria, Kioga, and Albert,* Entebbe, Uganda: UNDP/WMO, 1973; G. W. Kite, "Recent Changes in Level of Lake Victoria," "Analysis of Lake Victoria Levels," and "Regulation of the White Nile," *Hydrological Sciences Journal,* vol. 26, no. 3, 1981: 233–243, vol. 27, no. 1, 1982: 99–110, and vol. 29, no. 2, 1984: 191–201.

6. Garstin, ed., *Report upon the Basin of the Upper Nile,* p. 63.

7. Said, *The River Nile,* p. 152. Since beginning their migrations from their homeland on the Benue Plateau more than two thousand years ago, Africans speaking Bantu languages have occupied most of the continent south of the equator and have increased their numbers by hundreds of millions. They enveloped the Cushitic speakers in eastern Africa and pushed the Khoisan hunters and gatherers into the arid regions of southwest Africa. Although they speak four hundred languages that are seldom mutually understood, these all have a similar vocabulary and morphology. Dr. Wilhelm H. Bleek, who made linguistic studies in southern Africa in the mid nineteenth century, observed that these languages all have the same root, *ntu,* for *people,* and he gave this group of languages the name Bantu. The Bantu languages of the Benue-Congo region are a collateral branch of the larger Niger-Congo linguistic family, which includes the languages of West Africa, just as Cushitic is a collateral branch from northeast Africa of the larger Afro-Asiatic family in North Africa, Egypt, and the Middle East.

8. Jan Vansina, *Paths in the Rainforest,* Madison: University of Wisconsin Press, 1990, pp. 61–65.

9. Adolphus Fredrick, Duke of Mecklenberg, *In the Heart of Africa,* London: Cassel, 1910, p. 47; Hans Meyer, *Die Burundi,* Leipzig: Otto Spainer, 1916, p. 14. See also René Lemarchand, *Rwanda and Burundi,* New York: Praeger, 1970, pp. 18–19.

Chapter 3: The Sudd

1. A. E. W. Gleichen, Count von, ed., *The Anglo-Egyptian Sudan: A Compendium Prepared by Officers of the Sudan Government,* London: His Majesty's Stationery Office, 1905, vol. 1, p. 304.

2. Egyptian *Master Water Plan, Main Report,* UNDP/EGY/73/024, 1981. Said, *The River Nile,* gives an extravagant estimate for the Bahr al-Ghazal water at 400 billion cubic meters (p. 115), but see John Waterbury, *Riverains and Lacustrines: Toward International Cooperation in the Nile Basin,* Discussion Paper 107, Research Program in Development Studies, Woodrow Wilson School of Public and International Affairs, Princeton University, 1982, pp. 75–77; Collins, *The Waters of the Nile,* p. 298.

3. Sir William Garstin, *Irrigation Projects on the Upper Nile, Egypt, No. 2,* London: His Majesty's Stationery Office, 1901, pp. 117–118.

4. J. V. Sutcliffe and Y. P. Parks, *The Hydrology of the Nile,* Wallingford, U.K.: International Association of Hydrological Sciences, Special Publication no. 5, 1999; Collins, *The Waters of the Nile,* pp. 98–99.

Chapter 4: Land Beyond the Rivers

1. E. E. Evans-Pritchard, *The Nuer,* Oxford: Clarendon, 1940, p. 151.

2. Ferdinand Werne, *Expedition to Discover the Sources of the White Nile in the Years 1840, 1841,* trans. Charles William O'Reilly, London: Richard Bentley, 1849, vol. 2, pp. 252–253.

3. Air Vice-Marshall T. Twidible Bowen to Sir H. J. Trancard, Chief of Air Staff, 3 March 1928, Public Records Office, Foreign Office Archives, Kew, Great Britain, 141/519.

4. G. L. Elliot Smith, 28 April 1938, Private Papers, Sudan Archive, Durham University.

5. M. O. Yassin to Permanent Undersecretary of the Minister of Foreign Affairs, 30 March 1955, National Records Office, Khartoum, UNP, 1/47/347.

6. During the twentieth century the average annual flow reaching the White Nile from the equatorial lakes after the passage through the Sudd was 13.5 billion cubic meters. The average annual flow from the Sobat during the same century was 13 billion cubic meters, or 14 percent of the total Nile waters at Aswan. During the great rains of 1917–1918, the Sobat flow surged to 20 billion cubic meters, and in the first half of the 1960s it averaged more than 15 billion cubic meters. There were also years of low water, such as 1913, 1940, 1972, and 1982, when the flow from the Sobat was less than 8 billion cubic meters. These records are reasonably well documented.

7. "Note on Proposed Program of Work for the Upper White Nile Division for the Years 1920–1927," UNP I/9/75, Sudan Government Archives, Khartoum.

Chapter 5: The Blue Nile

1. Pedro Páez quoted in James Bruce, *Travels to Discover the Source of the Nile,* ed. A. Murray, 3d ed., Edinburgh: A. Constable, 1813, vol. 5, appendix 4, p. 445. See also John O. Udal, *The Nile in Darkness,* Wilby, Norwich: Michael Russell, 1998, pp. 99–106.

2. Siemens AG, *The Exploration of Lake Tana for Irrigation and Hydro-Electric Power,* Munich, 1956;

U.S. Bureau of Reclamation, *Land and Water Resources of the Blue Nile Basin,* vol. 5, *Power,* p. 219; Declan Conway, "The Climate and Hydrology of the Upper Blue Nile River," *Geographical Journal,* vol. 166, no. 1, March 2000: 49–62.

3. The average of the Dinder's five-day spate each August is 815 million cubic meters; the average for the Rahad is 630 million cubic meters. U.S. Bureau of Reclamation, *Hydrology,* vol. 3, Appendix, p. 150.

4. C. E. J. Walkley, "The Story of Khartoum," *Sudan Notes and Records,* vol. 8, no. 2, 1935: 23.

Chapter 6: From Khartoum to Kush

1. Sir Samuel W. Baker, *The Nile Tributaries of Abyssinia,* Philadelphia: J. P. Lippincott, 1868, pp. 52–53.

2. In 1977, eleven years after the completion of the Khashm al-Girba Dam, the capacity of the reservoir, 1.3 billion cubic meters, had been reduced to 0.8 billion cubic meters, or a loss of 40 percent. Agrar und Hydrotechnic, *New Halfa Rehabilitation Project: Phase 1,* Khartoum: Ministry of Planning, 1978, p. 13. The rate of siltation has not diminished, but the amount has varied depending on rainfall in Ethiopia.

3. William Y. Adams, *Nubia: Corridor to Africa,* London: Allan Lane, 1977, p. 32.

4. Quoted in J. S. Trimingham, *Islam in the Sudan,* London: Oxford University Press, 1949, p. 65.

5. Ibn Abd al-Hakam, *The Mohammedan Conquest of Egypt,* trans. C. C. Torrey in *Yale Biblical and Semitic Studies,* New York: Scribner's, 1901, pp. 307–308.

6. Adams, *Nubia,* pp. 461, 469.

7. Adams, *Nubia,* pp. 506–507; Hasan Yusuf Fadl, *The Arabs and the Sudan from the Seventh to the Early Sixteenth Century,* Edinburgh: Edinburgh University Press, 1967, pp. 22–24; Jay Spaulding, "Medieval Christian Nubia and the Islamic World: A Reconsideration of the *Baqt* Treaty," *International Journal of African Historical Studies,* vol. 28, no. 3, 1995: 577–594; Bruce Trigger, *History and Settlements in Lower Nubia,* New Haven: Yale University Press, 1965, p. 81.

Chapter 7: The Egyptian Nile and Its Delta

1. Said, *The River Nile,* pp. 59–61.

2. Said, *The River Nile,* pp. 59–60.

3. Janet L. Abu-Lughod, *Cairo: 1001 Years of the City Victorious,* Princeton: Princeton University Press, 1971, p. 18.

4. Said, *The River Nile,* pp. 66–68.

5. From Aswan to Cairo the Nile drops 243 feet in 595 miles, 2.5 feet per mile. In the delta the Damietta and Rosetta branches drop 39 feet in 150 miles, 4 feet per mile.

6. Michael A. Hoffman, *The Predynastic of Hierakonpolis,* Cairo: Egyptian Studies Association, no. 1, 1982.

7. Said, *The River Nile,* p. 205.

8. Said, *The River Nile,* p. 207.

9. Said, *The River Nile,* p. 191.

10. Said, *The River Nile,* pp. 196–200.

11. Karl W. Butzer, *Early Hydraulic Civilization in Egypt,* Chicago: University of Chicago Press, 1976, p. 210.

12. Said, *The River Nile,* pp. 213–214.

13. Justin A. McCarthy, "Nineteenth-Century Egyptian Population," *Middle Eastern Studies,* vol. 12, no. 3, October 1976: 29.

Chapter 8: British Engineers on the Nile

1. Sir Garnet Wolseley to Lady Wolseley, 15 September 1882, quoted in Thomas Pakenham, *The Scramble for Africa, 1876–1912,* New York: Random House, 1991, p. 139.

2. McCarthy, "Nineteenth-Century Egyptian Population," p. 25.

3. Brian Fagan, *Floods, Famines, and Emperors,* New York: Basic, 1999, p. 12.

4. R. Weaver, *Dictionary of National Biography,* London: Oxford University Press, 1937, p. 329.

5. Sir William Willcocks, *The Nile Reservoir Dam at Assuân,* London: E. & F. N. Spon, 1903, p. 4.

6. Sir William Garstin, *Report as to Irrigation Projects on the Upper Nile,* London: Parliamentary Accounts and Papers, 1901; Garstin, ed., *Report upon the Basin of the Upper Nile,* 1904.

7. C. E. Dupuis, "A Report upon Lake Tana and the Rivers of the Eastern Sudan," in *Report upon the Basin of the Upper Nile,* ed. Garstin, pp. 209–236; G. W. Grabham and R. P. Black, *Report of the Mission to Lake Tana, 1920–1921,* Cairo: Ministry of Public Works, 1925.

8. Lyons, *Physiography of the River Nile and Its Basin,* p. 2.

9. Sir William Willcocks to H.E. High Commissioner, Lord Allenby, 18 July 1918, Sudan Archive, Durham University, p. 2.

10. R. S. Stafford, Inspector of Interior, Tanta, to Adviser, Ministry of Interior, 24 February 1920, Public Records Office, Foreign Office Archives, Kew, Great Britain, 141/435/101844.

11. Report and Opinion of Judge Booth, in *Nile Projects Commission Report,* Cairo: Ministry of Public Works, 1920, p. 5.

12. Report on the Second and Third Terms of Reference by President and Dr. Simpson by H. T. Cory, *Nile Projects Commission Report,* pp. 57–58, 65, 66–68.

13. R. M. MacGregor and Abdel Hamid Suleiman, *The Nile Commission Report,* Cairo: Ministry of Public Works, 1926, para. 21, Sudan Archive, Durham University, 500/3/28.

14. H. E. Hurst, "Progress in the Study of the Hydrology of the Nile in the Last Twenty Years," *Geographical Journal,* vol. 70, 1927: 441.

15. A. D. Butcher, *The Sadd Hydraulics,* Cairo: Ministry of Public Works, 1938, p. 38.

16. Hurst, Black, and Simaika, *The Future Conservation of the Nile,* p. vi.

17. R. M. MacGregor, *The Upper Nile Irrigation Projects,* 10 December 1945, p. 8, Sudan Archive, Durham University, 589/14/48.

Chapter 9: Plans and Dams

1. W. N. Allan, *Note on the Equatorial Nile Project, 1 July 1948,* 580/5/1, Sudan Archive, Durham University.

2. Minutes of Third Meeting of the Jonglei Committee, 22 July 1947, UNP I/10/85, Khartoum: Sudan Government Archives; Paul Howell, Michael Lock, and Stephen Cobb, eds., *The Jonglei Canal: Impact and Opportunity,* Cambridge: Cambridge University Press, 1988, p. 39.

3. H. A. W. Morrice, *The Chasm: The Protest of an Engineer,* London: Alliance Press, 1945, pp. 24–25.

4. Paul Howell to John Winder, 16 May 1951, UNP I/9/80, Sudan Government Archives.

5. R. J. Smith to W. N. Williams, 11 July 1949, UNP I/9/80, Sudan Government Archives.

6. H. A. W. Morrice and W. N. Allan, *Report on the Nile Valley Plan,* 2 vols., Khartoum: Ministry of Irrigation, 1958; H. E. Hurst et al., "Discussion on Planning for the Ultimate Hydraulic Development of the Nile Valley," *Proceedings of the Institute of Civil Engineers* (U.K.), vol. 16, July 1960: 294, 314.

7. John H. Spencer, *Ethiopia at Bay: A Personal Account of the Haile Selassie Years,* Algonace: Michigan Reference Publications, 1984, p. 188.

8. Tom A. Clark, *Preliminary Reconnaissance Report on the Water Resources of the Blue Nile,* Washington, D.C.: United States Department of the Interior, Bureau of Reclamation, 1952; J. Seymour Harris, *Report on the Proposed Control and Utilization of the Waters of Lake Tana,* Birmingham: Seymour Harris and Partners, 1952.

9. *Ethiopian Herald,* 6 February 1956.

10. *Foreign Relations of the United States, 1958–1960,* vol. 14, National Security Council Report, NSC 6028, December 30, 1960, Washington, D.C.: Department of State, 1992, p. 203; see also Dedjazmatch Zewde Gabre-Sellassie, "The Nile Question, 1955–1964: The Ethiopian Perspective," Conference on the Nile Civilization, History, and Myths, 19–22 May 1997, Tel Aviv University.

11. *Land and Water Resources of the Blue Nile Basin: Ethiopia,* 17 vols., Washington, D.C.: United States Department of the Interior, Bureau of Reclamation, 1964; Dale Whittington and Elizabeth Mc-Clelland, "Opportunities for Regional and International Cooperation in the Nile Basin," *Water International,* vol. 17, no. 3, 1992: 144–154; Giorgio Guarsio et al., "Implications of Ethiopian Water Development for Egypt and the Sudan," *Water Resources Development,* vol. 3, 1987: 111.

12. *The Times* (London), 3 June 1959.

13. G. W. Furlonge to Rt. Hon. Selwyn Lloyd, 3 August 1959, enclosed in "Summary Report on Nile Waters, June 19, 1959, prepared by Bolton, Hennessey and Partners for the Economic and Technical Board of the Ethiopian Government," Howell Papers, Sudan Archive, Durham University; *Ethiopian Herald,* 10 June 1959. The article in the *Ethiopian Herald* was based on the report by Bolton, Hennessey and Partners.

Chapter 10: The Nile Ends at Aswan

1. Hurst, Black, and Simaika, *The Major Nile Projects.*

2. Tom Little, *High Dam at Aswan: The Subjugation of the Nile,* New York: John Day, 1965, pp. 69–82.

3. *Report by the Board of Consultants on Sadd el-Aali Project,* Cairo: Sadd el-Aali Authority, 1955, p. 1, quoted in Elizabeth Bishop, "Talking Shop: Egyptian Engineers and Soviet Specialists at the Aswan High Dam," Ph.D. dissertation, University of Chicago, June 1997, p. 16; see also Herbert Addison, *Sun and Shadow at Aswan,* London: Chapman and Hall, 1955. John Waterbury, *Hydropolitics of the Nile Valley,* Syracuse: Syracuse University Press, 1979, pp. 102–104; Mohamed Hassenein Heikal, *The Cairo Documents: The Inside Story of Nasser and His Relationships with World Leaders, Rebels, and Statesmen,* Garden City, N.Y.: Doubleday, 1973.

4. Bishop, "Talking Shop," pp. 253–254.

5. The technical matters and relationships between Egyptian and Soviet personalities during the construction of the Aswan High Dam are discussed with an extensive bibliography from Egyptian and Russian sources in Bishop, "Talking Shop," pp. 141–153, 170, 249–250.

6. Sunallah Ibrahim, quoted in Samia Mehrez, *Egyptian Writers Between History and Fiction: Essays on Naguib Mahfouz, Sonallah Ibrahim, and Gamal al-Gatani,* Cairo, 1994, p. 125.

7. M. A. Abdel-Khalik, "Water Management Strategies Under Drought and Flood Conditions in Egypt," *Proceedings, Seventh Nile 2002 Conference,* Cairo: Egypt, 15–19 March 1999, p. 1.2.

8. Little, *High Dam at Aswan,* p. 162.

9. Ismail H. Abdalla, "Removing the Nubians: The Halfawis at Khashm al-Girba," in *The Nile: Histories, Cultures, Myths,* ed. Haggai Erlich and Israel Gershoni, Boulder, Colo.: Lynne Rienner, 2000, pp. 235–243.

10. Said, *The River Nile,* p. 246.

Chapter 11: Jonglei

1. H. T. Möth, "Investigations into the Meteorological Aspects of the Variations in the Level of Lake Victoria," Nairobi: Meteorological Department, East African Common Services Organization, 1967, p. 6; B. S. Piper et al., "The Water Balances of Lake Victoria," *Hydrological Sciences Journal,* vol. 31, no. 1, 1986: 25–37.

2. Fagan, *Floods, Famines, and Emperors,* p. 37.

3. The permanent swamp increased from 1,053 to 6,318 square miles. The seasonal swamp was enlarged from 5,109 to 11,622 square miles. J. V. Sutcliffe and Y. P. Parks, "Hydrological Modelling of the Sudd and Jonglei Canal," *Hydrological Sciences Journal,* vol. 32, no. 2, 1985: 3.

4. Charles O. Okidi, "International Laws and the Lake Victoria and Nile Basins," *Indian Journal of International Law,* vol. 20, 1980: 422, 421; Earle E. Seaton and Sosthenes T. Maliti, *Tanzania Treaty Practice,* Nairobi: Oxford University Press, 1973, pp. 90–91. The Nyerere Doctrine was not a new idea. It had been proposed in the context of the 1929 Nile Waters Agreement by H. A. W. Morrice in 1959, when he was the hydrological consultant for East Africa.

5. Earthscan Press Briefing Document No. 8, International Institute for Environment and Development, London, April 1978.

6. The initial estimated cost for excavating southern Sudanese "cotton soil" was only 0.15 Sudanese pounds per cubic meter; the estimate for draglines was ten times higher, or 1.5 Sudanese pounds per cubic meter. "Cost Estimates of the Project," *The Jonglei Project: Phase One,* Khartoum: Executive Organ for Development Projects in the Jonglei Area (JEO), 1975, p. 71; *Jonglei Canal Project* (Agreement between the Ministry of Irrigation and Hydro-electric Energy and CCI/CFE), Nanterre, 1976, p. 4.

7. Abel Alier, "Statement to the People's Regional Assembly on the Proposed Jonglei Canal," Khartoum: National Council for the Development of the Jonglei Area, 1974, pp. 20–21.

8. "Presidential Order No. 284, October 1974," *Jonglei Project: Phase One,* Khartoum: Jonglei Executive Organ, 1975, pp. 93–98.

9. This incredibly low cost was based on the price of fuel in 1976. The dramatic rise in the price of petroleum made this cost unrealistic. The Sudanese pound was also highly overvalued at the time. The contract was renegotiated in 1980.

10. Professor Richard Odingo, Environmental Liaison Centre Press Conference, University of Nairobi, Nairobi, September 1977.

11. *Jonglei Environmental Aspects,* Arnheim: Euroconsult, 1978, p. 2.

12. Mefit-Babtie Srl., *Development Studies in the Jonglei Canal Area,* 10 vols., and *Development Studies in the Jonglei Area: Final Report,* 4 vols., Glasgow, Khartoum, and Rome: Mefit-Babtie, April and October 1983, respectively.

13. Ministry of Irrigation and Hydroelectric Power, *Jonglei Canal Project: Eastern Alignment to Bor* (Agreement between Ministry of Irrigation and CCI/CFE), Nanterre, 1980, p. 22; Permanent Joint Technical Commission for the Nile Waters, *Jonglei Project: Project Evaluation,* Khartoum, 1981, p. 22.

14. John Garang de Mabior, "Identifying, Selecting, and Implementing Rural Development Strategies for Socio-Economic Development in the Jonglei Projects Area, Southern Region, Sudan," Ph.D. dissertation, Iowa State University, 1981, p. 227.

15. R. K. Badal, "The Addis Ababa Agreement Ten Years After: An Assessment," in *North-South Relations in the Sudan Since the Addis Ababa Agreement,* Khartoum: Khartoum University Press, 1988, p. 32.

Chapter 12: Who Owns the Nile?

1. Boutros Boutros-Ghali, *Egypt's Road to Jerusalem,* New York: Random House, 1997, p. 327; *Ethiopian Herald,* 14 May 1978.

2. Wondimneh Tilahun, *Egypt's Imperial Aspirations over Lake Tana and the Blue Nile,* Addis Ababa: Addis Ababa University Press, 1979, p. 30.

3. Boutros Boutros-Ghali, "The Foreign Policy of Egypt," in *Foreign Policies in a World of Change,* ed. Joseph E. Black and Kenneth W. Thompson, New York: Harper & Row, 1963, p. 319. For a historical analysis of the convoluted relationship since 1971 between Egypt and Ethiopia over the Nile waters, see Erlich, *The Cross and the River,* pp. 145–225.

4. Boutros-Ghali, *Egypt's Road to Jerusalem,* pp. 321–322.

5. Boutros-Ghali, *Egypt's Road to Jerusalem,* p. 63.

6. Said, *The River Nile,* p. 273.

7. Fahay T. Dawood, Hassan M. A. Osman, and Omar H. Ahmed, "Geological and Hydrogeological Studies of the High Dam Lake Region and Its Vicinities, South Egypt," *Proceedings, Seventh Nile 2002 Conference,* 15–19 March 1999, Cairo, EGY-16.1–16.25; Abdel-Khalik, "Water Management Strategies"; M. A. Abu-Zeid and S. Abdel-Dayem, "Egypt's Programmes and Policy Options for Low Nile Flows," in *Climatic Fluctuations and Water Management,* ed. M. A. Abu-Zeid and A. K. Biswas, London: Butterworth-Heinemann, 1992, pp. 48–58; I. Murray, "The Mighty Cradle of Civilization Is Drying Up," *The Times* (London), 5 November 1987; T. E. Evans, letter to the editor, *The Times* (London), 14 November 1987.

8. The literature on El Niño and La Niña is enormous, but for their relationship to the Nile waters and their flow see Said, *The River Nile,* pp. 124–126; M. R. Glantz, R. Katz, and M. Krenz, eds., *Climate Crisis: The Social Impact Associated with the 1982–1983 World Wide Climate Anomalies,* Nairobi: United Nations Environmental Programme, 1987; M. Hulme, "Global Climate and Change and the Nile Basin," in *The Nile: Resource Evolution, Resource Management, Hydropolitics, and Legal Issues,* ed. P. P. Howell and J. A. Allan, London: School of Oriental and African Studies and the Royal Geographical Society, 1990, pp. 59–82; J. E. Janowiak, "An Investigation of Interannual Rainfall Variability in Africa," *Journal of Climate,* vol. 1, 1988: 240–255; B. B. Attia and A. B. Abulhoda, "The ENSO Phenomenon and Its Impact on the Nile's Hydrology," in *Climatic Fluctuations and Water Management,* ed. Abu-Zeid and Biswas, pp. 71–79.

Chapter 13: The Waters of the World and the Nile

1. Igor A. Shiklomanov, "World Fresh Water Resources," in *Water in Crisis,* ed. Peter H. Gleick, New York: Oxford University Press, 1993, pp. 13–24.

2. I. A. Shiklomanov and O. A. Markova, *Specific Water Availability and River Runoff Transfers in the World,* Leningrad: Gidrometeoizdat, 1987.

3. Shiklomanov, "World Fresh Water Resources," pp. 19–21.

4. Shiklomanov and Markova, *Specific Water Availability.*

5. United Nations Population Division, *Long-Range World Population Projections: Two Centuries of Population Growth, 1950–2150,* New York: United Nations, 1991.

6. Peter H. Gleick, "Water in the Twenty-first Century," in *Water in Crisis,* ed. Gleick, pp. 105–113; Robert Engelman and Pamela LeRoy, *Conserving Land: Population and Sustainable Food Production,* Washington, D.C.: Population Action International, 1995; Sam L. Laki, "Management of Water Resources of the Nile Basin," *Transboundary Resources Report,* International Transboundary Resources Center, vol. 11, no. 1, 1998: 4–6.

Bibliographical Essay

The literature about the Nile is voluminous, embracing every conceivable subject from anthropology to zoology. Some of it is of great antiquity: fiction begins in ancient Egypt and continues through the millennia from medieval mythology about Prester John to Hercule Poirot investigating murder on the Nile in the twentieth century. Its aggregate would fill many stacks in research libraries, let alone collegiate and public libraries. Aficionados can consult Robert O. Collins, *The Waters of the Nile: An Annotated Bibliography* (London: Hans Zell, 1991), and the more recent and complete bibliography by Terje Tvedt, *The River Nile and Its Economic, Political, Social, and Cultural Role: An Annotated Bibliography* (Bergen: Centre for Development Studies, 2002). During the past decade there has been a torrent of books and articles in a multitude of journals, newspapers, and the Internet on every imaginable subject. This enormous quantity of literature, historic and contemporary, is not much help for the general reader wanting to know more about the Nile. I have therefore restricted myself to the river rather than trying to cover its banks, the monuments, and the long cultural history of its people. This results in arbitrary but manageable categories of description, geology, hydrology, the search for the source, and Nile control.

Surprisingly there are few general descriptions of the Nile from its sources to the sea. The author of many popular books, Emil Ludwig, wrote a romantic, readable book, *The Nile: The Life-Story of a River* (London: George Allen & Unwin, 1936). This was followed by a pedestrian but more thorough description by the preeminent hydrologist of the twentieth century, Dr. H. E. Hurst, *The Nile: A General Account of the River and the Utilization of Its Waters* (London: Constable, 1951). There are several photographic books with limited text that follow the course of the Nile from source to the sea, the most dramatic being Kazuyoshi Nomachi, *The Nile* (Hong Kong: Odyssey, 1998). Robert E. Cheesman, the British consul in Gojjam Province in Ethiopia during the 1920s, wrote a readable account in *Lake Tana and the Blue Nile: An Abyssinian Quest* (London: Macmillan, 1936; reprint, London: Frank Cass, 1968). The fascinating story of the historic nilometers that measured the flood, particularly the famous one on the island of Roda, can be found in William Popper, *The Cairo Nilometer* (Berkeley: University of California Press, 1951). The best discourse on the Nile literature has recently been published in *The Nile: Histories, Culture, Myths* (Boulder: Lynne Rienner, 2000), edited by Haggai Erlich and Israel Gershoni.

The making of a river and the mysteries of its flow have inspired a flood of scientific literature that can intimidate even scholars, let alone the general reader. The classic account by Rushdi Said, former head of the geological survey of Egypt, *The River Nile: Geology, Hydrology, and Utilization* (Oxford: Pergamon, 1993), is a compendium of information covering the geologic evolution of the Nile and its hydrology, not surprisingly with greater emphasis on Egypt than the upstream riparian states and their history. Hydrology, as opposed to geology, has been the principal industry of Nile research and commentary. These include the famous government document by Sir William Garstin, *Report upon the Basin of the Upper Nile* (London: His Majesty's Stationery Office, 1904), which can be found in most research libraries and is recommended for its clarity and style, not often found in official records. Two other hydrologic studies of the Nile cross over from the bureaucratic to the readable. Sir Henry G. Lyons, director general of the Egyptian survey department, wrote *The Physiography of the River Nile and Its Basin* (Cairo: Survey Department, 1906). Karl W. Butzer and C. L. Hansen have described the geology and hydrology of Nubia in *Desert and River in Nubia* (Madison: Wisconsin University Press, 1968). A more contemporary and comprehensive discussion of Nile hydrology is *The Nile: Sharing a Scarce Resource,* edited by P. P. Howell and J. A. Allan (Cambridge: Cambridge University Press, 1994). A summary of Nile hydrology consummating fifty years of research can be found in J. V. Sutcliffe and Y. P. Parks, *The Hydrology of the Nile* (Wallingford, England: International Association of Hydrological Sciences, 1999). Although not for the general reader, the *Proceedings of Nile 2002 Conferences,* a record of the meetings held annually since 1992, contain the most contemporary thoughts on the Nile waters, particularly the contributions from Egyptian hydrologists and engineers.

The search for the source of the Nile has been a major mystery that obsessed individuals, scholarly societies, and the public since Herodotus. The first to provide an account of this saga was Sir Harry H. Johnston, *The Nile Quest* (London: Lawrence and Bullen, 1903), but the most popular and readable works on the search are by Alan Moorehead, *The White Nile* (London: Hamish Hamilton, 1960) and *The Blue Nile* (London: Hamish Hamilton, 1962), both of which have been reprinted in many subsequent editions. John O. Udal, *The Nile in Darkness: Conquest and Exploration, 1504–1862* (Wilby, Norwich: Michael Russell, 1998) provides the most authoritative account of those seeking the source of the Nile before the Victorians. Recently Christopher Ondaatje has retraced the steps of the Victorian explorers in *Journey to the Source of the Nile* (Buffalo, N.Y.: Firefly, 1999), but the reader should not neglect the handsome and colorful volume by Gianni Guadalupi, *The Discovery of the Nile* (New York: Stewart, Tabori, and Chang, 1997).

Dams, canals, and controversy, known as Nile control, are a central feature in discussions of the Nile. The phrase is derived from the title of Sir Murdoch MacDonald's controversial two-volume work, *Nile Control* (Cairo: Ministry of Public Works, 1921), which among other things advocated dams in the Sudan at Sennar and Jabal Auliya that were subsequently built. It represents the transition of Nile control from the brilliant perceptions of Garstin in 1904 to the more sophisticated proposals of H. E. Hurst, R. P. Black, and Y. M. Simaika in their famous work, *The Future Conservation of the Nile* (Cairo: Physical Department, Ministry of Public Works, 1946), volume 7 of the eleven-volume series *The Nile Basin* (Cairo: Ministry of Public Works, 1936–1966). Equally important but forgotten is H. A. W. Morrice and William Nimmo Allan, *Report on the Nile Valley Plan* (Khartoum: Ministry of Irrigation and Hydroelectric Power, 1958), containing even more sophisticated proposals based on computerized analysis. These reports are heavy in the arcane terminology of hydrology and are found only in research libraries. They are probably not for the general reader, but anyone interested in Nile control should know they exist.

The Aswan High Dam has generated a huge literature because of the controversies regarding its financing, construction, and impact on the environment. Tom Little, *High Dam at Aswan: The Subjugation of the Nile* (New York: John Day, 1965) describes with the clarity of an investigative journalist the negotiations that made it possible. Surprisingly there is no adequate assessment of the High Dam for the general reader, but the politics of Nile water after the construction of the High Dam were first explored in John Waterbury, *Hydropolitics of the Nile Valley* (Syracuse: Syracuse University Press, 1979). The controversial Jonglei Canal is one of the most studied water projects ever. Ecology, resource management, and environmental impact are clearly presented in *The Jonglei Canal: Impact and Opportunity,* edited by Paul Howell, Michael Lock, and Stephen Cobb (Cambridge: Cambridge University Press, 1988). The hydropolitics and construction of the canal are described in detail in Robert O. Collins, *The Waters of the Nile: Hydropolitics and the Jonglei Canal, 1900–1988* (Oxford: Oxford University Press, 1990; Princeton: Markus Wiener, 1996). The Ethiopian connection has been less well explained, but the most readable account is Zewdie Abate, *Water Resources Development in Ethiopia: An Evaluation of Present Experience and Future Planning Concepts, A Management Method for Analysing a Key Resource in a Nation's Development* (Reading, U.K.: Ithaca Press, 1994).

There is also the vast volume of literature on climatic change and the availability of freshwater, including El Niño and La Niña. A popular discussion of these phenomena is found in Brian M. Fagan, *Floods, Famines, and Emperors: El Niño and the Fate of Civilization* (New York: Basic, 1999). Scientific literature about climate anomalies and global freshwater have appeared in the last decade with hurricane force, but summaries for the world that include the Nile are in *Climate Crisis,* edited by Michael Glantz, Richard Katz, and Maria Kreng (New York: United Nations Publications, 1987), and *Water in Crisis: A Guide to the World's Fresh Water Resources,* edited by Peter H. Gleick (New York: Oxford University Press, 1993).

Index

Aba Island, 86

Abay Wanz. *See* Blue Nile

Abbai Bridge, 96

Abboud, Ibrahim, 173, 187, 188

Abd Allahi, Khalifa, 57, 58

Abd Allah ibn Sad Abu Sarh, 116

Abu al-Raddad, 16

Abu Hamed, Sudan, 111–112

Abu Hamed Reach, 112, 113

Abu Klea, 111

Abu Simbel temple, 186–187

al-Abyad, Bahr. *See* White Nile

Adams, William Y., 120, 186

Addis Ababa Agreement (1972), 79, 210

Adonga, Sudan, 75

Adulis, 40

Adura, Khor, 81

Africa: Corridor to, 105, 115, 118, 121;
   dissemination of Islam in, 57; impact of
   independence on countries of, 197–198;
   management of water resources in, 46,
   222–225, 232–233; and Nubia as link with
   Egypt, 120–121. *See also* Egypt; Ethiopia;
   Sudan; *and names of other African nations*

Agam Dildi (Portuguese Bridge), 94, 95

Agha, Ali Khurshid, 104

agriculture in the Nile Valley, 130, 131–134,
   138–139, 142, 219

Ahmad, Muhammad. *See* al-Mahdi

Ahmad, Samir, 224

Ahmad Grañ (Ahmad ibn Ibrahim al-Ghazi),
   100, 217

Aïda (Verdi), 23, 104

Akobo River, 75, 76, 81

Akwei-wa-Cam, 77

Al-Ahram, 216

Albert, Lake, 2, 31, 32, 34, 35, 37, 144–145, 149,
   154, 157–158, 196, 220

Albert Nile, 2, 37, 47

Aleksandrov, Aleksandro, 183

Alexander the Great, 19, 135

Alier, Abel, 199–201, 202, 203, 204

Allan, W. Nimmo, 158, 160, 166, 168

Allaqi, Wadi, 20, 111

Allen, George, 170

Allenby, Lord, 150–151

Al-Siyasa al-Duwaliyya, 216

Amda Seyon (Ethiopian emperor), 92

Amenemhet I (pharaoh of Egypt), 18, 133

Amenemhet III (pharaoh of Egypt), 18

Amhara people, 93, 98, 100

Amin, Muhammad, 158, 166

Amosis, 113

Amr ibn al-As, 21, 125

Amun, Temple of, 114

Anger River, 99

Angereb River, 110, 111

Anglo-Egyptian Condominium, 71

Bito, 44–45
Bjerknes, Jacob, 196
Black, Eugene, 179
Black, R. P., 151–152, 153, 156, 157
black land *(kmt)*, 123
Blanc, Pierre, 202
Blashford-Snell, John ("Blashers"), 101
Blemmyes, 106
Blue Nile, 1, 3, 4, 13, 74, 80, 86, 87, *map* 90, 145, 146; bridges over, 93, 94, 95; canyons of, 94–99; cataracts of, 94; control of, 169; exploration of, 101; fords of, 96–97, 98–99; hydrology of, 152, 170–171; at Khartoum, 103–104, 106; and the Sennar Dam, 102–103, 147; sources of, 88–92; as trade route, 93; tributaries to, 91–92; volume of, 99, 103
Blue Nile Basin Study Plan, 170–171
Bolton, Hennessey and Partners, 174
Bor, Sudan, 49, 62, 66
Bor Conference (1983), 211–212
Boulé, M. E., 144
Boutros-Ghali, Boutros, 215–217, 224, 228
Broken Bridge, 96
Bruce, Fort, 81
Bruce, James, 8, 91
Brun Rollet, Antoine, 54, 56
Bucketwheel, 202, 205, 206, 208, 209, 212
Buganda, 36, 45, 46
Bulaq, 126
Bunyoro-Kitara, 45
Burns, Robert, 157
Burullus, Lake, 128
Burundi, 1, 27, 42, 43, 198, 222, 224
Bushmen, 39–40
Busseri River, 58, 63
Butana Plain, 106, 110
Butcher, A. D., 66, 153, 154, 155
Butiaba, Uganda, 34
Bwimba, Ruganzu, 42
Byzantine empire, 20–21, 135–136

Cairo, Egypt, 125–126
cataracts, Nile, 3, 29, 94, 105, 111, 113, 114, 116, 117–118, 119
Catholic missionaries, 54, 90

Central Treaty Organization, 179
century storage, 154, 156, 157, 159, 164, 176, 178
Chad, Lake, 129
Chara Chara, 93
Charlière, Guy, 202
Chasma Jhelum Link Canal, 202
Chay River, 96
Chick, A. L., 162
Chirol, Sir Valentine, 147
Christianity. *See* Catholic missionaries; Coptic Christians; monasteries
Churchill, Sir Winston, 177
Clark, Tom A., 169
Claudius Ptolemaeus. *See* Ptolemy
Compagnie de Constructions Internationales (CCI), 205
Congo, 198
Constantinople, 20
Cooper, Gary, 149
Coptic Christians, 15, 20, 22, 90, 215
corvée, 139–140
Cory, Harry Thomas, 149–150
Cory award, 149–150, 166, 174–175
cotton cultivation, 138–139, 148
crocodiles, 7
Cromer, Lord (Sir Evelyn Baring), 24, 59, 126, 141–142, 144, 146
Crophi, 32
Cushitic people, 39, 40
Cwezi people, 41
Cyr, Leo, 170
Czechoslovakia, Egypt's ties with, 179

Dabana River, 99
Dabus River, 89, 92, 99
Dakhla oasis, 217–218
Dal Cataract, 118
Damazin, Sudan, 101
Danaqla, 116
Dandur, temple from, 186
Daninos, Adrian, 163–164
Dar, Bahr, 93, 146
date palms, 8
dead storage, 185, 189
Debre Mariam monastery, 92

Pibor River, 76, 80–81
Podgorny, Nikolai, 184
population explosion, 230–231
Portuguese Bridge, 94, 95
Prenile, 127, 128–129
Prompt, Victor, 58
Ptolemies (Greek rulers of Egypt), 132, 133–134,
135
Ptolemy (astronomer/geographer), 8, 32

al-Qahira. *See* Cairo, Egypt
Quz Rajab, 107–108

Raga River, 63
Rahad River, 89, 92, 103
rainfall, 230; impact of El Niño on, 195–196;
role in formation of the Nile, 12–13
ra'is, 69
Ramses II (pharaoh of Egypt), 18, 114, 186–187
Ramses Square (Cairo), 126
Ras Tafari. *See* Haile Selassie I
razzias, 72, 115, 120
Red Sea, 108
Reisner, George Andrew, 186
reth, 74
Revolutionary Command Council (Egypt), 163,
164, 177, 179
Rhodes, Cecil, 201
Ribb River, 92
Riesner, George Andrew, 120
Rift Valley, 30–32, 47–48, 158
Ripon Falls, 9, 36, 37
Robertson, Sir James, 163
Robinson, George Frederick Samuel, 36
Roda, Island of, 126, 136
Roda nilometer, 16–17
Romans, 15; nilometers used by, 19; in the Sudd,
53
Roseires Dam, 89, 101, 166, 174, 175, 176
Rosetta Stone, 137
Roue-pelle. *See* Bucketwheel
Royal Geographic Society, 207
Rubin, Arin, 101
Rugaamba, Ntare, 43
Rushatsi, Ntare, 43

Russia. *See* Soviet Union
Rusumu Falls, 2, 29, 35, 223
Ruvubu River, 27–29
Ruvyironza River, 27
Ruwenzori Mountains (Mountains of the
Moon), 5, 7–8, 32, 33–34
Rwabugiri, Kigeri, 43
Rwanda, 42–43, 198, 222, 224
Rwogera, Mutara, 43

Sabaluqa gorge, 48, 105–106, 107
Sabara Dildi (Broken Bridge), 96
Sabtiya district, 126
el-Sadat, Anwar, 184, 213, 214, 215, 216, 217
Sadd al-Aali. *See* Aswan High Dam
Sahara desert, 5, 129, 191–192
Sahel, 5, 105, 110
Said, Rushdi, 193, 218, 225
Said Sughaiyar, 57
Saint Gabriel, Church of, 92–93
Saint George, Church of, 93
Saint Michael and Zarabruk, Church of, 90
Saint Stephen, monastery of, 92
Sakala, spring at, 88–90
Saladin, 125
Salih, Umar, 57
Salim, Salah, 173
Salim Qapudan, 53, 54, 71
Salisbury, Lord, 59
Salt, Henry, 187
sandstorms, 112, 191–192
Santab and Skamba, 187
saqia, 20, 133–134, 138
Satana Ford, 98
Scorpion (king of Egypt), 130
Scott, Robert D., 170
Scott-Moncrieff, Sir Colin, 24, 126, 142, 143
Semliki River, 31–32
Semyen Mountains, 108–110
Sennar, Sudan, 101–102, 104
Sennar Dam, 89, 102–103, 147–148, 150, 165
Setit River, 110
Shabaqo (king of Kush), 115
shaduf, 133, 138
Shafartak Ford, 96–97

258   Index

Shakespeare, William, 122

Shambe, Lake, 50, 53

Shankalla people, 6

Shari'a, 211

Shayqiyya people, 113

Shendi Reach, 106, 107, 108

Shepilov, Dimitri, 180

al-Sherif, Amin, 183

Shewa, canyons of, 95, 98

Shilluk people, 6, 44, 74–75, 84, 107

shoebill stork, 7, 50

Shubra district, 126

Shukriyya people, 110–111, 189

Siemens, 100

silt, Nile, 123, 139

Simaika, Y. M., 156, 157

Sir Alexander Gibb and Partners, 166

Siwa oasis, 218

slave trade, 55, 63, 72, 119–120

Sneferu (pharaoh of Egypt), 120

Sobat River, 3, 4, 62, 65, 76, 78, 80, 81, 82–83, 201

Sopo River, 63

Southern Provinces Regional Self-Government Act (Sudan), 199

Southern Regional Government (Sudan), 199–201, 203

Soviet Union: and the Aswan High Dam, 180–183; influence in Africa, 79–80

Speke, John Hanning, 8, 36

Stack, Sir Lee, 150

Stanley, Henry Morton, 8, 33

Stegner, Wallace, 229

Sudan, 37, *map* 73; and the Aswan High Dam, 165–168, 173–176; border with Egypt, 119; border with Ethiopia, 76–78, 100; British rule in, 71; civil war in, 69, 71, 72, 77–79, 100, 199, 209–212; conflict with Egypt over water usage, 149–151, 213–214; dams in, 89, 101, 102–103, 147–148; efforts to control the Nile, 112–113; human diversity of, 6–7; independence of, 173. *See also* Blue Nile; Jonglei Canal; Sudd

Sudan People's Liberation Army (SPLA), 79, 211, 212

Sudan Railways, 108

Sudd, 1, 2, 8, 49–69, *map* 61, 145, 154; hydraulics of, 65–69; lagoons of, 51–53; Muslim reformers in, 57; as obstacle to flow of the Nile, 49–51, 54–56, 59–62, 145; peoples of, 67, 69; water loss in, 49, 66. *See also* Jonglei Canal

Sue River, 58, 63

Suez Canal, 24, 57, 141, 142, 180

Suleiman, Abdel Hamid, 151

Suleiman, Sidki, 183

Suna II (kabaka of Bunyoro-Kitara), 46

Susenyos (Ethiopian emperor), 90

Sutcliffe, J. V., 66

Tafari Makkonen. *See* Haile Selassie I

Taharqo (king of Kush), 115

Tammai River, 96

Tana, Lake, 3, 9, 80, 89, 92, 94, 101, 145, 156, 217; churches of, 92–93; dam proposals for, 146, 149, 151, 152, 165, 168, 169–170, 173–174; hydrological surveys of, 146, 151–152

Tanganyika, 174, 197, 198

Tanganyika, Lake, 8, 30–31

Tanwetami (king of Kush), 115

Tanzania, 46, 197, 222, 224

Tapari River. *See* Gel River

Tawfiqiyah, 83

Tekeze River, 110, 111

Tekla Haymanot II (Ethiopian emperor), 91

Tel el-Kebir, 141

Temcha River, 98

Terzaghi, Karl von, 178, 179, 182

Tessama, 80

Thabit, Thabit Hasan, 185, 186

Thadewos, Saint, 92

Thinis, Egypt, 130

tiang, 7

Tilahun, Wondimneh, 215, 225

Tis Abbai hydroelectric power station, 93

Tisisat Falls, 89, 94

toic, 67, 196

Tonj River, 63, 64

trade winds, 13

Tscheborarieff, Gregory, 182